SELF-MADE SUPERSTAR

"David Bowie, the real man behind the image, is a wily operator, a hardheaded businessman, knowledgeable about the Hollywood studio system, and thus the first rock star to market himself as if he were a movie star. A consummate showman, he is the Barnum and Bailey of his time; a man with a magpie mentality—the living embodiment of T. S. Eliot's famous line 'Good poets copy, great poets steal'—a cruiser of all aspects of popular culture; a synthesizer of the arts, style, and fashion; and, above all, the Emperor of Rock."

—From *Bowie*, the biography hailed in 2014 as one of
Parade Magazine's 17 Great New Music Books!

"Wendy Leigh highlights the adult exploits and other hijinks that preceded his settling down with supermodel Iman."

—*Parade Magazine*

"Explosive details. . . . A blockbuster book."

—*National Enquirer*

"Entertaining and informative. . . . Leigh is good on how the peculiarities of Bowie's family background shaped him—and on what they cost him."

—*The National*

"Was David Bowie merely a sexual adventurer or an actual sex addict? . . . In *Bowie*, more than one observer characterizes Bowie as a sex addict."

—*New York Daily News*

"Shocking. . . . Bowie leaves nothing behind closed doors."

—*FDRMX*

BOWIE

THE BIOGRAPHY

Wendy Leigh

GALLERY BOOKS

NEW YORK   LONDON   TORONTO   SYDNEY   NEW DELHI

Gallery Books
An Imprint of Simon & Schuster, Inc.
1230 Avenue of the Americas
New York, NY 10020

First Gallery Books trade paperback edition February 2016

GALLERY BOOKS and colophon are registered trademarks of Simon & Schuster, Inc.

For information about special discounts for bulk purchases, please contact Simon &
Schuster Special Sales at 1-866-506-1949 or business@simonandschuster.com.

The Simon & Schuster Speakers Bureau can bring authors to your live event. For more
information or to book an event, contact the Simon & Schuster Speakers Bureau at
1-866-248-3049 or visit our website at www.simonspeakers.com.

Interior design by Jaime Putorti

Manufactured in the United States of America

10   9   8   7   6   5   4   3   2   1

Library of Congress Cataloging-in-Publication Data is available for the hardcover edition.

ISBN 978-1-4767-6709-3
ISBN 978-1-4767-6707-9 (hardcover)
ISBN 978-1-4767-6711-6 (ebook)

For Dr. Erika Padan Freeman

BOWIE

INTRODUCTION

June 6, 1992

Villa La Massa, Florence, Italy

David Bowie's allure has always partly been due to his capacity for confounding expectations, and the day of his wedding to Iman was no different.

His friends and family initially assumed that the wedding reception would take place inside the secluded compound of Britannia Bay House, David and Iman's Balinese-style estate on the tiny private Caribbean island of Mustique, overlooking the ocean and completely hidden from view of prying paparazzi and besotted Bowie fans alike. More than practically anywhere else in the world, Mustique is akin to a fortress, its borders closely guarded by officials who, if necessary, are quick and effective in banning journalists, photographers, and sundry undesirables from ever setting foot on its hallowed soil.

Such was the high degree of security and the absence of intrusive press on Mustique that, some years before, Britain's Princess Margaret was able to throw caution to the wind and cavort freely on the beach with London gangster and accused killer John Bindon (who, coincidentally, was also an intimate of David in the seventies). An enclave for only the very rich and famous, for kings and queens, princesses, billionaires, politicians, and tycoons, Mustique (which, despite its elite, jet-set allure, or perhaps because of it, Iman does not particularly like) is an airtight world of privilege and privacy.

But regardless of the beauty of David's Mustique home, and the security he'd be guaranteed by holding his wedding on the island, he instead opted for the cliché of throwing a public, celebrity-style wedding that would be immortalized in the pages of *Hello!* In deciding to sell his wedding to the magazine for a sum that might have been as much as four million dollars and agreeing to pose for photographs with Iman for hours, David opted for cold cash—yet also drove such a hard bargain that although he and Iman were photographed throughout the wedding ceremony at Saint James Episcopal Church in Florence, Italy (after which eight photographs were published in the magazine's twenty-three-page coverage), and at the reception, he insured that the privacy of most of his sixty-eight guests was preserved, so that very few of them were photographed for *Hello!*

Awarded pride of place at the wedding reception in Florence's beautiful Villa La Massa, as befits her status as David's mother, the regal Margaret Jones, an imposing woman of seventy-eight, though struggling with bad health, graces a plush, ornate, red velvet and gold cherub–garlanded throne. As Margaret—or Peggy, as she is known—gazes forthrightly into the camera, her blue eyes are clear, with a far-seeing psychic quality to them (she was said to have a talent for mental telepathy, one that David has claimed he shares). Her warm smile displays her snaggled front tooth, a twin to David's (before he had it fixed through the miracle of cosmetic dentistry), and her palpable star quality and commanding presence are a testament to how close the apple has fallen to the maternal tree.

Peggy had always been a brave and fearless pioneer, who in 1940s England wore pants long before they were acceptable attire for ladies. And like her son David—the world's first rock star to publicly out himself, to talk to the press about his open marriage, to wear makeup, stark white nail polish, and dresses—Peggy was also a rebel, a woman born to flout the bourgeoisie. The mother of three illegitimate children (including David) at a time when a girl could have been ostracized by society for having even one, Peggy was never afraid to dance to a different drummer. Nor—and again the similarity to David is remarkable—was she afraid to embrace two diametrically opposed camps in a relatively short time span.

Peggy briefly became enamored of Oswald Mosley's British Union of Fascists (the British equivalent of the Nazi Party) and in October 1936, when she was twenty-three years old, attended one of their rallies in the prosperous spa town of Tunbridge Wells. However, according to Peggy's sister Pat, when protesters flung rotten fruit and vegetables at Mosley's followers, Peggy was far more transfixed by the macho swagger of the Fascists in their fetching black shirts than by the fracas surrounding her.

Yet though an acolyte of the British Union of Fascists, which routinely terrorized Jews all over Britain, less than ten years later, Peggy had a love affair with Jack Isaac Rosenberg, the son of a wealthy Jewish furrier, and bore him a son, David's half brother Terry, nine years his senior.

A similar dichotomy is evident in David's own history. In 1976, he was accused of making the Nazi salute, while standing up in an open Mercedes convertible (an accusation that he went on to deny), and around the same time also threw out a few positive remarks about Hitler, proclaiming of him, "His overall objective was very good, and he was a marvelous morale booster. I mean, he was a perfect figurehead."

So that just as his mother was once seduced by the glittering visual image of Mosley's Blackshirts, David clearly was as mesmerized by Nazi style, swagger, and sharp tailoring. Yet his good friend Marc Bolan was Jewish, and so is the second most important woman in his life (after Iman), his best friend and faithful retainer in every area of his private and public existence since 1974, Corinne "Coco" Schwab, an American who was born in the stock room at Bloomingdale's, after her mother went into labor in the store's linen department.

At David's wedding reception, Coco is all radiant smiles, her thick, efficient-looking, shiny black bob creating a helmet around her face, a reminder that she invariably plays bad cop to David's good. As his gatekeeper and protector, Coco is legendary for her fierceness in eradicating from David's universe all those whom she considers to be undesirable (including his first wife, Angie) and protecting him 24/7 at a cost to her own life and authentic existence. Coco's dedication to David has always been unimpeachable, right through his drug-addled years and his divorce from Angie up to and beyond 2013, when she was on hand to assist in the making of his video for "Love Is Lost," which premiered at the Mercury Music Awards.

But during the wedding ceremony, as Iman glided up the aisle and joined him at the altar to the tune of "April in Paris," the song with which David serenaded her when he proposed, it was inevitable that informed onlookers would speculate on the possibly troubling emotions simmering behind Coco's poised and perfect smiling mask as she witnessed David's wedding and the start of his second marriage.

For Coco isn't just David's personal assistant, and her importance to him transcends such categorization, as does her enduring passion for him. Originally a receptionist/secretary at MainMan, Coco was employed by the company to work with David. As the years went by, she became his chief cheerleader, hand-holder, best friend, and has been thought to secretly harbor passionate desire for him.

A vestal virgin catering to the high priest? Or a flesh-and-blood woman with a carnal appetite for him? Tony Zanetta, president of MainMan during those years, remembers Coco saying of David, "I really do love him. I love him so very much."

German fashion designer Claudia Skoda first met Coco in 1976 when David, Coco, and Iggy Pop visited her at the Berlin commune where she was then living and working. "David didn't introduce Coco to me, and I initially assumed that she was Iggy's wife. She isn't a beauty queen, but she is intelligent, with sex appeal of a kind. People have said that she was a mother figure to David, but I couldn't see that. She looked after him as if she was his girlfriend. With intimacy. I surmised that they were having an affair," Claudia said.

Whatever the truth, Coco has been in David's life for forty years. In 1987, he wrote "Never Let Me Down," a song inspired by her friendship and her loyalty to him, and on her sixtieth birthday, he recognized Coco's stellar service to him by gifting her with a ring studded with rose-colored diamonds.

However, Coco's loyalty sometimes translates into a fierceness that other people find intimidating. As someone who has worked closely with Bowie for some years has revealed, even his venerable British publicist, Alan Edwards, who has masterminded Bowie's publicity for decades, is still slightly apprehensive when Coco sweeps into London, and makes it clear to everyone who deals with her, "Whatever you do, don't set Coco off. . . ."

Coco has never failed David. And David remains loyal to her, and kind, as he has been to Ken Pitt, his manager in the late sixties, and who recalled last year, "I'm ninety now, and hadn't seen David for years, but about four years ago, there was a knock at my door and it was David. He didn't seem that well, but we talked for over an hour. It was a lovely thing to do."

Not only that, but each year since they first met, and right up till now, David has sent Ken Pitt a Christmas present, and also regularly sends him editions of rare secondhand books that he feels Ken might relish.

David is also generous with his advice to other up-and-coming artists, and additionally has spent considerable time and energy helping young people who are struggling with drug habits, as he himself once did. Costume designer Ola Hudson, with whom David had a three-year affair, begged him to talk to her son Saul (Slash of Guns N' Roses) about drugs.

"David was engaging and wise in the ways of chemical abuse. He asked me about what I was doing drug-wise and what I was going through emotionally, psychically, and with the band," Slash said. "I rambled on for a while, but once I started talking about my little translucent friends, David interrupted me.

"'Listen to me,' he said, 'You are not in a good way. If you are seeing things every day, what you are doing to yourself is not good at all. You are at a very spiritual low point when that begins to happen. You are exposing yourself to the darker realms of your subconscious being. You are making yourself vulnerable to all kinds of negative energy.'"

Slash wasn't the only person struggling with addiction whom David tried to help. Famously, Iggy Pop was another, but David didn't just try to rescue those close to him. Makeup artist Carolyn Cowan was in Dublin in 1991, working with David on a video he was shooting there. She was battling with her addiction to crack cocaine and drinking far too much, as well. Though he hardly knew Carolyn, David immediately sensed that she was in trouble. From then on, every day of the shoot, he asked her if she had managed to stay sober the night before. The truth was that she hadn't, and David knew it.

"By the third day, he had persuaded me to go to an Alcoholics Anonymous meeting. Everything he'd said had finally got through to me and now I'm so grateful for his intervention," she said. "David Bowie saved my life. I have no doubt about it. He was never judgmental—just kind," Carolyn said.

And photographer Joe Stevens, who first met him in the days of Ziggy Stardust, also remembered his kindness and generosity: "A close friend had a triple bypass operation, and as he was an uninsured artist, he was unable to pay his medical bills. Bowie covered them, secretly," he said.

David's kindness manifests itself in other contexts as well, and he never pulls rank over others less successful than he is—which means just about the entire world. In the early 1990s, iconoclastic Indian singer Asha Puthli attended a party at David's Mustique house. "He came up to me and said, 'Asha, I have your first album.

It's in my special collection. I shall always keep it,'" she said. "I recorded that album in 1973. David is the kindest musician I have ever met."

He is also one of the most polite. His manners are impeccable, even under the most trying of circumstances. Even as far back as October 1972, in Los Angeles, David demonstrated an innate noblesse oblige. Following David's Santa Monica Civic Auditorium concert, DJ Wolfman Jack threw a party at his home, during which the guest of honor, David, fixed on a girl on the dance floor swirling around sexily with legendary wild man of rock six-foot-four-and-a-half Kim Fowley. When the dance was over, David tentatively approached Kim, and the following dialogue ensued:

"Is she with you?" David inquired politely.

"No," Kim said.

"Are you in love with her?" David probed.

"No."

Empowered, he asked Kim if he intended to have sex with the dancing girl. On being assured by Kim that he did not, David put all his cards on the table, as it were, and confessed to him that *he* wanted to have sex with her.

"Can you escort me across the dance floor?" David asked.

Kim complied and watched as David moved closer to the dancing girl.

"My name is David Bowie," he said quietly, and then added, "Would you like to accompany me to the bathroom?"

She didn't think twice and followed David immediately. Together, they walked into the bathroom. They locked the door and did not emerge until after quite some time. At that point, David kissed her on the cheek, shook her hand, and said, "Thank you," and off she went, charmed to the toes by David and his good manners.

So was Kim Fowley.

"Thank you very much" were David's last words to him that night.

• • •

Another important guest at David's wedding was yet another strong woman in the mold of Iman and of Coco Schwab. John Lennon's widow, Yoko Ono, was an honored guest at the wedding, primarily because David nurtured warm memories of John and, from their first meeting, respected him immensely. That respect was mutual. For although John did once crack, "Meeting David Bowie is always interesting, because you never know which one you are meeting," John was always fond of David and was wholehearted in his support of his career. So much so that in the very last interview of his life, on the Friday before he was slaughtered, John had dinner at Mr. Chow with BBC broadcaster Andy Peebles, who was also in Manhattan to interview David, then starring on Broadway as John Merrick in *The Elephant Man*.

"John Lennon was very interested that I was talking to David the next day, and said that he thought David was a very talented man, and very gifted. He said that it was amazing that David was doing *The Elephant Man*," Andy Peebles said.

Playing John Merrick, a man born with a tragic facial deformity, was a triumph for David. Yet at the same time, his decision to play a misfit in his Broadway debut tells a tale about David Bowie, the man. The only child his parents had together, David was born left-handed, which in 1950s England was considered a disgrace, an aberration that had to be corrected at all costs. "At school, I remember very distinctly kids laughing at me because I would draw and write with my left hand," David said.

His schoolmates yelled that he was "the devil," simply because he wrote with his left hand. Worse still, "the teacher used to smack my hand to try and make me right-handed," he said.

The teacher tried her utmost, but in spite of her frequent attempts to force David to favor his right hand over his left, he instinctively resisted and continued to use his left hand regardless. Nonetheless, the battle had left him scarred and also served to forge iron in his soul. He said, many years later, "It put me outside of others immediately. I didn't feel the same as the others because of that. . . . So I think it might have been one of those tips of how I was going to evaluate my journey through life: All right, I'm not the same as you motherfuckers, so I'll be better than you."

His deep-rooted sense of isolation and drive toward nonconformity were cemented yet further when he was thirteen and was almost robbed of the sight of his left eye, causing him to suffer the medical condition anisocoria, so that he emerged with two markedly different-looking eyes. Not an easy condition for a young boy to cope with, especially in the rough-and-tumble environment of growing up on the fringes of South London. Consequently, David felt like an outcast, a pariah, and his sympathies have always veered toward the underdog, those who walk on the wild side. "It's a subject I'm fascinated in . . . gigolos, male escorts, male hookers," he once said.

His fascination with sexual outlaws is natural, given his own history. David, initially celebrated for his androgyny, has always been the ultimate sexual liberator, trumpeting sexual freedom and diversity openly and proudly. He did so first in his songwriting, one of the many facets of his genius (along with performing, painting, and art directing every element of his entire existence), and wrote lyrics dealing with gender-bending in "Rebel, Rebel," "Suffragette City," "Queen Bitch," and "Oh, You Pretty Things."

On a personal level, by declaring to the press that he was gay at a time when even Elton John was still in the closet, then amending the announcement by saying he was bisexual, by wearing a dress in public, and by being consistently unafraid to cite his various sexual proclivities to interviewers, Bowie smashed through the accepted barrier of what was considered "normal" sexuality and, in the process, freed many a fan from his prison of sexual aloneness.

The truth is that, rather like a latter-day Tom Jones in Henry Fielding's book of the same name, David has adventured his way from sexual experience to sexual experience, embracing gay sex, threesomes, group sex, straight sex, then, perhaps most startlingly of all, monogamous marriage.

David's amorous exploits through the years amount to an extremely multifaceted sexual odyssey, which can be attributed not only to his good looks, his trim, toned, and flexible body, his high-octane libido, his impressive, much-vaunted endowment, his star quality and massive powers of attraction, but also to the fact that Bowie has always been an equal-opportunity lover. Neither age, race, religion, nor the looks of his lovers has ever prevented him from following the siren's song of his lust, wherever it might lure him.

A brief, kaleidoscopic overview of his conquests: Bette Midler (reportedly an isolated incident in a closet); record executive Calvin Mark Lee; *Playboy* model and actress Bebe Buell; Nina Simone (who inspired him to record "Wild Is the Wind," which she had recorded first); Charlie Chaplin's widow, Oona, (twenty-two years his senior); dancer Melissa Hurley (twenty years his junior); singer Ava Cherry; Jean Millington, of the rock band Fanny; and model Winona Williams, whom he invited to live in Berlin with him.

Along the way he paid court to Monique van Vooren (twenty years his senior), had an affair with Dana Gillespie (who was then fourteen to his sixteen) and a dalliance with Cyrinda Foxe (a glamorous Monroe doppelgänger who sported a string of pearls she put to good use during their last sexual encounter), and—in the spirit of his continuing rivalry with Mick Jagger—toyed with Jagger's onetime girlfriend Marianne Faithfull, backing singer Claudia Lennear (the inspiration for Mick Jagger's song "Brown Sugar," and about whom David wrote "Lady Grinning Soul"), and briefly dated Mick's first wife, Bianca Jagger.

According to David's ex-wife, Angie, who has hawked a variety of negative stories about David since their divorce, there may also have been more than a moment with Mick Jagger himself. In Angie Bowie's version of the alleged event, first published in her 1981 autobiography, *Free Spirit*, she returned from a trip to find Mick and David in bed together, only not sleeping, something which David has taken the rare step of denying. However, David's girlfriend in the early seventies, Wilhelmina model Winona Williams, also says, "I remember walking in on David and Mick, and tending to think that they had just finished doing something together."

Other of his conquests—never denied—include Susan Sarandon; Tina Turner; Lulu; Ronnie Spector of the Ronettes; one of the Three Degrees; Ralph Horton, his second manager; and possibly Ken Pitt, his third manager, who was clearly in love with him, although there is no conclusive evidence that their relationship was ever consummated.

Sexually voracious, David conducted simultaneous affairs with dancer and mime artist Lindsay Kemp and Natasha Korniloff, Kemp's costume designer. He also had a much-publicized affair with transsexual Romy Haag, and affairs with sundry staff employees of MainMan (the company that spearheaded his onslaught on America), consolidating a pattern repeatedly characterized by observers as being David's way of marking out his territory, and with an array of groupies both male and female, as well. As he put it in a 1997 BBC radio interview, "I was hitting on everybody. I had a wonderfully irresponsible promiscuous time."

David's sexual adventures—some partly cocaine-fueled, all ignited by his unbridled appetites and his propensity to cast a wide net, coupled with his unlimited opportunities—typifies his generation's newfound ability to live out their wildness. His sexuality aside, David Bowie, the real man behind the image, is a wily operator, a hardheaded businessman, knowledgeable about the star-making factory that was the Hollywood studio system, and thus the first rock star to market himself as if he were a movie star. A consummate showman, he is the Barnum & Bailey of his time; a man with a magpie mentality—the living embodiment of T. S. Eliot's famous line "Immature poets imitate; mature poets steal"—a cruiser of all aspects of popular culture; a synthesizer of the arts, style, and fashion; and, above all, the Emperor of Rock.

Yet while his unrivaled sense of style and cool may well be the product of an innate iciness within his deepest nature, throughout his life he has also formed abiding relationships with a number of people, and in this, as in his art, he exhibits yet another contradiction. Through it all, to paraphrase the *La Cage aux Folles* anthem "I Am What I Am," Bowie has definitely always been his own special creation.

But here at David's wedding to Iman, there isn't the slightest whiff of the cross-dresser, the chameleon, or the unconventional about him. He is dashing in his Thierry Mugler black tie and tails, with Iman breathtakingly beautiful by his side. The only sign that David isn't a five-times-married Beverly Hills billionaire banker or a dissolute Russian oligarch pledging his troth in a romantic, opulent wedding ceremony is the diamond stud in his left ear, and his openhearted love for his wife, his joy at their union.

"This for me is so exciting and so invigorating," David said. "I have such great expectations of our future together. I have never been so happy."

Twenty-two years after their marriage, David Bowie and Iman are still happy together, their initial conjugal bliss complete with the birth of their daughter, Alexandria, in 2000. Today, David and his family spend most of their time in Manhattan, with David, the consummate husband and father, besotted by both his wife and his daughter, as well as with Duncan (born Zowie) his grown son by his first marriage, who is now an award-winning movie director and very much part of David's life.

Professionally, he still hasn't lost his touch. Out of the blue, at 5 A.M. on the morning of his January 8, 2013, his sixty-sixth birthday without any prior warning, he unleashed "Where Are We Now?" on an unsuspecting public to great acclaim, followed in just two months by his much-feted album, his first in ten years, *The Next Day*. And the subsequent outpouring of praise for and adoration of David amongst the press, the public, and most of all his peers was unprecedented.

"In the music business there is an aura of great respect around David," says music publicist Mick Garbutt, who has worked with him sporadically through the years.

David Bowie has climbed so very far, to the heights of fame and fortune, in every field that he has succeeded in conquering: He is a rock god whose story may seem like a moonlit fairy tale but simultaneously echoes the path, the choices, the triumphs, the disasters, and the lives lived by so many of his generation.

And it all began for him so long ago when he was just a kid in South London, where he began the journey that, by dint of his genius, his persistence, and his sheer hard work, would transform him into a global icon whose name, image, music, and artistry would endure forever.

ONE

ABSOLUTE BEGINNING

David Bowie's first hit, "Space Oddity," followed by "Life on Mars?" and "Starman," insured that he would be forever associated with the planets, space, the moon, and the stars—and later on, when he made his cinematic debut in *The Man Who Fell to Earth*, with aliens and other worlds. Yet David Bowie was born in what in 1947 was one of the most mundane, down-to-earth, run-down communities in Britain: Brixton, in the London borough of Lambeth, a poor, grimy, working-class enclave. Yet stark and ordinary as Brixton was in those days, in true contrasting Bowie fashion, David's birthplace also carried the visual blueprint of some of his creative dreams, his fantasies, his lyrics, his future.

As history tells us, during the Second World War German bombs didn't drop on London's historic landmarks, like Westminster Abbey, the Houses of Parliament, the Tower of London, St. Paul's Cathedral. Documents have revealed that after double agents planted deliberate misinformation within the Luftwaffe, the Germans set the coordinates of the flying bombs so they didn't fall on Central London and destroy England's most hallowed historic edifices, but rather on the East End and South London, which bore the brunt of the bombing.

Between October 1940 and June 1941, 1,215 bombs fell on Lambeth, an area three miles wide and seven miles long. And there was worse to come. Toward the end of the war, the lethal V-1 pilotless flying bombs (aka buzz bombs or doodlebugs) wrought havoc on London. At exactly 7:47 A.M. on July 16, 1944, a V-1 bomb hit Rumsey Road just one street north of Stansfield Road, where David Robert Jones (aka David Bowie) would be born just over two and a half years later, and in the process, demolished twelve houses and damaged forty others.

The ravages of that deadly attack (along with the hundreds of other bombs dropped on the Brixton area during the Second World War) were in evidence within a few miles' radius of David's home and would remain there well into the early fifties, when most of the houses were replaced with prefabricated reinforced concrete bungalows, known as "prefabs." Hurriedly thrown-together eyesores with seemingly paper-thin walls, prefabs rose up from bombsites that resembled the desolate craters on the surface of the moon: forbidding, barren, like some bleak mysterious planet—all grist for David's creativity.

Then there was the dark and sinister men's prison, Brixton Prison, situated 0.8 miles from David's home, where no less a luminary than Mick Jagger would be incarcerated for three nights after his drug bust, and where Anthony Newley, one of David's earliest musical influences, spent twenty-eight days after being convicted of driving with a suspended license.

And the local movie theater, the Astoria, was a palatial mock renaissance-style monstrosity, complete with marble foyer and mosaic fountain, that may well have been the first example of architectural excess and opulence David would have encountered in his young life. Perhaps even more of a dramatic and lasting influence, located ten minutes by foot from David's birthplace, was Brixton Market, the hub of Brixton's thousands of Jamaican immigrants, the first wave of which first arrived in London in the year of David's birth, all bringing with them the sounds, textures, and colors of the Caribbean.

Just across from the hallowed halls of Bon Marché, Brixton's sober department store, Electric Avenue and Granville Arcade were at the heart of acres and acres of covered market filled with stalls spilling over with mangoes, plantains, yams, pineapples, bolts of crimson lace, purple linens, coral lipsticks, glistening cocoa butter, and platinum nylon wigs, all sold by Jamaican barrow boys to the tinkling sound of Caribbean steel bands.

The spiritual, cultural, and commercial center of the Jamaican immigrant community in Brixton, Brixton Market was also a hive of beautiful Jamaican women, selling, buying, or just simply stalking through the market like Rocketts sporting multicolored flared feathers: all, short, young, old, hips swaying, voluptuous bodies swathed tightly in Technicolor cotton clothes, intoxicating, mesmerizing, and indelibly memorable.

A segue back to America, to Hollywood, and to a vignette from the life of David Bowie, age thirty, an artist at the top of his game, an Adonis at the height of his physical beauty, and a rock star still intent on sampling as great an assortment of the sexual fruits of his stratospheric success as possible.

By 1977, Elizabeth Taylor and David had bonded, and consequently, when he was performing in Los Angeles, she invited him to meet one of her close friends. Her name was Loretta Young, and in her day she was one of America's most beloved movie stars, and an Oscar-nominated actress. Her costars included Cary Grant and Clark Gable, who was also her lover, and with whom she had a daughter.

Once a household name, due to her eponymous TV show, Loretta Young was now sixty-four, long past her prime, yet still a great, if faded, beauty. She was vibrant and vivacious and, despite her age, her sexual appetites remained undimmed.

Moreover, her considerable carnal desires were now directed

obsessively at David Bowie. "All she had seen was his photographs, but she was enamored by him, fixated on him, and said to me, 'I want to meet him. I want to *be* with him. Can you arrange it?'" Elizabeth Taylor confided to Kim Fowley, who then went on to detail her response. "I told Loretta that David wasn't due in L.A. for a few months, and she said, 'Good, that gives me time to prepare,'" Elizabeth Taylor reported.

According to Elizabeth Taylor, the David-obsessed Loretta proceeded to spend the next few months feverishly preparing herself for her first meeting with him.

"She started an exercise regime, she had her hair restyled, had some nips and tucks on her body and her face; then the big day came," Elizabeth said. "I took Loretta to meet David. And assuming that it would be a foregone conclusion that she and David would immediately disappear into the night together, Loretta was very aggressive and said, 'I've gone to a lot of trouble to meet you tonight, David.'"

Whereupon David, who had always had a propensity for strong women, but not aggressive ones, declared to Loretta Young in his polite English gentleman's tone, "You shouldn't have gone to the trouble, my dear. I only like black women and Asian men."

Long after David's birth at 40 Stansfield Road, a three-story terraced house, mythology had it that the midwife who delivered him swooned about his "knowing eyes" and insisted that the newborn baby had "been here before." The baby David's otherworldliness is the first of the many myths attached to David Bowie, perhaps by his father, John Haywood Jones, a seasoned public-relations man who devoted his considerable talents to raising David's profile, or by subsequent publicists, or possibly by David himself, always his own best publicist, willing to spin untruths into truth, all in quest of lending luster to his image and his career.

But even if the midwife's reaction was contrived and merely a publicity ploy, the truth is that David's birth did have an otherworldly significance to it, one that would become clear only a few months before his tenth birthday, when Elvis Presley burst onto the scene with "Heartbreak Hotel" and "Blue Suede Shoes," thus becoming the world's first rock idol whose megawatt rock-god appeal has never waned: David Bowie was born on January 8, 1947, Elvis Presley's twelfth birthday. David's mother, Peggy, no mean judge of male charisma, was overcome when Elvis flooded the radio with hits, and she viewed the fact that David shared his birthday as a positive omen. As David said, "She never let me forget it. She was enthralled by the idea."

David himself was not immune to the significance of sharing a birthday with Elvis, and it added to his sense of his own destiny, his own specialness. Consequently, when he watched his aunt Una's daughter, his cousin, Kristina, dance to "Hound Dog" soon after it was released in 1956, his passion for music was ignited. "It really impressed me, the power of the music. I started getting records immediately after that," he said.

Even when David was on the threshold of stardom, Elvis continued to exercise a sway over him to such a degree that, in the face of the King, he would instantly be reduced to the level of fandom. In June 1972, David and his guitarist Mick Ronson took a midday flight from Heathrow to New York and arrived just in time to catch Elvis headlining Madison Square Garden. Or so they hoped. In fact, they arrived there after the show had begun.

As RCA was David's record label at the time as well as Elvis's, David had been given the best seats for the show. Which made it even worse that he and Mick arrived while Elvis was in mid-act. He was in the throes of "Proud Mary," when David, hobbling on Kabuki platform heels, his hair dyed bright red, and in full Ziggy regalia, practically stopped the show. "I could see him thinking: *Who the fuck is that? Sit the fuck down.* It was really humiliating—but unmissable," David said years later.

Although the idea was floated that David work with Elvis in a production-writer capacity, which David has said he would have loved, nothing ever came of it. But he still cherishes a note that Elvis sent him, wishing him a good tour—and his imitation of Elvis's Southern drawl is perfect, mimicry being yet another of David's manifold talents.

David may have cloaked himself in a mystical, magical, other-worldly image on his rise to stardom, but the reality is that his father came from solid Yorkshire stock, and it is likely that David inherited his financial savvy from him (witness the Bowie Bonds, shares in his back catalogue that David put on the stock market), his shrewdness, and his ability to remain grounded even while studiously projecting the opposite impression.

Born in Doncaster, South Yorkshire, and brought up in Tadcaster, John was orphaned in early childhood and raised by an aunt. Although he came from a working-class background (his father sold shoes and boots, and his maternal grandfather was foreman of a wool mill), like some hero out of Charles Dickens, John rose in the world after his wealthy aunt sent him to British public (private, in American terms) school, where he was drilled in good manners, thus emerging with the veneer of an English gentleman, to the manner born.

David claimed that his father received the call to work with orphans in a dream, and John did go on to do all he could to help them by taking a job at the children's charity Dr. Barnardo's Homes; he began working there in 1935 and continued until his death thirty-four years later.

But saintly as John's work in his latter years might have been, and true to his son's propensity for ringing the changes in the most dramatic way possible, he had also lived out a wild, anarchic side in his youth. After inheriting a substantial sum of money when he was only sixteen years old, he had bought a theater club and then a nightclub on Charlotte Street, London, which was patronized by boxers, wrestlers, and gangsters. Both failed dismally.

Before Peggy came into his life, John had married a cabaret performer known as Hilda, the Viennese Nightingale, but he was unfaithful to her with a nurse who gave birth to his daughter, Annette, whom Hilda, clearly a remarkable woman, agreed to bring up as her own. In fact, when her marriage to John was spiraling downward, Hilda persuaded him to buy a house that Annette could one day inherit. That house was 40 Stansfield Road, and when David was born, Annette would help care for him.

However, in 1956, Annette met and married an Egyptian engineer and moved to Cairo with him, became a Muslim, and coincidentally changed her name to Iman. She last saw David when he was fifteen years old and she'd flown back to London for a visit. "When David walked into the room, it all came flooding back. I threw open my arms to hug him, but he just flinched. I was hurt because I suddenly realized he cut me off in his mind the moment I walked out the front door when he was nine," Annette said.

After a chance meeting with Peggy Burns in her hometown of Tunbridge Wells, where she was working as a waitress at the Ritz movie theater café, John Haywood Jones fell in love with her. Both strong individuals, they had David in 1947 when they were in their midthirties, and by the time he was eight months old, they decided to marry, thus legitimizing him. They remained married until John's death, and different as he, a placid and contemplative man, was from Peggy, who managed the unique feat of being alternately tempestuous and cold, he stayed the course with her.

From his father, David got his love of reading (even in his darkest drug days he traveled the world with trunks containing his vast library of books); he got his first taste of Hemingway from his father's readers' book club, which sent him a book a month, each of which David eagerly devoured. "My father opened up my world because he taught me the habit of reading. I got so much information, so many of the things I wanted to do came from books," he recalled.

Another, less salutary habit that David picked up from his father was chain-smoking, and despite undergoing hypnosis and aversion therapy to break the habit, for a great part of his life, he was unable to quit. John's favorite brand of cigarette was Player's, which he chain-smoked, and David followed suit, making Player's his own cigarette of choice. In later years, though, he switched to Marlboros, making sure that Coco always carried a secret stash in her handbag, just in case he ran out.

Another legacy from his father, according to David, was religious tolerance. "My father was one of the few fathers I knew who had a lot of understanding of other religions. He encouraged me to become interested in other religions," he said. His tolerance was enhanced as well by the fact that his half brother, Terry, nine years his senior and his mother's son by her former lover, Jack Isaac Rosenberg, was half Jewish.

An adventurous and liberated woman, Peggy was the daughter of Jimmy Burns, a professional soldier of Irish descent who fought with distinction during the First World War. However, when he returned home to England virtually penniless, he resorted to what he did best: playing the clarinet in the streets of Tunbridge Wells, as passersby threw coins into his hat in appreciation. Music was a Burns family passion and all six of Jimmy's children—Peggy, the eldest; Nora; Vivienne; Una; the youngest girl, Pat; and their brother, Jimmy, all sang and played an instrument.

When David was a little boy, every Sunday during lunch, he and his parents would listen to the BBC Light Programme's *Family Favorites* together. Peggy's most beloved song was "O for the Wings of a Dove," sung by soprano boy singer Ernest Lough, and she would sing along with him, transported.

"Her voice would soar in ambitious unison, effortlessly matching Ernest note for note as she delivered the gravy boat to the table," said David, who went on to remember that his mother told him: "'All our family could sing. We couldn't do much else but we all loved music. It was thought I'd have a career in music at one time.'"

Apart from sharing her son's musical talent, he and Peggy had something else strikingly in common: Throughout her life, Peggy composed poems—lush, introspective poems—which, even though she left school at fourteen, were quite literate. In addition to writing poetry, like John, she also read a great deal. Sometimes it seemed to visitors that she was so involved in whatever book she was reading that it was as if she were alone in the room and David wasn't there at all. Terminally self-involved, Peggy didn't bother herself with encouraging David's burgeoning artistic talents. "A compliment from her was very hard to come by. I would get my paints out and all she would say was, 'I hope you're not going to make a mess,'" David remembered.

According to Ken Pitt, David confided that his mother never kissed him. "There was no sign of affection any time," Dudley Chapman, one of David's childhood friends, confirmed. "It was a very cold household. She'd feed him, clothe him, do all the mother's things, but there was no cuddling."

Peggy's lack of warmth toward David would take its toll on his emotions for her. So that when he grew up and left home, he would virtually sever contact with her and his family. In 1992 David's aunt Pat, Peggy's youngest sister, tracked his unhappy relationship with his mother and recalled, "David started out as a fun-loving, beautiful little child. But he grew up in a cold atmosphere and by the time he was five he was extremely quiet and serious.

"I remember David coming home from school when he was fourteen upset by something which had happened that day. He ran upstairs and threw himself onto his bed sobbing his heart out. I asked Peggy if she was going to see what was wrong. She went up, but, being such an unemotional person, she was unable to give him a hug or a cuddle to make him feel better.

"David turned to her and said quietly, 'You know, Mum, sometimes I think you hate me,'" his aunt Pat said.

Although Peggy did do the requisite amount of cooking and cleaning and washed David's clothes into his teens, her deep-seated remoteness, her strangeness, her inability to relate closely to David are highly likely to have been a slight manifestation of the schizophrenia from which her sisters Una, Nora, and Vivienne also all suffered. For as much as David might try and joke about it, cracking of his family, "Most of them are nutty—just out of, or going into an institution," the reality was dark and serious.

In September 1950, Una was sent to a mental hospital, Park Prewett, where she was diagnosed as a schizophrenic. She was thereafter subjected to archaic treatments for the condition, and died in her thirties. Vivienne suffered from schizophrenia. Nora was also hospitalized, diagnosed with manic-depressive psychosis, and, most horrifying of all, underwent a lobotomy. Then there was Terry, David's half brother, whom David idolized, but who would also be felled by the family curse of schizophrenia.

It was inevitable, then, that David would grow up haunted by the specter of mental illness and petrified of losing his wits. "He told me so, quite often and quite clearly," his first wife, Angie, confided.

"He told me about the insanity that ran through his family and that it scared him," model Winona Williams, who had a two-year relationship with him in the early seventies, said.

"There's a lot of madness in my family," David told biographer George Tremlett, who proceeded to suggest to him that he was merely talking about eccentricity. "No, madness—real fucking madness," David shot back. "It worries me sometimes, because I don't know whether it's in my genes and if I'll end up that way, too."

David's salvation would prove to be his love of reading, which led him to R. D. Laing's seminal reappraisal of schizophrenia, *The Divided*

Self, published when David was thirteen, and which became one of his all-time favorite books. In it, Laing wrote, "It is the thesis of this study that schizophrenia is a possible outcome of a more than usual difficulty in being a whole person with the other, and with not sharing the common-sense (i.e., the community sense) way of experiencing oneself in the world." Or, put more simply, Laing also said, "Insanity—a perfectly rational adjustment to an insane world."

Laing's book, a sensation upon publication in Britain, was the first bulwark against David's fear of inheriting his family's insanity. The second was his ability to submerge his fear in his lyrics and thus disarm it.

But he was a winsome baby, with blue eyes, blond hair; his photogenic little face is wreathed in smiles, and the only intimation of the future captured in the earliest photographs of him when he was ten months old, is his charisma. In short, he is the epitome of a happy bouncing baby. But as always, with David, everything is not what it seems.

A quintessential moment in his childhood: "The very first memory I have is of being left in my pram in the hallway of 40 Stansfield Road, facing the stairs. It seemed to be a very, very long time and I was very scared of the stairs. They were dark and shadowy," he recalled.

TWO

STARBOY

When David was about three years old, his mother caught him putting on makeup for the first time. Not hers, but makeup belonging to the tenants in the apartment upstairs; lipstick, eyeliner, and face powder, which he daubed all over his little face.

"When I finally found him, he looked for all the world like a clown," Peggy Jones remembered in 1986.

Shocked and amused, she rounded on David and told him in no uncertain terms that he shouldn't use makeup. If that edict had been handed down to him by his father, whom he idolized, and whose calm temperament he appeared to have inherited, he might have accepted it. Instead, David said, somewhat reproachfully, "But *you* do, Mommy. . . ."

In the spirit of fairness, Peggy agreed, but then hammered home her point that makeup was definitely not for little boys. It doesn't take Sigmund Freud to analyze the ripple effect that Peggy's ruling had on the three-year-old David when he grew up, feeling as ambivalent about her as he did. . . .

However, only a few years later, Peggy did back down and encourage David's childish tendency toward theatricality, perhaps because

own passion for singing reflected in him, and perhaps also
intuited his nascent talent. After she sewed David a robe
s, and his father made him a crook for his role as a shep-
the nativity play put on by Stockwell Infants School, which he
first attended when he was almost five, Peggy observed how much he
loved dressing up. "It was then that we realized that there was something in David," she said.

That realization was compounded by David's reactions when he
listened to the radio, in particular to American entertainer Danny
Kaye's "Inchworm."

"He would tell everyone to be quiet and listen, and then fling
himself about to the music," said Peggy, adding, "In those days we
thought he might become a ballet dancer."

However, David's exhibitionist tendencies did not find favor with
his aunt, Peggy's sister Pat, who sniped, "He was a vain child, and
he always tried to look different." Clearly irritated by David's childish vanity, Pat targeted his hair: "He always liked to comb it his way,
forward, with a quiff by his ear. If you combed it, he always had to do
it again himself. He looked at himself a lot in the mirror," she said.

David may have looked in the mirror a good deal, but only child or
not, he wasn't in love with himself. Instead, his hero as a small boy was
his half brother, Terry. Space in Stansfield Road was at a premium, and
Terry and David shared the ground-floor bedroom. Consistently kind
and loving to David, Terry compensated in part for Peggy's coldness
and inability to express her feelings.

Nonetheless, David's pain at his mother's failure to demonstrate
maternal warmth toward him inevitably took its toll. "I was cut off
from my feelings since I was maybe four years old," he revealed.

Even then, as a very small child, David was already attracted to
the limelight, and the limelight, in turn, appeared to be attracted to
him. When David was five, his father had a brief stint working at Dr.
Barnardo's office in Harrogate, Yorkshire, and David and his mother
stayed there with him. Taken to an agricultural show that the new

Queen and Prince Philip were attending, David managed to elude the adults with him and end up right in front of the Queen, who looked down at him, and said, in the kindest tones possible, "Oh, hello, little boy," when a local photographer immortalized the moment.

Consequently, David made his debut in the media by appearing on the front page of a Yorkshire newspaper, which (according to him) ran the picture of him and the Queen, looking down at the little boy, slightly bemused. Sadly, that picture has proved to be untraceable.

And back in London, when his father took him to see a Christmas pantomime at a local theater, little David slipped out of his seat in the stalls and ran backstage, where he positioned himself behind the curtain, drinking in all the activities, watching the stagehands and, most important of all, the audience—and then, of course, there was the applause. Mesmerized by his first live show, David was equally enthralled by television. In early-fifties Britain, owning a television, even a black-and-white one, was a luxury, but John Jones, with his important job at Dr. Barnardo's, as well as his abiding interest in show business, didn't balk at getting one for the family. Almost immediately, it became clear to anyone visiting that David had commandeered the television; the choice of program the family watched depended on him.

Until 1955, when ITV—the Independent Television channel (which, unlike the BBC, transmitted commercials) was launched—British television consisted of just one channel, the BBC, which broadcast only in black-and-white, starting in the afternoon. With only one channel available, there were also very few programs, particularly for children. David's favorite show, *The Flowerpot Men*, a children's program featuring the puppets Bill and Ben, the flowerpot men, and their sidekick, Little Weed, was to become the highlight of his day.

He also developed a fascination with the science-fiction series *The Quatermass Experiment*, followed by *Quatermass II*, but which his parents decreed was far too adult for him, and forbade him to watch. Undeterred, while his parents watched the program, the resourceful David hid behind the sofa and watched wordlessly, most likely secure in the knowledge that even if his parents did discover him there, he would suffer few consequences.

He was undoubtedly his father's favorite, and poor Terry generally had to sit on the sidelines when John arrived home from work and recounted his day in detail to David, and just David. Even Peggy, as cold and remote as she was, nonetheless, favored David over Terry, as well.

When David was six, his parents sold 40 Stansfield Road, and after a year in Bickley, outside Bromley, in Kent (one of England's "home counties," with South London its northern border and the English Channel its southern one), moved to Clarence Road, Bromley. Finally, in 1955, David and his family moved to 4 Plaistow Grove, Sundridge Park, Bromley, a terraced house with four rooms, a kitchen, and an attic, where they would remain for fifteen years.

David's bedroom overlooked the back of a pub, but even though the noise of carousers could be deafening, especially on a Saturday night, he could always lose himself in his dreams, and in reading. "I was a kid that loved being in my room reading books and entertaining ideas. I lived a lot in my imagination. It was a real effort to become a social animal," he said.

When he was ten, he enrolled at Burnt Ash Primary School, in Bromley, joined the church choir, and was popular with classmates, who dubbed him a leader, not a follower, and he refused to take part in roughhousing with the other boys.

"I felt very protective toward him," said his neighbor, Barrie Jackson, who lived across the street from him. "He was very small and when all the boys gathered together . . . telling rude jokes, David sat in the corner mostly, not at all impressed."

Rude jokes might not have impressed him, but at the young age of ten, he was already aware of girls, and claims to have fallen head-over-heels in love with one of them. "She was the first girl in the class to get tits," he said succinctly: Clearly, he always remembered her—and them. "I went out with her years later, when we were about eighteen—but I fucked it up. On our second date, she found out that I'd been with another girl, I could not keep it zipped," he said.

Although David's thoughts may have started to stray toward girls when he was very young, those thoughts and anything else in his life were dwarfed by his rising passion for rock music. David was eight years old when Bill Haley & His Comets' "Rock Around the Clock" hit the top of the charts and swept Britain with its revolutionary sound, aimed exclusively at teenagers. And young as he was, David was set on fire by "Rock Around the Clock." As a result, he fixed his already considerable will on amassing a record collection. Fortunately for David, unlike most kids in Britain at that time, most of whom had to save up six shillings and eight pence in order to buy a 45 rpm of their chosen hit, he was in the privileged position of getting them for free, as his father, chief publicist at Dr. Barnardo's Homes, routinely brought him the latest records that well-wishers had donated to the charity.

And when Little Richard (complete with gold lamé suit, glittering from top to toe with gold jewelry) broke into the hit parade with "Tutti Frutti," David was in the seventh heaven when his father presented him with the disc. Little Richard became his idol, and David remained true to him and as an adult would always cite him as of one of his favorite artists.

Little Richard and the other American singers whose discs John Jones gave David also provided him with his first taste of America, that far-off wonderland that seemed a million miles away from Britain. "I had America mania when I was a kid," David recalled, adding, "but I loved all the things that America rejects; it was black music, it was the beatnik poets, it was all the stuff that I thought was the true rebellious subversive side. What makes America great is its pioneer, independent spirit."

From the time when he received his first Little Richard disc from his father, America became his fantasy home, and from then on, at night he would often slide under the covers and listen to the American Forces Network radio station playing the top ten records and broadcasting plays based in Springtown, USA. "I would put myself into the play in my head and be living there, and drink sodas and drive a Cadillac and play sax in Little Richard's band and all that," he once said.

Little Richard didn't just represent the advent of rock and roll in Britain, or personify America for David, but as Richard also played the sax, David, who never did anything by halves, resolved to follow in his footsteps and those of Terry, who had always been a huge jazz fan and favored iconic saxophonist John Coltrane.

Determined to learn to play the baritone sax, David was not a little disappointed when his father gave him a white acrylic Grafton alto—not baritone—sax. Still, undeterred, he picked up the local telephone directory, found a number, and called renowned baritone sax player Ronnie Ross, who had performed with Woody Herman and other jazz greats—and, better still, as far as David was concerned, lived just a few miles away from him in Orpington, Kent.

Following the Pied Piper of his sense of destiny, David wasn't in the least bit shy in asking Ronnie to give him lessons. As he remembered: "I said, 'Hi, my name is David Jones, and I'm twelve years old, and I want to play the saxophone. Can you give me lessons?'"

Ronnie was taken aback by the request—his first instinct was to refuse. But somehow or other, David convinced him to meet, and when they did, he won the sax player over. David's Saturday morning lessons with Ronnie, which cost him the princely sum of £2 a lesson, lasted for three months, during which Ronnie was impressed by his pupil's diligence, persistence, and talent. And David, returning the compliment, judged Ronnie to be cool, and always remembered him fondly.

"Much later on," David recalled, "when I was producing Lou Reed, we decided we needed a sax solo on the end of 'Walk on the Wild Side'; I got the agent to book Ronnie Ross."

After Ronnie flawlessly completed his solo in one take, David, who rarely forgets anyone who has treated him well in the past, smiled and said, "Thanks, Ron. Should I come over to your house on Saturday morning?"

"I don't fucking believe it!" Ronnie Ross exclaimed when he discovered that David Bowie had once been David Jones, his talented pupil, the twelve-year-old with so much love for the sax, and so much ambition.

From the first, John Jones, the former nightclub owner, who had once been married to Hilda, the Viennese Nightingale, was fascinated by show business, and passed his passion for greasepaint on to his son, David, as if by osmosis.

"Uncle John enjoyed all the celebrities and . . . that touch of glamour," David's cousin Kristina observed.

As soon as David was old enough, John Jones gave him an autograph book and did all he could to help him fill it with the signatures of stars. And as Dr. Barnardo's press officer in charge of recruiting celebrities to help raise funds for the charity and also to interact with the children in it, he also was able to afford David an early glimpse of stars and stardom. When David was still a child, his father took him to see entertainer Tommy Steele onstage and took him backstage to see Tommy afterward. Born Tommy Hicks, like David, south of the Thames, Tommy Steele would become somewhat of an inspiration for David, and the blueprint for a facet of his initial show business image: the cheeky, chappy Cockney singer, part Tony Newley, part Lionel Bart, essentially a slightly disreputable character of the ilk of the Artful Dodger, of *Oliver Twist* fame.

The outing to see Tommy Steele was one of many that John Jones arranged for David. "Uncle John wanted David to be a star," David's cousin Kristina noted.

"He thought his son was absolutely marvelous. He always said he was going to do something great and talked about him all the time," said John's secretary, Winifred Bunting.

In short, instead of having a classic show business mother, a Mama Rose, exhorting him to "sing out," David was blessed with having a show business *father*, one who would, through his teens, guide him, help him, and teach him the ways of self-promotion and image making.

As David dreamed of Little Richard and America, he dreamed from the perspective of postwar Britain, where he grew up. America became his Mecca, seemingly as far away from Bromley as Earth was from the moon. For although it may seem hard to believe today, Britain in the late fifties and on the cusp of the sixties still resembled a war zone. Food wasn't particularly plentiful, and steak was a rare treat in a country where food rationing only ended in 1954, so as a ration-book baby, David would have been fed dried eggs and other ersatz produce.

When it came to music, artists like Ernest Lough, Danny Kaye, and Petula Clark dominated the radio waves. Rock music wasn't played at all on the BBC Light Programme, and apart from the American Forces Network, only Radio Luxembourg aired rock music on Sunday nights at 11 P.M., when Pete Murray spun the top twenty records. It wasn't until the pirate station Radio Caroline was launched in March 1964 that rock really exploded in Britain.

By then, David, characteristically, was ahead of the game, having seen Little Richard perform onstage in person. Moreover, he was also well aware of the band opening for Little Richard, the Rolling Stones, and its lead singer, one Mick Jagger, who had an instant impact on him.

"I'll never forget this," David recalled. "Some bloke in the audience looked at Jagger and said, 'Get your hair cut!' And Mick said, 'What—and look like you?' It was so funny."

As David fell about in his seat, laughing at Mick's bon mot, he couldn't know that he had come face-to-face with the man who was destined to become his friend and his rival, and, now and again in certain arenas, including his choice of lovers, his doppelgänger. Only four years apart in age, and coming from the middle class, not the working class, as they so often projected themselves, David and Mick actually grew up less than ten miles apart—Mick in Dartford, Kent, and David in Bromley, Kent, and both of them had fathers of Yorkshire descent.

. . .

Away from his show business ambitions, David grew up in much the same way as many an English schoolboy of his time. At ten, he enrolled in the Wolf Cubs (the American equivalent of Cub Scouts) signing in with the 18th Bromley Cubs at St. Mary's Church, where he was to meet his lifelong friend George Underwood, a good-looking local boy, the son of a greengrocer, who also nurtured ambitions of becoming a singer. Tall, cool, and stylish, with his hair arranged in a hot and happening Elvis style, George had charm and self-confidence, and, his classmates agreed, was tipped to the top of any career he chose to follow.

With George and their fellow Wolf Cubs, David spent one vacation at a summer camp by the seaside in Bognor Regis, Sussex, and another with his parents and George staying in a caravan in Great Yarmouth, on the Norfolk coast. He also went on vacation to a family holiday resort called Pontins, in Camber Sands, where his next-door neighbor was the then well-known British comedian Arthur Haynes.

"I used to go over and try and get his autograph. I went over three mornings running and he told me to fuck off every day," David recalled in a conversation with Alexander McQueen, published in *Dazed and Confused*. "That was the first time I met a celebrity and I was so let down. I felt if that's what it's all about . . . they're just real people."

It was an early lesson he would never forget, and when he became famous, he would always endeavor to stay true to it and remain real.

At eleven, David took the 11-plus exam, which British children then took in the last year of primary education, and the result of which governed their admission to various types of secondary school, and won entrance to Bromley Technical High School. An above-average student, he still counted music as his main interest.

Meanwhile, John Jones continued to encourage David to raise his head above the parapet, and, young as he was, to make his mark on the world. When the thirteen-year-old David developed a passion for American football games, which he monitored religiously on the short-wave radio purchased for him by his father, John encouraged him to write to the U.S. Navy's London headquarters, detailing his passion for football and asking if they could send him some magazines about the sport.

David's letter, as masterminded by his father, elicited not only American football magazines but the gift of a helmet, a set of shoulder pads, and a football. Whereupon John immediately wrote a press release and sent it to a local newspaper, which duly published the story about young David Jones and his fascinating preoccupation with American football.

Fortunately for David, one of his other primary interests, art, was fueled by the head of Bromley Technical High School's art department, Owen Frampton, whose son, Peter Frampton, would find fame as a guitar player and go on the road with David on his Glass Spider tour, and also play on his *Never Let Me Down* record.

"David was quite unpredictable," Owen Frampton remembered. "He was completely misunderstood by most of my teaching colleagues, but in those days, cults were unfashionable and David, by the age of fourteen, was already a cult figure.

"I was thoroughly used to very individualistic pupils and was rarely surprised by anything that occurred. Even when David varied the color of his hair or cropped it short, or plucked his eyebrows, I accepted his actions as a means of projecting his personality, and of that he had plenty!"

By the age of thirteen, David was engaging, handsome, and charming, and girls were already flocking to him like homing pigeons. On a school trip to Spain, such was his sex appeal that afterward, in a school magazine article, he was dubbed "Don Jones, the lover, last seen pursued by thirteen senoritas."

Aware of his power over girls, even in his early teens, David manifested a streak of ruthlessness whenever a girl took his fancy, riding roughshod over any competition. When he double-dated, he thought nothing of jettisoning the particular girl he was with in favor of the girl who was with the other boy in the foursome, whereupon that girl immediately went off with him, lamblike, leaving the girl he was supposed to be dating feeling rejected, lost, and alone.

However, his propensity for assuming that any girl was fair game for him, no matter who else had already laid claim to her, led to one of the most seminal events in his life. In the spring of 1961, when David was just fourteen years old, a girl named Carol would inadvertently be the architect of the first tragedy of his life—one that would ultimately become the cornerstone of his image, and in many ways would lend him his unique trademark aura of dreamy otherworldliness.

His classmate and best friend George Underwood had fixed his amorous attentions on Carol, then still at school, and arranged a date with her. David, who had designs on Carol himself, told a massive lie to George, declaring that Carol wasn't interested in George and therefore wouldn't be going on the date he had set up with her.

When George learned the truth, outraged, he took a swing at David and caught him in the eye. David stumbled and fell down. At first, George assumed that he was kidding, as the punch hadn't been hard. But by some malevolent quirk of fate, his punch had caught David's left eye at an odd angle and scratched the eyeball, causing the muscle that contracts the iris to become paralyzed.

The end result was that, even to this day, David's left pupil remains permanently dilated, giving that eye the appearance of being a different color from his right eye. It also left him with damaged depth perception, so that when he drove, cars didn't come toward him but just appeared to get bigger.

His unmatched eyes also lent his gaze a hypnotic quality, and although it took him some time to adjust to the fact that his eyes were no longer identical, and he thought that he looked "weird," he admitted, "I quite enjoyed that as a badge of honor."

THREE

SELLING HIMSELF
TO THE WORLD

Although George Underwood's punch had damaged his vision irrevocably, David knew that his own nefarious plotting had provoked the attack, and that fact, coupled with his good nature, caused him to forgive George, and their friendship continued, undiminished. By the time he was fourteen, George, who was handsome and talented, had already sung with a local band, the Kon-rads, who played pop covers. A year later, in June 1962, David became the band's saxophonist, calling himself Dave Jay, and also provided some backing vocals, while George was lead vocalist.

Soon David was playing gigs with the band, sometimes as Davie Jones, other times as David Jay. His first public performance with the Kon-rads took place at his school's summer fete. He was nervous but the show went without a hitch, as the band performed covers of Little Richard's "Lucille," Sam Cooke's "Twistin' the Night Away," and more. Although David was the youngest member of the Kon-rads, his creativity was already aflame, and he was constantly suggesting new songs and new outfits for the band, as he pushed to be allowed to write songs for them.

After leaving school in July 1963, on August 29, David made his first professional studio recording, singing backup on the Kon-rads'

"I Never Dreamed," a landmark event in his young life. An assistant to Eric Easton, a manager of the Rolling Stones, had seen the band onstage and invited them to audition for the Decca Records label, who then invited them to make a studio recording of the song. Decca's reaction to it, however, was negative.

So David, never one to cling to the wreckage of a sinking ship, moved forward on his own, and with George Underwood formed the rhythm and blues band the King Bees, and set about trying to get financing for them. In April 1964, in an enterprising move, which more than likely was orchestrated by his father, David decided to make an appeal to one of Britain's richest men, washing machine tycoon John Bloom, and ask him to invest in him and the King Bees.

"His father probably helped him concoct the letter," John Bloom says today. "In it, he wrote, 'Brian Epstein's got the Beatles, you should have us. If you can sell my group the way you sell washing machines, you'll be on to a winner.'"

David's chutzpah impressed Bloom, who, as it happened, had met the Beatles, liked music, and said to himself, "This is just another young kid, but then what was Ringo?"

"So I thought I'd give David a chance, and called my friend Leslie Conn, who ran Doris Day's music publishing company and was also a talent scout for the Dick James Organization," John Bloom said.

One of the few music industry figures instrumental in David's early career who wasn't gay, Leslie Conn, who also managed a young singer from Stamford Hill named Marc Feld (later Marc Bolan), invited David to audition at his Marble Arch, London, apartment. Upon hearing David perform, Conn decided that the teen had potential and signed David and the King Bees on the spot.

"He was as broke as any of the kids in those days, but he walked around like a star and was prepared to work for success," Leslie Conn said, years later.

Unfortunately for David and the King Bees, the first gig that Leslie booked for them was singing at John Bloom's wedding anniversary party.

As John remembers, "I'd invited Roger Moore, Vera Lynn, Adam Faith, Shirley Bassey, and all the top London show business impresarios to the party, and invited David and the King Bees to perform as I thought it would be good for him. David took the stage wearing blue jeans and a white T-shirt. His hair was relatively short and dyed a cornflower blond with a Tony Curtis quiff. He looked like a young waiter who had blown his first check on a bad haircut," John Bloom said.

The party was held at the Jack of Clubs nightclub in London's Berwick Street, and when David and the King Bees started their set, the guests were in the middle of eating and ignored them, chatting away to each other instead.

"I did not realize how tiny Bowie was until I saw him on the stage that night. The thing I noticed was that he had really small feet. He was very pleasant but subdued: He seemed tired, even a bit nervous," John Bloom said. "But most of the people in the room were in their sixties, and they didn't understand or like the kind of songs David and the King Bees were singing. I wanted the party to be special for my wife, and I was worried that it would turn out to be a disaster.

"So I went up to Billy Wright, who captained England at football, and before David and the King Bees launched into their next song, on my request, Billy went up to them and told them nicely to pack up. I was very sorry, and I gave Leslie £100 for David and the King Bees on the spot. Then Vera Lynn came on next and sang, 'The White Cliffs of Dover,' " John Bloom said.

Fortunately, David's failure to wow the establishment at John Bloom's anniversary party didn't sour his new manager, Leslie Conn, on him at all. Despite the fiasco of his anniversary party, John Bloom also somehow still retained his belief in David as well.

He remembered, "I sent Leslie another £400 for David and the King Bees, and the next thing I knew, Leslie called me and told me he had got a record deal for them."

That record deal was with Decca Records, and, on June 5, 1964, David's first record, "Liza Jane," an arrangement of the old standard

"Li'l Liza Jane," produced by Leslie Conn, was released as a single. By then, David had left Bromley Technical High School and was working in an advertising agency called Nevin D. Hirst on London's tony Bond Street, where he was employed as a junior visualizer (now known as a storyboard artist, a freelance artist who sketches out commercials and advertisements at the behest of the company's art director.)

David worked in advertising for a year and along the way was able to glean the basics of advertising and marketing, drinking in the ethos of the industry as epitomized by the words of the adman in Hitchcock's *North by Northwest*: "In the world of advertising there's no such thing as a lie, there's only the expedient exaggeration."

All of this would color his future dealings with the media, so that Ken Scott, who produced several of his early albums, would go on to observe, "You never quite knew when he was being honest. It's not something I realized at the time, but seeing various explanations in interviews of something I'd known about, I'd think, 'Ah, so that's what you're like.'"

David's schooling in the mores of advertising, marketing, and self-salesmanship would color his future pronouncements (most likely his slick explanation of the choice of Bowie as a last name), which meant they were not always strictly accurate. At the time, though, he kicked against the conventionality of his working life.

"He only took the job for his father's sake. His father thought that all this business with groups and music could well be a passing fad and that, at least if he spent a year or so at work, it would give him some stable grounding to fall back on," his mother, Peggy, remembered, adding: "So David went to work there, though not without protest. I can remember him coming home and moaning about his 'blooming job.'"

On Saturdays, he had a morning job at a local record store, Vic Furlong's, but it didn't last long—Furlong fired him because he considered him to be a dreamer who talked too much. Nonetheless, music remained his goal, his raison d'être. "I never, ever thought about the big house or the big car or anything like that. It never entered my mind," he once said of his youthful ambitions.

In his spare time, he was single-minded about his music, so dedicated and determined that he ran the risk of alienating his peers. "What made him different was he would pass a party or anything up if there was something he needed to do for his music," observed one of his contemporaries.

Through Leslie Conn's persistence, "Liza Jane" was played on the BBC's *Juke Box Jury*, in which a panel of four celebrities listened to a song—while the artist who recorded it was hidden behind a screen—then voted on whether it was a hit or a miss.

Sadly for David and the King Bees, the *Juke Box Jury* members' vote was a resounding "miss"—but David wasn't about to give up yet. Nor was his father, John Jones, who resorted to contacting former Dr. Barnardo's boy Leslie Thomas, then a music columnist for the *London Evening News*.

Leslie Thomas recalled, "John called and told me that his son was now a pop singer who had just produced his first record. 'I think it's terrible,' John said. Then he added, 'But would you listen to it?'"

Leslie obliged. He wasn't particularly impressed, but wrote a small column item plugging David and "Liza Jane." Still, his efforts came to no avail, and the record sank without a trace. By the summer of 1964, the King Bees were history for David, as he had moved on to become the lead singer and tenor sax player in the Manish Boys, a rhythm and blues band that mostly performed their own material and was based in Maidstone, Kent.

David disliked the band because it was too big; he also hated living in Maidstone, and when he cut a record with the band—the blues song "I Pity the Fool" and. on the B side, the first song he had ever written and composed, "Take My Tip," a jazz-based song for EMI's Parlophone—he was furious when the band refused to give him an individual credit on the label.

He might have been part of the Manish Boys, but inside, David had always seen himself as a star who stood on his own. So he was heartened when his father came up with a masterstroke—one that would solely focus on David, and him alone. John Jones swung into action and, applying his well-honed PR skills, along with David's input, concocted a cause designed to thrust David into the limelight and—John hoped—win him some notice. Along the way, of course, David had the opportunity to observe and study his father's PR techniques, which he would one day adopt.

Consequently, in November 1964, at John Jones's behest, the ever-obliging Leslie Thomas published an article in the *Evening News* titled, "For Those Beyond the Fringe," announcing the formation of a new society, the International League for the Preservation of Animal Filament, whose founder and president was none other than David Jones.

On November 12, 1964, in his second TV appearance after his brief moment on *Juke Box Jury*, David appeared on the prime-time BBC program *Tonight*, pontificated with polish and great self-possession about the trials and tribulations of sporting long hair, and announced, "You've no idea the indignities you have to suffer just because you've got long hair." After the *Evening News* feature, in the interest of clarity, the name of the International League for the Preservation of Animal Filament was changed to the much more media-friendly Society for the Prevention of Cruelty to Long-Haired Men.

Declaring that he was targeting P. J. Proby and the Beatles as potential members, David also cited the Rolling Stones as prime candidates to join the society. In mentioning the Rolling Stones, David may well have left a clue as to the whole genesis of the Prevention of Cruelty to Long-Haired Men Society: his memory of seeing Mick open for Little Richard, then being taunted for his long hair and cleverly defending himself, something that David said he would never forget, and most likely had imparted to his father in detail.

Following in Mick's footsteps—something he would at times do in the future—and determined to expose the outrages inflicted on him and others with long hair, David, already a consummate performer, laid on the drama as heavily as possible. "Dozens of times I've been politely told to clear out of the lounge bar at public houses. Everybody makes jokes about you on a bus, and if you go past navvies digging in the road, it's murder," he said. Then he delivered a final punch line, "We've had comments like 'Darling' and 'Can I carry your handbag?' thrown at us. And it has to stop!"

The following year, when David and the Manish Boys were scheduled to appear on the BBC's *Gadzooks! It's All Happening*, producer Barrie Langford took one look at David and demanded he cut his hair. Seizing the moment for its PR value, David flatly refused, and Leslie Conn promptly arranged for a few fans to demonstrate outside the BBC Television Centre, waving banners that read "Be Fair to Long Hair."

Although the protest didn't capture the interest of the nation, the BBC relented and booked David and the Manish Boys on the condition that if there were any protests from the public, the group's fee for the show would be donated to charity. None materialized. And that was the end of the Society for the Prevention of Cruelty to Long-Haired Men. But it had served its purpose by putting David in the spotlight once more, and Leslie Conn, at least, felt that he was fulfilling his obligations to him.

In dealing with David, he had always done everything by the book, driving to Plaistow Grove in his Jaguar to meet with Peggy and John before signing David to his management contract. There, he found Peggy to be "narcissistic"; in contrast, he judged John Jones to be a concerned father, and a conservative businessman.

Toward the end of 1964, in an act billed as Davie Jones and the Manish Boys, David made his first appearance at the fabled Marquee Club in Soho, London. Clad in a Robin Hood–style shirt with billowing sleeves, jeans, knee-length fringed suede boots, his hair long and flowing, he was handsome and dashing, and instantly captivated fourteen-year-old Dana Gillespie, who was in the audience.

"I was a very forward fourteen-year-old girl," Dana remembered. "David looked great, and after the show, when I was in the bathroom, brushing my hair, which was waist-length and dyed blond, he came up behind me, took the brush from my hand, and carried on brushing it. And when he asked if he could take me home that night, I said that he absolutely could. So I took him home to my house. I had a single bed and I guess we fiddled about. It was exploration sex.

"In the morning, I introduced him to my father. Afterwards, he said he didn't know whether David was a man or a woman until he actually opened his mouth."

From then on, whenever possible, David would pick Dana up from school.

"It's often said that he carried my ballet shoes, which sounds kind of romantic, but he actually did sometimes, if I was carrying a whole load of things," Dana said, then recalled her first visit to David's parents' home. "I'll never forget it. His parents were sitting and staring at a black-and-white TV. We sat down and had tuna-fish sandwiches. It was a cozy little room, but there didn't seem to be any love in the house, and I realized that David didn't love his parents like I loved mine," Dana said. "It was a very depressing experience. When his parents went out of the room, David turned to me and said, 'Whatever it takes, I am going to get out of here.'"

Unaware of David's deep discontent, his father, concerned about his son's lack of success in the music business and his struggles to keep afloat financially, remained the archetypical stage father, watched over David's career diligently, dealt with all his correspondence, and even handled his bank account. John Jones was tirelessly supportive of David's career and resolutely uncritical of him, to his face, at least. Forever afterward, on a professional level, David would automatically expect the same unconditional love and support from anyone who worked closely with him.

Even though David was still living at home with his parents in Bromley, he was broke and Leslie Conn did his best to help him get by, even giving him a job repainting his Denmark Street offices, along with his other protégé, fellow musician Marc Bolan. Bolan, then still Feld, was almost seventeen; David, then still David Jones, was almost eighteen; and both of them were struggling musicians, determined to make it to the top.

"They were very similar, in so many ways. They could have been brothers," Keith Altham, who was publicist for both of them at different times through the years, said.

"Both Marc and I were out of work, and we met when we poured into the manager's office to whitewash the walls," David remembered, adding, "So there's me and this mod whitewashing the office and he goes, 'Where'd you get your shirt?'"

And so. almost immediately, they launched into a conversation about clothes and then and there bonded. Both David and Marc were good-looking and exuded charm, ambition, but from the first, there was a certain amount of rivalry between them, as each began to outdo the other with boasts of the golden professional future he assumed was in front of him. "I'm gonna be a singer and I'm gonna be so big you're not gonna believe it, man," Marc said.

David attempted to counter Marc's boasts, but Marc wasn't about to yield to him, either in ambition or in talent.

As Brooklyn-born producer Tony Visconti, who had originally been an acclaimed guitarist, then moved to London in 1968 and went on to produce both David and Marc, put it years later, "Marc was in rivalry with everybody. He simply couldn't stand attention going in anyone else's direction. He was a total megalomaniac, God bless him. David, on the other hand, is a very gregarious, open-minded person, and apart from a normal, healthy type of rivalry, he was never obsessed with Bolan."

In the first innocent few days after their initial meeting, David and Marc painted Leslie's office together, taking breaks in a nearby café, La Gioconda, in bustling Denmark Street, London's Tin Pan Alley, a street occupied almost exclusively by music publishers, agents, record studios, and a hangout for musicians, unemployed or otherwise. The street was not only the epicenter of Britain's music business but was adjoined Soho, the city's red-light district, which lent the area a patina of illicit sin, reinforced by a plethora of strip clubs and sex-magazine emporiums. Nonetheless, the music business dominated, with Ronnie Scott's Jazz Club, the 100 Club, 2i's Coffee Bar, and, of course, the Marquee, a musician's Mecca.

Four record labels ruled the roost in Britain at that time: EMI, Decca, Philips, and Pye. Beatlemania was rife, with the Beatles managed by Brian Epstein, the prototype for London's gay music managers like Kit Lambert, who managed the Who. That David was so determined to make it as a rock star in the London of those days was in part due to the Cinderella aura of the music business in that era. For while every American boy grew up believing he could one day become president and every American girl that she could make it as a Hollywood star, the British equivalent was to dream of becoming a rock star.

On the threshold of Swinging London, as *Time* termed it—when youth, fashion, photography, and pop converged in a highly colored Niagara of possibility, Carnaby Street was the heartbeat of the sixties scene, dominated by the Beatles, the Stones, the Who, and the Kinks, by Twiggy, David Bailey, Mary Quant, Jean Shrimpton, Vidal Sassoon, and Barbara Hulanicki, founder of the iconic Biba store, where David would eventually shop—becoming a rock star appeared to be an attainable dream for David and for Marc.

In May 1965, now jaded with the Manish Boys, when David heard through the grapevine that the rock-and-roll band the Lower Third was looking for a new member, he auditioned for them and beat Steve Marriott, (who went on to front the Small Faces) and was invited to join the group, which consisted of Dennis Taylor on lead guitar, bass guitarist Graham Evans, and, soon after David joined as lead singer, drummer Phil Lancaster.

Before Phil was hired, David was enlisted to vet him over coffee at La Gioconda. Phil remembered his first impression of David: "He was quite striking because he was just skin and bones. He had shoulder-length hair, which had been bleached but had grown out. We had a good chat over a cup of tea. We talked about music. He even did a Bob Dylan impression for me—and it was very good."

David warmed to Phil immediately and told him he'd made the band without even having to audition for it. For the next seven months, David and Phil worked together closely.

"The Lower Third had this ambulance we used to drive around in, which was great. It still had the bell and sign. Me and Dave used to sit in the back together and think of wacky ideas to get us noticed more," Phil said. "David suddenly said: 'How about wearing makeup?' I thought he meant clown makeup so I was well up for it. But when I shouted it over to Graham in the front of the ambulance he wasn't impressed. He told us, 'Not fucking likely.'"

Despite what would soon transpire, Phil had no doubts whatsoever that David was heterosexual. "We were playing in a club, and a waitress offered us a night's accommodation. I was in the same room as David and the waitress, who were in bed together. I knew from the noises that he was having sex with her. He wasn't shy about doing it in the same room as me," Phil Lancaster said.

After David and the Lower Third secured a record deal with Parlophone and recorded two tracks, "You've Got a Habit of Leaving" and "Baby Loves That Way," David had a chance meeting with Ralph Horton, a former booker for the King Agency, then a roadie/driver for the Moody Blues. Ralph pitched himself to David as a manager. Impressed, David, in the kindest way possible, broke the news to the long-suffering Leslie Conn that he was leaving him and hiring another manager instead.

Aware that he had probably taken David as far as he could, Conn graciously stepped aside, and in July 1965, Ralph Horton took over as the manager of the Lower Third. In his late twenties, Horton was relatively open about being gay—a courageous stance in the midsixties, when the Sexual Offences Act, which decreed homosexuality to be a criminal offense, was still the law in Britain, and would only be repealed in July 1967.

"Ralph was babyish, chubby-cheeked, and borrowed money so he could spend it on promoting David and the band," said Kenny Bell, who worked for the Terry King Agency and shared an apartment with Ralph Horton in Warwick Square.

At first, as he booked the Lower Third for nationwide gigs, Horton's sexuality didn't come into play in terms of his style of management. But after a few months, it became clear that his interest in David was more than professional.

"Dave became a little more aloof and would go off with Ralph quite a lot. He stopped helping us load up the gear onto the van to and from gigs," Phil Lancaster remembered, adding, "It had always been a joint effort, but now he'd just sit down and watch. Instead of coming back from gigs in the ambulance with us, he would go back with Ralph in his Jaguar."

"Ralph Horton was uptight and tense. He was probably in love with David. He fancied David," said John Hutchinson, who played with David in the Buzz, the band he formed after the Lower Third.

"David certainly slept with Ralph. He often stayed over at Warwick Square, where there were only two bedrooms. I slept in one and Ralph and David slept in the other one," Kenny Bell said.

Clearly enthralled by David, Ralph openly favored him over the rest of the band, which, at the end of September 1965, he would rename Davie Jones and the Lower Third, in the process teaching David exactly how far his own sexual charisma could carry him in the London music scene.

As Derek Boyes, who went on to join the Buzz with David, put it, "In the business, agents, impresarios, ninety-nine percent of them were bent anyway. There was no point in getting uptight."

David had never been uptight about sex, and now he was about to exploit his lack of inhibition to his full advantage. After all, he had spent more than three years fighting to make it in the business, but to no avail. Ralph Horton's passion for him had finally shown him the way.

Toward the end of the summer of 1965, Ralph Horton, then managing seventeen-year-old Davie Jones (as David was then calling himself), was broke. Desperate for financing, he set about searching for a business partner to help him manage Davie Jones and the Lower Third. Consequently, Ralph invited rock manager Simon Napier-Bell for a meeting at his home/office, a rented basement apartment at 79A Warwick Square, intending to offer him a fifty-fifty deal if he agreed to become Davie Jones and the Lower Third's comanager.

At the time, Napier-Bell, then managing the Yardbirds, and who went on to manage Marc Bolan and, much later on, Wham!, was far more of an established manager than Ralph Horton. Hence Ralph's invitation to Simon, with whom he wanted to split his representation of David, in exchange for an injection of cash.

Today, Simon Napier-Bell still remembers every detail of what happened when he arrived at Horton's apartment to find him and David waiting there for him. "Davie sat demurely in a corner," Simon remembered. Then, without so much as introducing Simon to David, Ralph took him aside and, according to Napier-Bell, without making any bones about it, put forward the following proposition to him: "[Horton] said that if I were to agree to come in on the management, he would allow me to have sex with his young protégé.

"I had no idea whether [David] was in on the proposition or not," Napier-Bell said afterward.

Given that David was in the room at the time Ralph Horton made the proposal to Napier-Bell, it seems highly unlikely that Horton would have offered him sex with David unless David had agreed in advance to honor that offer. It would seem that, at seventeen, David Jones had traveled inordinately far from the tousle-haired, winsome, saxophone-playing thirteen-year-old boy who was already his school's Casanova, and whose desires had in those early days appeared to be directed exclusively at girls, and only girls.

Then again, according to Alan Dodds, who was the guitarist in the Kon-rads and wrote the lyrics to "I Never Dreamed," when David was sixteen, "he was telling everyone that he was bisexual."

FOUR

SEXUAL LABYRINTH

After Simon Napier-Bell rejected Ralph Horton's proposal, Horton turned to another manager for help. His name was Ken Pitt; he was in his early forties and had worked as a publicist for Frank Sinatra, and with Liberace, Vic Damone, Mel Tormé, and none other than Anthony Newley, David's then idol.

But at that stage, Pitt simply wasn't interested in signing any clients and refused Horton's request. As a parting shot, he advised Horton to change David's name, as another Davy Jones, an actor who had already won acclaim as the Artful Dodger in the theatrical production of Lionel Bart's *Oliver*, and who'd found fame as one of the Monkees, was doing extremely well, and he felt that there could be confusion between them.

Ralph Horton took Ken's suggestion to heart. "He came into the Roebuck Pub on Tottenham Court Road (where we always rehearsed) one night and told David that he should change his name and we should change ours, and that we all should go away and come up with a new name," Phil Lancaster said. "David went away and the next morning came back and told us his new name was 'Bowie,' but didn't say anything about it being do with a knife."

Given that David still lived at home, it was certain that he had consulted his father, who micromanaged every detail of his career, about the choice of his new name. And, as it happened, at Dr. Barnardo's, where John had worked for many years, one of the most important supporters was named Norman Bowie, a war hero who'd won the Burma Star and was a well-established businessman as a trustee of the charity and later became head of Barnardo's council. So it's highly likely that David's father may well have suggested the name Bowie and that David, who implicitly trusted his father's instincts, instantly took up his suggestion.

"I came home to Warwick Square early one afternoon, and David and Ralph were in the living room," Kenny Bell recalled. "And David said, 'Oh, I've got myself a new name.' I said, 'What is it, then?' And David said, 'I'm calling myself 'David Bowie.' So I said, 'That's a stupid name. That's a knife. The Bowie knife. It's American.'

"David didn't say 'I know.' He just shrugged and said, 'Well, I'm going to call myself 'Bowie' anyway. . . .' I was the one who, after he'd changed his name to Bowie, first told David about the Bowie knife," Kenny Bell said.

Naturally, it would follow that either Ralph or Ken Pitt or David's father would likely seize on Kenny Bell's explanation of the name Bowie, and decide that claiming David's last name had been inspired by a knife, rather than by an executive of a children's charity, would play far better in the media.

So David soldiered on under the name Bowie, and "Can't Help Thinking About Me," a rock song that he wrote, then recorded with the Lower Third, was released. But after Ralph Horton refused to pay the other members of the band for a gig, telling them that he'd had to recoup his expenses, all the Lower Third, except for David, refused to play anymore. The end result was that the Lower Third, who were also annoyed that David had higher billing than they did, finally split up in January 1966.

Almost immediately afterward, David formed a new group, the

Buzz, along with Derek "Dek" Fearnley, Derek Boyes, and John Eager. At Ralph Horton's suggestion, they were all transformed into new-look mods, and although the change in their image was radical, there was very little tension between Ralph and the members of the Buzz.

"Ralph could be very funny, the way he took people off and minced around," Boyes recalled before he passed away in 2011.

Ralph was less than amused, or amusing, though, when he learned of David's romantic involvement with Dana Gillespie, whose career David was trying to help by teaching her guitar chords and arranging for her to make a guest appearance on the TV show *Ready Steady Go!*

Using an alibi that would pay dividends for David in the future, whenever he intended to spend time with Dana, he told Ralph that he was going to visit his parents in Bromley. When Ralph discovered the truth, he hit the roof, claiming that Dana was a bad influence on him, but David carried on seeing her regardless.

At the same time, now that David was in full flower of his good looks, according to Leni and Peter Gillman's seminal 1986 book, *Alias David Bowie*, he had become a magnet for gay men and was surrounded by a coterie of male admirers, all of whom clustered around him in Horton's basement. "One suitor was an actor who plied David with barley wines at the Marquis of Westminster in Warwick Square; another was a journalist who managed to insert regular items about David in *Melody Maker*; a third was a commercial radio disc-jockey who played his records with embarrassing frequency," Leni and Peter Gillman said.

Lionel Bart, creator of *Oliver* and a musical giant, was also charmed by David, sending him congratulations on his record releases, making it clear that he was firmly on his team, and appearing so regularly in his company that Paul Trynka, author of *Starman*, described Bart as being often seen "with a rent boy in tow, or snuggled up to David."

Whether or not David made himself sexually available to Lionel so that he could take advantage of having such a famous gay man as his admirer, or how far he allowed Lionel to go with him sexually, is not on record. Clearly, though, the two were good friends, so much so that in April 1973, when Lionel was in a car accident, according to Bart's biographer, Caroline Stafford, David went to visit him in the hospital.

"David was exactly Lionel's type. He was beautiful and not too young," Stafford said.

But if David had traded on the rich, famous, and influential Lionel Bart's inclination toward beautiful boys in the music business, he may not have been totally alone. For none other than Mick Jagger also seems to have formed a close relationship with Bart on the way to rock superstardom. As Mick's biographer Philip Norman confirmed, in 1965, when Mick found himself homeless for a while, Lionel invited him to stay at his apartment in Bryanston Mews, Marylebone, and Chrissie Shrimpton, Mick's then girlfriend, moved in with him.

"Chrissie was more worried by other new friends that Mick was attracting," Philip Norman wrote, adding, "Lionel Bart, whose roof they now shared, was ostentatiously gay and, despite the draconian antihomosexuality laws, made no secret of his florid and expansive sex life. Prominently displayed throughout the flat were tubes of KY lubricating jelly, which Chrissie in her innocence mistook for hair gel."

According to Norman, Bart was also extremely close to Lord Montagu of Beaulieu, who had been jailed for what were then known as "homosexual offenses," but was released after a year. As Chrissie Shrimpton confided to Norman, "He was always trying to persuade Mick to go and stay at his country house. I objected to all these people being after my boyfriend. . . ."

Whatever the cause, as Norman put it, "Mick was constantly simmering. It was not only the habit of addressing males and females alike as 'darling' or 'dear' and his fascination with celebrity mega-queens like Lionel Bart."

Like Mick, David was adept at playing London's gay elite. Peter and Leni Gillman, who interviewed Dek Fearnley before he passed away in 2008, tell of a night when a bemused Horton received a call informing him that he was about to receive a visit from an "international recording star." Whereupon a chauffeur appeared at the door, made the announcement, "Miss Garland is here," and there was David, in full drag, wearing makeup and a ball gown.

But though Horton and Bowie shared a sense of fun, as well as a passion for show business, and though he was dedicated to David, Ralph was small-time, and David knew it. Fortunately for David, both his luck and his management were about to change. On the afternoon of Sunday, April 17, 1966, Ken Pitt attended the second of David's "Bowie Showboat" shows at the Marquee and virtually fell in love with him at first sight.

His book, *The Pitt Report*, paints a portrait of David so homoerotic in quality that there can be little doubt about the true nature of Ken's feelings for him. "I could see that he was wearing a biscuit-colored, hand-knitted sweater, round-necked and buttoned at one shoulder, its skin-tightness accentuating his slim frame. . . . He oozed confidence and was in total command of himself, his band and his audience. His burgeoning charisma was undeniable," Ken Pitt wrote.

Ken was undoubtedly smitten and, without any further preamble, made a deal with Ralph Horton to manage David jointly with him.

Though David was now catnip for a variety of powerful, often older, gay men, his allure for women hadn't diminished a jot. One afternoon, over coffee at La Gioconda, David chanced to meet the then notorious Mandy Rice-Davies, the glittering blonde who, with Christine Keeler, had been at the heart of the John Profumo/Stephen Ward scandal, which two years before had brought down the Conservative government.

"I thought he was really interesting and good-looking, and his eyes fascinated me. I think he was quite sexy, and if I hadn't been married at the time, I may well have fallen for David," Rice-Davies says today.

At La Gioconda to scout for an entertainer to perform at Mandy's, her newly opened nightclub in Tel Aviv, Mandy invited David to lunch and promptly offered him the job of singing in the club. "He was very keen on going to Israel," Mandy remembered. "He was a very self-confident young man. And he asked me a question I've never forgotten: 'What is the best thing about being famous?' I said, 'You never have to buy your own lunch.'"

Mandy came back to the Gioconda two weeks later, ready to make the arrangements for David's Tel Aviv gig, only for him to tell her really apologetically, "I'd love to come, but I can't. I've got a recording contract."

Now jointly managed by Ken Pitt and Ralph Horton, David had also formed a friendship with singer-songwriter Jonathan King, who had a major hit with "Everyone's Gone to the Moon" when he was eighteen years old, and also had a regular column in *Disc and Music Echo.*

"I loved 'Can't Help Thinking About Me,' and gave it the whole lead of my column and said it was fabulous," Jonathan recalled. "That thrilled David, and he immediately got in touch with me and came round to my place. He was desperately trying to be a star, but he wasn't. I thought he was very sweet, and I think he fancied me. But I didn't fancy him because of his different colored eyes.

"It never got to a point where I rejected him, I just had the vibes that if I had wanted to . . . David was bisexual, but was predominantly heterosexual. Looking back now, I've got the feeling that his gay experiences were part of wanting to get on," Jonathan said.

By the end of the year, David had ended his relationship with the Buzz and, along the way, had signed with Deram Records, a subsidiary of Decca, to cut "Rubber Band"/"The London Boys," then, utterly inexplicably, "The Laughing Gnome." The last was a novelty song that he wrote after performing in a venue in Eastbourne on the south coast of England and, afterward, going back to the house of five-foot-one Malcolm Diplock, where the pair spent the evening laughing uproariously together. Hence, "The Laughing Gnome."

The record was quirky and would haunt David throughout his career, much to his distaste. As British DJ Tony Blackburn revealed to

Dylan Jones, author of *When Ziggy Played Guitar*, he once told David he loved "The Laughing Gnome." "And he turned and very gently said, 'Oh, that's not me,' and walked off," Tony Blackburn said.

But despite David's disdain for "The Laughing Gnome," one of the most fascinating elements of the recording is that on it, David's voice is almost an exact voiceprint of Anthony Newley's. His fascination with Newley was born when, at the impressionable age of fourteen, he saw him onstage in *Stop the World, I Want to Get Off*, which Newley wrote and performed. A singer, actor, songwriter, mime, and dancer, Newley was the prototype of the star David longed to become. "I was Tony Newley for a year," he once admitted.

However, David being David, he flew too close to the flame by aping Newley's voice with such unerring accuracy that, at the time, Newley was said to be genuinely annoyed by his uncanny imitation of him, particularly in June 1967, when David's first solo album, *David Bowie* (for which he wrote and sang all fourteen tracks) was released, still with a big dollop of Newley about it.

"I think Bowie liked that irreverent thing, and his delivery was very similar to mine, that Cockney thing," Newley observed long afterward, then hastily added, "but then he went on to become madly elegant and very, very original."

Ten days after David's first album was released, he made the monumental decision to move out of his parents' home and into Ken Pitt's book-filled fourth-floor apartment on London's elegant Manchester Square. There, David was to be exposed to one of the seminal musical influences of his career: the Velvet Underground. It all began when Pitt went to America in November 1966 and returned with a demo of the Velvet Underground's first album and gave it to David, telling him it was hideous but probably the kind of thing David would like.

"I adored it," David said, "and—this is a funny thing—started doing a couple of the songs from the album onstage. So I was actually doing Velvet Underground covers before the album came out."

By now, Ralph Horton was completely out of the picture, and Ken Pitt was managing David on his own—and acting as his cultural mentor, as well, although David's knowledge of literature was already well developed. In fact, the first time David walked into Ken's apartment, he headed straight to the bookcase and ran his fingers over the spines of the works of Oscar Wilde and Antoine de Saint-Exupéry, thus demonstrating that he was already well acquainted with both authors. Pitt was instantly impressed by his erudition.

"He was a great lodger, never a problem, except for the joss sticks," Ken Pitt said, doing his best to obscure the truth about the full extent of his relationship with David.

For David was far more than a lodger, far more than a client to him. Journalist George Tremlett, author of *David Bowie: Living on the Brink*, whose father was one of Ken Pitt's friends for many years, observed David and Ken together at the Manchester Square apartment. "They probably did have a sexual relationship—but one that was never as important to Bowie as it was to Pitt," George said, adding, "I believe Pitt genuinely loved him, but Bowie was always a chancer—and within days of him moving into the apartment Pitt was left in no doubt that Bowie would happily sleep with women as well."

However, Peter and Leni Gillman, who interviewed Ken Pitt, are adamant that Ken was never able to fully consummate his passion for David. Whatever the truth, he was patently in love with David, and, despite his awareness that David swung both ways, he clearly adored the fact that once David moved into his apartment, he habitually walked around stark naked.

"David derived comfort from leaving off his clothes, sometimes sitting cross-legged on the floor encircled by blaring hi-fi speakers," Ken began somewhat primly in his book, but then went on to salivate, "sometimes loping around the flat, naked, his long, weighty penis swaying from side to side like the pendulum of a grandfather clock."

Far from being shy about his considerable genetic gifts, David happily flaunted his endowment as often as possible, and both onstage and off would take to wearing the tightest trousers possible in order to display it. As well-respected writer, Lisa Robinson, commented in the magazine *After Dark*, "More unearthly than his face is his crotch, which seems unusually large, almost inhuman."

In her second autobiography, *Backstage Passes*, Angela Bowie labeled David's endowment "the Lance of Love," but as far as he was concerned, love had very little to do with it. In those early years of clawing his way up the ladder to success, his impressive endowment would prove to be one of his most valuable assets when it came to dealing with a series of gay men in the music business, all of whom would be riveted by him and his vast advantage in life. Moreover, he was free and open with his charm and his ability to seduce, whether the target was female or male.

Director Michael Armstrong was a twenty-one-year-old former Royal Academy of Dramatic Art student turned director, about to cast a film, *A Floral Tale*, when he spotted David's album in a shopwindow and was struck by something about his face on the cover. He immediately purchased the record, decided then and there to work with David, and so contacted Ken Pitt.

"I spent two or three hours with David and Ken, and I fell in love with David. He was absolutely amazing and did a wonderful Elvis impersonation," Armstrong said.

Although Michael's film didn't get made, he arranged for David, on November 19, 1967, to sing at the Stage Ball in aid of the Catholic Stage Guild. The event was held at the Dorchester Hotel. "He was fabulous, but the audience didn't know what to make of him, so he died onstage. He was so upset that he ran out in tears," Armstrong remembered.

Nonetheless, there was a positive outcome of David's Dorchester Hotel performance after all, as celebrity female impersonator Danny La Rue was in the audience, became enthralled with him, and afterward wrote him a long letter proposing a collaboration of some sort. Whether or not David actually ever met Danny La Rue is not on record, but if he did, there is no doubt whatsoever about David's approach to Danny.

"David was a terrible flirt in the way in which he dealt with you," Armstrong said. "He did that with me. He was flirtatious, not in a sexual way, but in a kind of come-on way. It was part of him.

"He always seemed to be playing a cat-and-mouse game with you. He flirted, he really did. I said that he would either be a gigantic star or make a lot of money in the Piccadilly men's loo," said Michael Armstrong, who went on to cast David in *The Image*, a highly praised short film that he directed and shot in June 1967.

One of the by-products of David's appearance in *The Image* was that it helped him get a highly prized equity card, allowing him to work in British theater, although producers weren't lining up to hire him.

"Ken tried everything to get David's career going, but nobody seemed to want to know about him, and it was extraordinary to me, as his star quality was so obvious," Michael Armstrong said.

As Ken struggled to promote David's career and garner him success at last, he palpitated with an altruistic, almost aesthetic adoration of David, particularly when David serenaded him with his guitar, then spent hours writing reams of lyrics, and, when he had finished, handed them to him, desperate for his opinion. Ken constantly assured David that he was destined to be a star, and together they spent hours contemplating the prospect, imagining it, tasting it.

In anticipation of David's inevitable ascent to stardom, Ken, eminently experienced publicist that he was, taught him how to handle a press interview so that the journalist interviewing him would warm to him. Although he had faith in David's good looks, intelligence, natural charm, and innate ability to win over any journalist who interviewed him, Ken nonetheless gave him some tips, such as never to argue with an interviewer, but to tell the interviewer exactly what he or she wanted to hear, and tailor his answers to the type of media outlet the interviewer was representing.

David was intent on absorbing all of Ken's advice, and hour after hour assiduously eavesdropped on Ken's telephone calls as Pitt employed all his public relations skills in promoting his charge to the press. In fact, David was so set on grasping every aspect of the PR business that Ken sometimes found him riffling through the letters on his desk, in quest of further knowledge of PR and marketing. By studying a seasoned publicist like Ken Pitt so intently, David was able to build on what he had already learned from his father about public relations. Consequently, when success finally hit, David would become renowned amongst the press for being the most intelligent, polite, and interesting rock star they'd ever interviewed.

Aware that David's talents were multidimensional, Ken threw himself into finding him work in a variety of creative fields and arranged for him to audition as host of ITV's children's program *Play School*, and for the Amsterdam run of the English touring company of the rock musical *Hair*. But as much as he wanted to succeed, David failed to get either part.

Later on, out of financial necessity, in June 1968, he took a part-time job at Legastat, a photocopy shop near London's High Court, which was primarily patronized by legal professionals working nearby. There, according to owner John Eddowes, David was "a nice, studious guy. We all liked him."

Along the way, in January 1969, he also appeared singing in a thirty-second TV commercial for LUV ice cream, which was shot by Ridley Scott.

Meanwhile, Ken Pitt never lost faith in him. "I'm going to make him a star," he announced to London booking agent Harry Dawson, who had said to his face that David would never get anywhere. But if Ken Pitt was David's biggest champion, he was also his Boswell, immortalizing their year of living together with a combination of perception and adoration, afterward writing of David, "He had a way of sitting in a chair and looking at you with a certain intensity. He managed to look at you as though his eyes were slightly closed, but then you realized that they were in fact wide open and you got the impression that, as you were talking to him, he was analyzing and dissecting every word you said and forming an opinion in his mind."

During his time living with Ken, perhaps prompted by his hero worship of Anthony Newley, who performed mime in *Stop the World, I Want to Get Off* so successfully, he began to study mime with former stripper, comic, dancer, and mime artist Lindsay Kemp—with whom, unbeknownst to Ken, he also conducted an affair.

In Lindsay Kemp, David had found a kindred spirit.

"I like to do most everything fully. I drink until I'm drunk. I eat until I'm full, frequently until I'm sick. I don't fancy people, I fall in love with them," Lindsay once proclaimed.

Lindsay had perfected a performance that successfully combined drag with mime and dance. After Pitt sent Kemp a copy of David's single, from his album, *David Bowie,* entitled "When I Live My Dream," Lindsay took to playing it before his show, then on at the Little Theatre Club, off St. Martin's Lane in London. He invited David to come and see the show. Apart from being riveted by Lindsay's artistry, David, who was nine years Lindsay's junior, was highly flattered that Lindsay had introduced the show by playing his song. Naturally, one thing led to another, and soon David was studying dance and mime with Lindsay, and sharing his bed, as well.

After David began his affair with Lindsay, which he kept secret from Ken Pitt, he also launched on a simultaneous affair with Lindsay's costume and set designer, Natasha Korniloff. And then there was also Lesley Duncan, who introduced him to the music of Jacques Brel and also became his lover.

Scott Walker had been his predecessor in Lesley's life, and long afterward, David cracked, "I went out with a girl who used to go out with Scott Walker and she preferred him to me. I had to listen to all his songs night after night. She wouldn't play my music."

Through all of David's romantic escapades, Ken Pitt became accustomed to what he termed "David's walkabouts," the times when he disappeared and didn't offer up any explanations designed to justify his whereabouts. But the fact that David was simultaneously juggling male and female lovers couldn't have been a complete secret to Pitt, who exhibited a well-developed sense of irony when he arranged for David to audition for director John Schlesinger, then casting *Sunday, Bloody Sunday*. The part? That of Bob Elkin, the handsome bisexual man having concurrent affairs with the character played by Peter Finch and the one played by the young and beautiful Glenda Jackson (whom David would go on to eerily resemble in the video for "Life on Mars?") and with Peter Finch.

Yet perfect as David might have been for the role, and however uncannily closely the plot of the film mirrored his current sexual relationships and however much the character of Bob Elkin could easily have been based on him, he failed to get the part; Murray Head played it instead. And after Decca refused to renew David's record contract, news of which reportedly caused him to break down and cry, in despair, he called Stuart Lyons, who ran the Hampstead Country Club, and asked him if he could do a gig there.

"David used to call me all the time," said Stuart, echoing one of the complaints of music writer Penny Valentine, who reviewed his work with passion but became exasperated when he kept calling her, pushing her to write about him.

"He was very persistent, and more pushy than most artists," Stuart remembered. "But I did book him at The Country Club."

Fortunately, David's father's contacts also came in handy once more, again in the shape of Leslie Thomas, whose novel *The Virgin Soldiers* was being made into a film at Twickenham Film Studios, and who arranged for David to be cast as an extra in the tiny nonspeaking role of one of the "virgin" soldiers.

"Typecast again," David cracked at the time.

Playing a larger part in the movie, Scottish actor Alex Norton hung out with David during filming. "We got on very well . . . we both played guitar and had little jam sessions together. David introduced me to the songs of Jacques Brel. He sang them to me and I was amazed," Alex remembered.

With his brief movie acting stint behind him, David continued his mime classes, and his relationship with Lindsay, who commented on his progress: "He wasn't a very good mover, but he was equipped with the essential thing: a desire to move. And I taught him to exteriorize, to reveal his soul. And he had all this inside him, anyway."

Producer and musician Tony Visconti, who has played a major part in David's career, right up through today, started working with him around this time and remembered seeing David "go to a mirror just to check a head angle, or he would brush his hair back in a particular way. At the time I thought he was just incredibly vain; later I realized that he was always working on himself, constantly honing his stage persona."

With Lindsay and Jack Birkett, in December 1967, David appeared in the play *Pierrot in Turquoise*, for which Natasha designed the set and the costumes. Besotted by David, she classified him as "a wonderful lover," and, to top that, really seemed to understand him.

"He's not an acquisitive person at all. He doesn't care for possessions very much," she said.

At the same time, while Natasha clearly got close enough to David to understand him perfectly, Lindsay still brandished a torch for him, as well, and swooned that he was "an angel."

David was playing fast and loose with his assorted lovers by resorting to the most rudimentary of schoolboy tricks. As Lindsay (who later allowed that "David had an enormous sexual appetite,") remembered, "Frequently there were notes from his mother to say he had earache or something, but later on I realized of course that those notes had been faked."

It was only matter of a time before David's entire house of amorous cards collapsed completely. On one night while David, Natasha, and Lindsay were on tour together in Whitehaven, as Lindsay recently remembered, "I heard noises through the wall: It was David and Natasha, who hadn't known that I was seeing David. After that, he couldn't go to Natasha's bed and he certainly couldn't go to mine, so he spent three nights sleeping in a chair, the tortured martyr."

In the heat of the moment, Natasha took an overdose of aspirin, and Lindsay, even more dramatically, cut his wrists. Both of them survived, but neither of them forgave David, at least not at the time.

But perhaps if they had read one of his first interviews, the one he gave to Barbara Marilyn Deane of *The Chelsea News* in which he said, flatly, "I do not believe in love in its possessive form," they might have understood his attitude toward love, sex, and relationships.

Fortunately, in the near future, he would meet the one person in the universe who would understand and share those attitudes completely.

FIVE

MODERN LOVE

Although David's betrayal of both Natasha and Lindsay had tarnished his relationship with them, albeit temporarily, he still carried on seeing them—in particular, Lindsay, who had awakened him to the world of Kabuki, to Jean Genet, and even the music hall. In return, David introduced him to Buddhism, which he was then exploring. Still, no matter how cavalier David's behavior to him had been, Lindsay still loved him. Years later he would continue to revel in the fact that those who learned of their affair would be lost in wonder: He imagined them asking themselves, "Can this bald-headed old queen have been Bowie's boyfriend?" he said.

As David's work with Lindsay's mime group wound down, Ken Pitt was still struggling manfully to promote David's career and get him bookings, but he was increasingly finding that David was defying him by ignoring his professional advice and disappearing for days on end. Finally, David moved out of Ken's apartment, ostensibly returning to live with his parents again in Plaistow Grove.

The truth, though, was that David had fallen hard for a woman, a fragile, beautiful English rose named Hermione Farthingale. They met for the first time at one of Lindsay's dance classes in London's

Covent Garden, and in the spring of 1968, they both danced in *The Pistol Shot*, a BBC TV play. So it was that, for the first time in his life, David was in love in a conventional way, with a relatively conventional woman, one who came from a prosperous middle-class family, a cut above his own.

Away from performing, David and Hermione, a trained classical ballet dancer, swiftly became close, despite the fact that her father, an attorney, didn't particularly approve of David. Her father's approval, however, didn't matter much to Hermione.

"We were twin souls, very alike. I was fascinated by him, this fey, elfin creature," she said.

For a while, Ken didn't learn about the advent of Hermione in David's life. "David used to tell Ken he was going to go to Hampstead Heath to watch for flying saucers and UFOs, when he was actually going to see Hermione," Michael Armstrong said.

David managed to sustain his deception for a while, but soon it became clear to him that he needed to escape from Ken's jealous possessiveness of him. Consequently, he moved into the house that Hermione shared with other aspiring artists at 22 Clareville Grove, in London's Kensington district. He was now twenty-one, and Hermione nineteen. They were both beautiful, and Hermione, in her natural incarnation, and David in his freshly acquired current one, were idealistic and determined to live a bohemian lifestyle together.

For a few months, their love and life together appeared to be idyllic. So much a product of the Summer of Love, of hippie ideals, their joint enterprise, Feathers (a multimedia group comprised of David, Hermione, and John Hutchinson, singing the songs of Jacques Brel and of David doing mime), and their youth itself attracted the attention of the media. They were selected as two of the subjects for a prestigious feature for *the Times* titled "The Restless Generation," written by Sheila More and published on December 11, 1968.

Ironically, none other than Mick Jagger was also featured in the same article as typifying his generation, along with his then girlfriend,

Marianne Faithfull, and Tony Visconti's future wife Mary Hopkin, who had just hit the charts with her wistful "Those Were the Days."

While Mick railed against convention and the older generation ("When you grow up, you become a thinking person, you can't stay a child, and some parents just can't take that."), David came off as more nihilistic: "We feel our parents' generation has lost control, given up, they're scared of the future," he said, adding, "I feel we're going to make an even greater mess of it. There can only be disaster ahead."

His relationship with Hermione would endure for more than a year. Then, after she came back from Norway, where she was filming the small part of a dancer in *Song of Norway*, she announced to David that she had fallen in love with one of the dancers on the movie and went on to end her relationship with him. His heart was broken, and even in 2000, he still had her letters. Devastated by this once-in-a-lifetime romantic rejection—his first and last—he would turn to Dana Gillespie for comfort, turning up at her South Kensington cottage in floods of tears.

Despite his heartache over losing Hermione, professionally he knew he had no choice but to move on. By the next year, he was running the Beckenham Arts Lab and trumpeting it in suitably politically correct terms. "I run an arts lab, which is my chief occupation," he declared to *Melody Maker*. "I think it's the best in the country. The people who come are completely pacifist . . . we started our lab a few months ago with poets and artists who just came along."

Steve Dube was a young reporter when he covered David and the Arts Lab. "I remember his eyes in particular because they were a different color. He was wearing bell-bottom trousers and a flowery shirt and looked like a hippie," Steve said. "I remember thinking that I liked him. He was a nice guy and was straight with me. Some people bend over backwards to create a good impression on a journalist. I didn't think that David was trying to create a favorable impression. He wasn't trying to sell himself; he was interested in what he was doing and in the people he was doing it with. I liked that."

However, David was still looking for work, either in the theater or in movies, and he got a part in a live TV two-character play, *My Country 'Tis of Thee*, with Lesley Joseph, then a student at the London Academy of Music and Dramatic Art.

"We were playing two hippies who were at a police station, and I can't remember much more about the play. David was a typical working actor," Lesley said. "I remember that he invited me to the Arts Lab, but I didn't go."

By now David was living in Beckenham with a new girlfriend, journalist Mary Finnigan, a divorcée with two children, a free spirit who came from a middle-class background but who also had a subversive streak that had led her to experiment with drugs and which ended with her serving a short time in London's Holloway Prison for women.

Radical and liberated, Mary fell hard for David, and soon he was singing in a local folk club and taking hash with her in his spare time. However, little though Mary knew it, true to form, David was not faithful to her. Apart from still dallying with Ken Pitt, who continued to be his manager, once a week, David would also spend the night in London with thirty-three-year-old Chinese-American A&R man Calvin Mark Lee, a flamboyant, flirty, effeminate character from San Francisco who wore a glittering red love jewel on his forehead and was a doctor of pharmaceutical chemistry.

Looking back at his affair with David, Lee often questioned whether or not David's interest in him had been prompted by the fact that he was the influential assistant head of record label Mercury's European office. Calvin and David first met in 1967, after Calvin sent David fan letters, care of Ken Pitt, some of which were laced with passionate love declarations. David was not immune to Calvin's sentiments and was flattered by the strong emotions he had aroused in someone who had never even met him.

Their affair, which began during David's relationship with Hermione, and continued after he had replaced her with Mary, was beneficial to David, not just because of Calvin's record company role, but also because Calvin's flamboyant image had made its mark among London's glitterati and he was renowned as one of the best network-ers around town—thus he was in a prime position to introduce David to powerful and important people.

According to informed observers, Calvin was madly in love with David and wanted a deeper relationship with him than the casual fling that David had in mind. By now, David was an accomplished sexual juggler, an emotional tightrope walker, living out a duplicitous exis-tence. What with Ken Pitt's continuing passion for him, Hermione, then Mary, and now Calvin, as well, the pressure on David escalated and finally took its toll on him in the form of debilitating migraine headaches. Yet despite all the convoluted problems he was juggling in his personal life, his creativity remained untarnished, and he contin-ued to be prolific in writing songs.

One night, he called Dana Gillespie and asked if he could come over and sing her his latest song. Naturally, she agreed, and, arriving at her South Kensington cottage with his guitar, he proceeded to strum to the words "Ground control to Major Tom." After Dana expressed her approval of "Space Oddity," David telephoned Shirley Wilson, a Bromley girl who had started his fledgling fan club, and played her the song, and she liked it as well. Then David went over to Ken Pitt's, and, on his twelve-string guitar, played the song for him. And, love-struck or not, Pitt recognized a hit when he heard one, and proceeded to finance "Space Oddity" every step of the way.

Calvin Mark Lee, of course, was on hand, pushing for David, doing all he could to get the song released on Mercury. However, his boss, Lou Reizner, remained unconvinced of David's talent and of the potential of "Space Oddity." In truth, his indifference to David and his work was not rooted in professional grounds but in the fact that David had stolen his girlfriend. Her name was Angela Mary Barnett.

A whirlwind of manic energy, with a view of herself so inflated that her bumptiousness knew no bounds, at nineteen, Angie, as she always called herself, was highly strung, creative, kindhearted, and the daughter of an American colonel, who'd fought the Japanese in World War II but was now running a mill for a mining company in Cyprus, and his wife, Helen.

Educated in America, Angie was expelled from school in Connecticut when it was discovered that she was having an affair with another girl. Nonchalant in the extreme about her expulsion and the reasons behind it, she developed a devil-may-care, attention-seeking sexual persona that would become the primary driving force in her life. After attending finishing school near Montreux, Switzerland, and emerging with show business aspirations, she met entertainer Liberace while traveling on a grand ocean liner, and was dazzled by his glittering sequined jackets and his charisma. She decided that he was the epitome of show business, the world of which she longed to become a part.

In 1966, Angie moved to London to take a secretarial course and then enrolled at Kingston Polytechnic to study economics and marketing. By 1969, she was working at the Nomad Travel Club, a travel agency in Paddington, where she lived above the shop and yearned for bigger and better things. Then fate took a hand and, in the elevator at Leonard's, the trendy hair salon in Grosvenor Square, she met and caught the fancy of Lou Reizner, the big boss of Mercury Records in London.

In love with life, with her own talent, with her own energy, and, above all, with herself, Angie used Lou's power and contacts to storm London with a vengeance, bolstered by her masculine, pragmatic, boisterous attitude toward sex. Now openly bisexual, when Lou Reizner introduced her to Calvin Mark Lee, on learning that he, too, was bisexual and was cutting a swathe through both men and women all over town, and not a little because she was curious about what it would be like to go to bed with a Chinese man, Angie embarked on an affair with him.

At the time, she was fully aware that she was merely one of his lovers—as a photo gallery of all his various lovers, male and female, on display above his bed attested. She was not prone to jealousy and had already acquired a taste for young and beautiful men, so when she flung herself on Calvin's bed one night and closely examined the assorted photographs of his lovers, inevitably, she fixed on the most beautiful, the most alluring, the most sexual of them all, stark naked from the groin up, and in his entire glory: David Bowie.

David and Calvin were best friends, Calvin initially said, but upon realizing that part of Angie's charm was her nonjudgmental, nonpossessive attitude to sex, he changed his mind, plunged ahead, and told her the truth about his affair with David, as she listened and filed the information away in her razor-sharp brain, saving it for later. She and Calvin were having fun together, and that was all that counted. And there was always Lou Reizner, powerful, well-connected, wealthy Lou, who remained excited by her brashness, her joie de vivre, her American go-getting energetic attitude to life and to love.

However, once Lou had introduced her to Calvin, he realized that all bets were well and truly off. Worse still, he was forced to stand by while Angie fell instantly, wholly, and completely in love with David. She first saw him onstage at the Roundhouse, when Calvin took her to see him in a Feathers performance. Observing how enthralled Calvin was by David, she at first felt sorry for him, perhaps even then intuiting that, as she would later say, "David was a serial player."

That night, at the Roundhouse, where The Who topped the bill, marked the night of Angie's first rock concert. She was overcome with excitement, and, when she looked at David, sheer lust.

"A lean, blond, enigmatic figure in a pastel-striped sweater and mustard-colored sailor's flares and a voice so compelling that no one could turn a head, David captivated every single member of the audience. Every move, every gyration quickened the pulse. His steel-blue eyes burned with mystery that defied the searching spotlights and his whole performance exuded an eroticism," she wrote afterward, unknowingly evoking the breathless style of Ken Pitt's description of his first sight of David.

David was living with Mary and involved with her, but nonetheless, Calvin suggested that Angie join him and David for supper in Chinatown. Aflame with excitement, she threw herself wholeheartedly into playing the role of potential girlfriend to a rising rock star. Determined to make an impression on David, she dressed from head to foot in a masculine fuchsia and purple pantsuit, perhaps as a way of subliminally signaling her bisexuality to him. Aware that David was having sex with Calvin, just as she was, as far as she was concerned, in revealing her bisexuality Angie may well have hoped to forge a unique, if profane bond between them.

"When we met, we were both fucking the same bloke," David would phrase it to the press some years later, and so they were.

Soon enough, David told her about the existence of Mary in his life, as well. "We work together, but we don't belong to one another. People don't belong to each other. She has her life and I have mine," he said blithely.

Fortunately for Angie, Mary wasn't around to elaborate on the intimate details of her relationship with David. "I found him incredibly attractive right from the start," Mary said later in a newspaper tell-all, revealing, "He was slim with this pale, pale skin, but he was very well endowed."

Then, putting her recollections on a more decorous plane, she went on: "The room would be all warm, there would be incense burning and a joint ready to smoke. . . . The atmosphere was so heady and sensual, it was inevitable we'd end up in bed. David seemed to love the ritual. He was not the kind of man who had to make love every night, but when it happened it lasted for hours and hours."

Her other recollections of David were not so sanguine. "I would go so far as to say he's a slob. He always expected other people to clean up after him. He was totally oblivious of mess and basically needed an army of servants keeping things organized around him," she said.

Although Angie was nonplussed on learning about the existence of Mary, determined not to demonstrate any sexual jealousy (a trait that she despised and always would), she maintained her sangfroid. After supper, she and David and Calvin moved on to the Speakeasy Club, where she and David took to the dance floor and jived together in complete unison. Sometime during the evening, she confided in him that she had been expelled from school because she'd had a sexual relationship with another woman. Unlike most men to whom she had revealed the same story, David didn't bat an eyelash, just as she had hoped that he wouldn't.

"You only did what you felt. That's how love is. You can't control those kinds of feelings," he said reassuringly.

The following night, he and Angie dined together again, only this time alone. And after dinner, they went back to Angie's apartment and consummated their relationship.

"Sex with David was nice, and encouraged intimacy, but it wasn't the kind of overwhelming experience sex can be," she wrote. "He was a stud, not a sensualist, and I found myself in a situation all too common among young women: the sex frequent and vigorous, but the ultimate pleasure elusive or, as in my case, unattainable."

This verdict, given long after their divorce, and immortalized in her 1993 memoir, *Backstage Passes*, differs considerably from that which she gave in her 1981 memoir, *Free Spirit*, where she deemed making love to him a "fulfilling experience."

But whatever the truth, from the time of their first shared sexual exploration, she was sufficiently aroused by him so that when, the very next day, he called, told her he had the flu, and asked her to come to his house and minister to him, she did just that. Mary Finnigan was away on a journalistic assignment at the time, and Angie eagerly threw herself into her self-imposed role of mother to David, and so it would continue between them.

She had inadvertently stumbled on an important truth about him. As his onetime fling Natasha Korniloff once put it, "He's always either hungry or tired or cold, or any combination of the three, and if you can satisfy his immediate demands, like put another coat on him or feed him something, of which he will eat only a bit, or make him a little nest to sleep in, he's absolutely and totally happy. Then he wakes up and goes to work."

But much as Angie might baby David on occasion, part of her lure for him was that she was as freewheeling about sex as he was. In the future, they would happily switch sexual identities, with Angie playing the male, and David the female. Soon Angie had made a friend of Mary to such a degree that, with Mary's consent, Angie moved in with her and David, Angie and David sleeping in one room and Mary in another.

Professionally, too, David's career was finally proceeding apace. In July, before releasing "Space Oddity," he sent Pete Townshend of the Who a copy. "He had the goodness to write me a note afterwards, saying that he liked the song very much," David remembered, and then said, "I thought, 'If I ever get really big, I'll try to be as nice as that to people.'"

The song was quirky, unusual, somewhat of a novelty number, and when David sang it at a disco at London's Imperial College, he was almost booed off the stage.

"I was so angry, I took the microphone and said, 'Remember the name David Bowie. He's going to be a star and you'll remember the day you booed him offstage,'" DJ Bob Harris, who accompanied David to the gig, remembered.

David was indeed destined for stardom, but not with the initial release of "Space Oddity." Though the song gained notice when, five days after its release, Neil Armstrong took his first steps on the moon, it was felt by some critics to be too downbeat, with its suggestion that Major Tom would never return from space.

However, some writers, like Penny Valentine, one of David's strongest supporters amongst the media, came out in favor of "Space Oddity." Valentine raved, "I listened spellbound throughout, panting to know the outcome of poor Major Tom and his trip into the outer hemisphere." She then compared the record to the Bee Gees' "New

York Mining Disaster," an unerringly accurate perception on her part. The record had been released on the Mercury label, but not without some help from an unexpected quarter, as David admitted in a subsequent interview.

Referring to Lou Reizner and to Angie, David said, "He hated me. She thought I was great. Ultimately, she threatened to leave him if he didn't sign me. So he signed me."

In Angie, David had found a loyal champion who would fight for him till the end, and who would be by his side until she was no longer useful to him. Discarding those who had outlived their usefulness to him was one of David's less palatable traits, as Angie and quite a few others who crossed his path, would subsequently discover.

SIX

ON THE WILD SIDE

Although "Space Oddity" wouldn't hit the charts until September, when it climbed to number 48, and reached a peak in November, when it soared to number 5 in the hit parade, it appeared that David's future—both professional and personal, now that he was happy with Angie—was assured. However, less than a month after the song's release, David was in Europe with Ken Pitt, competing in a song contest; right after he won, he learned that his father was sick and in critical condition. As soon as he heard the news, David flew home and rushed to his bedside.

"David handed the statuette to his father, telling him that he'd won the contest, and his father told him that he knew he would succeed in the end. He died not long afterwards," Peggy Jones told broadcaster Kerry Juby.

"David and his father were devoted to each other," Ken Pitt told George Tremlett. "He was genteel and eloquent . . . and always concerned that David should behave properly in every situation."

In years to come, David was to say that he regretted that he had never been able to talk openly to his father. "He just died at the wrong damn time, because there were so many things I would have loved to have said."

However little he may have communicated with his father during his lifetime, David had always been clear about his debt to him. John Haywood Jones had introduced him to reading and a love of books, and by example, had demonstrated the intricacies of PR and dealing with the press and had supported his son's career every step of the way. And now he was gone. When David heard the news of his father's death, he was in the midst of recording, and momentarily broke down in tears, but then carried on.

Ken Pitt, who had always respected John Jones, immediately rushed to David's side and later recalled that he "was very shaken, but calm. He was crying a bit, which was understandable." Then he and David set about the sad task of dealing with John Jones's business affairs, aware that he had always been a tidy and organized man and that they would be able to sort things out very quickly.

Looking back, Ken said that the thing he most remembered was "David turning to me, as we stood by the desk looking at John's dentures, and David saying, 'I know it sounds a silly question, Ken, but what do I do about his teeth?'"

On Ken's advice, he dropped them into a wastepaper basket. Meanwhile, in the kitchen, a relatively calm Peggy was downing cup of tea after cup of tea. Even under the circumstances, David had enough self-control not to turn on her. But in the deepest recesses of his heart, he blamed his mother for his father's death, reasoning that she hadn't called the doctor soon enough.

From then on, the tension between mother and son escalated. Although David was on hand to help arrange his father's funeral, he found the prospect of looking after his mother unpleasant, particularly as she had taken a strong dislike to Angie and routinely screamed that she was "a slut."

Despite that fact that he was in mourning for his father, or perhaps because of it, David threw himself into his work with a vengeance. In November, he appeared at the Purcell Room, and afterward, Tony Palmer, *The Observer*'s well-respected reviewer, enthused, "On stage he is quite devastatingly beautiful. With his loofah hair and blue eyes, he pads around like every schoolgirl's wonder movie star. He smiles; you melt. He winks; you disintegrate."

Back in Plaistow Grove, where Angie and David were staying with his mother after the funeral (David sleeping alone in one bedroom, and Angie forced to sleep in another with Peggy, simply because Peggy considered it an outrage that her son was living in sin with Angie), the situation was close to the breaking point. As the weeks went by, David's relationship with his mother downward spiraled further, no matter how much he and Angie tried to pacify her. (One tactic included buying her a mink coat, which Peggy automatically accepted, but without gratitude, complaining publicly that, as she was a retiree, she had no use for it.)

Despite the fact that Angie and David paid for her to go to Cyprus and spend six months there with Angie's parents, she still loathed Angie and rued the day that she'd come into David's life. In the end, the ever-resourceful Angie took matters into her own hands and found somewhere else for herself and David to live. Haddon Hall, the Edwardian mansion at 42 Southend Road, Beckenham, where she and David moved in September 1969, would have made the perfect rock star palace had it not been divided up into apartments.

Meanwhile, they found an apartment for David's mother in nearby Albemarle Road, Beckenham, which they helped her to furnish. Not in the least bit mollified, Peggy took to calling Angie at Haddon Hall on a daily basis, berating her. Rattled in the extreme, Angie focused instead on creating a life for herself and David in their new home.

They had rented Haddon Hall's ground floor apartment 7 for a sum of money reportedly between £8 and £14 a week. A minstrel's gallery at the top of the stairs, which would come in handy down the line when David's band members needed a place to crash, was one of Haddon Hall's most striking features. The apartment was blessed with a large entrance hall, and a dramatic staircase at the end of it, rather like something out of an antebellum mansion. An ornate stained-glass window reflected light into the building and lent Haddon Hall an air of grandeur.

A Gothic monstrosity, part decaying mansion and part church, Haddon Hall came alive when Angie and David got to work and dedicated their creativity to decorating it, a task made easier when Angie's parents gifted her some money with which to fund the work. Before that, though, they furnished Haddon Hall from cellar to rafters with nothing but orange crates, which, David confessed, "we nick from the market after it closes."

Armed with her parents' money, Angie masterminded Haddon Hall's new look. The sitting room and bedroom ceilings were painted silver, the living room walls were daubed a dark green, and the bedroom walls were painted pink. The bedroom was dominated by a huge seven-foot wide Regency bed, which David had discovered in one of the local junk shops he had taken to haunting. Angie, revealing herself to be practical and able to turn her hand to a multitude of tasks, not only reupholstered a group of Gothic-style chairs in crushed red velvet but also dyed twenty-six lace drapes exactly the same shade of red.

David's burgeoning collection of Art Deco and Art Nouveau pieces, which he had assembled since his late teens, was also on display all over Haddon Hall. Eventually, Angie and David would manage to convince their landlord to allow them to build a recording studio in the basement, and their rock star haven was finally complete.

By the end of the year, Tony Visconti and his girlfriend Liz would rent the ground-floor back bedroom and share the living room with the big open fireplace with David and Angie. Haddon Hall was now a seductive cocoon, one that some judged to be decadent and louche, but which those close to the couple considered the perfect setting in which to nurture and compound David's mystique. (In fact, the photo on the cover of *The Man Who Sold the World* was actually shot among the red velvet chairs and lace drapes of Haddon Hall, with David, fetching in a dress, reclining on a chaise longue with a crushed-velvet throw on it.)

Now that she was queen of her own domain, Angie quickly established herself as hostess with the mostest, a cross between mother hen and Playmate of the Month, and the atmosphere at Haddon Hall was hot and steamy, with girlie magazines dominated by pictures of voluptuous, big-breasted black girls in evidence all over the bathroom. In the living room and bedroom, an ever-changing cast of boys, girls, men, and women explored their sexuality in every conceivable permutation.

David had launched his relationship with Angie by putting all his cards on the table and bluntly telling her he didn't love her—he warned her not to expect anything conventional of him.

"Because it can't be that way," he said, "I'm not made like that. I do things that other people might not subscribe to and I think it's only fair that you should know that before we set out."

Angie absorbed his words with a sense of mounting excitement. After all, hadn't she been expelled from school for having a lesbian affair? Wasn't she avant-garde, uninhibited, the ultimate sexual adventuress? Dazzled by the image of her own sexual bravado, Angie flung herself into an open relationship with David with abandon.

Afterward, in an interview with me conducted in the midseventies for my book *Speaking Frankly*, she would make the somewhat contradictory boast, "I kept a man like David by proving that he would never get anyone as magnificent—but it had nothing to do with bed. Although it is sexual, inasmuch as everyone else wanted you so he could always think: 'Well, I am very fortunate, seeing as how I've got her.'"

In the early days at Haddon Hall, David would bring home boys, and Angie would bring home girls. Some Angie dressed in leather and fishnets and photographed in a variety of positions. Others, she and David enjoyed together, in the same bed.

Dana Gillespie, the schoolgirl who had been in David's life since she was fourteen years old, was one of the girls who regularly had threesomes with David and Angie. In fact, Angie and Dana bonded to such a degree that today, Dana characterizes their relationship as being that of "bosom buddies."

"It was always known that Angie and David were in an open relationship, that they were good pals, like brother and sister. She and I landed up in bed with him, but it wasn't her and me," Dana said, intimating that she and Angie had both catered sexually to David.

Another schoolgirl swept up in the world of Haddon Hall was seventeen-year old Nita Bowes, who went to school nearby and had first met David when he was singing at the Three Tuns.

"David was always very nice and openhearted, and was very supportive of the Arts Lab," Nita remembered. "When Angie came along, she was far more exotic than David, and influenced the way in which he dressed. We all hung out together at Haddon Hall, and lots of people were always staying there.

"There was nothing predatory or improper about Angie and David. They didn't lure me into bed; I wasn't a groupie but just part of the art scene, and although we did have a cuddle in bed, it wasn't wild, but just affection between the three of us, just friends. Fundamentally, David is just a sweet South London boy," Nita said.

But despite their freewheeling lifestyle, Angie and David still tried to sustain an element of romance in their lives. In front of other people, they held hands, gazed into each other's eyes, and whispered, "In your ear" to one another, their code for "I love you."

Nonetheless, they were sometimes blatant about weaving a sexual web around those who took their fancy. Barbara Fulk, a secretary working for RCA, David's record label at the time, was summoned to the Park Lane Hotel, only to be greeted by a braless Angie, in flimsy lingerie, and a naked David, lying on the bed, seemingly asleep, and stark naked. Before Barbara could make her apologies and leave, Angie made a pass at her.

Judy Cook, widow of British comedian Peter Cook, recalled a night when Angie and David invited her and Peter to a club. In the limousine, with blacked-out windows, as Judy remembered, "David was wearing lots of makeup and looked highly exotic, while Angie, tall, skinny, and muscular, looked masculine in a trouser suit.

"We joined them in the back of the car, and the driver covered our laps with rugs. Angie told me she liked my hair and suggested I dress like a boy, too. Almost immediately, I felt someone's foot rubbing against my leg."

Judy had no doubt whatsoever that footsie was going on, but she didn't know whose foot it was. At the club, Angie asked her to dance.

"It was quite sexy and we carried on for a few dances," Judy said, adding that on the way back in the limo, more footsie went on, but didn't lead anywhere.

As Angie wrote in her books, she was also David's advisor and his road manager, and accompanied him on an assortment of gigs, supporting him every step of the way. They would stay together, she vowed, and work toward making him into a pop idol, and then once he'd arrived at the very top, they would turn their attention toward making her into the star of stage and screen she firmly believed she was destined to be. David, too, for a time appeared to have genuine faith in her potential, later writing "The Prettiest Star" for her.

She was, he said, "one of the very few women I'd be capable of living with for more than a week. She's remarkably pleasant to keep coming back to. And for me she always will be. There's nobody more demanding than me. Not physically, necessarily, but mentally. I'm very strenuous."

At times, she felt that he was more interested in his own future than in hers, and, disillusioned by him, at one point she escaped to her family in Cyprus, until, bereft, he sent her a postcard announcing, "This year I promise we'll marry."

He was true to his word, and proposed to her. In her first book Angie described in some detail the basis of their marriage, enthusing how much she had loved David and how much he reciprocated her emotions. At the time, Angie may well have had superstars in her eyes, because when George Tremlett attempted to interview David about his love for Angie, he laughed and said he didn't see it like that. According to Ken Pitt, David repeatedly confided that he was only marrying Angie to stop her being deported from Britain, and that he didn't love her.

After she and David were divorced, in a radio interview later to be reproduced in *David Bowie: The Starzone Interviews* Angie contradicted her original assertion that she and David had married for love and admitted that he had primarily married her to prevent her from being deported from England, and that when she was gone, he missed her managerial and organizational skills.

"David's no fool," she said. "He realized that every time I got sent out of the country he got two weeks behind.

"We got married because I was an American who needed to stay in London and he was a weak Brit who needed me to break down the doors and turn him into a star. I was wild and he needed me to help him be wild. It worked," Angie said.

On March 18, 1970, she and David went to Kensington Market, where vintage clothes, as well as outfits by new designers, were on sale, and selected a 1920s silk dress for her to wear at her wedding. Then, on the spur of the moment, they decided to pay a call to their friend, a female artist. Angie and David ended up in bed with her, and, as a result, as both of them would boast afterward, they were late for their wedding the next morning.

The female artist, who to this day remains a friend of David and Iman, was witness at the Bromley Register Office ceremony, at which, in the eleventh hour, Peggy materialized, though David hadn't invited her.

"She turned up on the day and I was delighted," Angie said of Peggy's surprise appearance afterward. "I thought David had a really silly attitude about his family. He thought he could get rid of them when he didn't want them. And I kept explaining to him you can't get rid of family."

Resigned to his mother's uninvited presence David graciously stood back and let her sign the register. And using four Peruvian silver bracelets instead of wedding rings (they would wear two each on their wrists) David Robert Jones married Angela Mary Barnett.

Ken Pitt, who had known about the wedding, was not invited. He was still besotted with David, so David, who had always used his sexual allure to manipulate Ken, and Ralph Horton before him, (the exact modus operandi of many a starlet winning fame and fortune via the casting couch) was quick to deny to Ken that he had emotions for Angie and to disparage their marriage.

Ken, however, was not naïve: "David was leading this double life," he said. "It was rather Jekyll and Hyde–ish. He put on a different hat at Haddon Hall and when he came to see me."

Although Ken was sanguine about David's juggling of their relationship with his marriage to Angie, Angie, who encouraged sexual but not emotional promiscuity in David, had no intention of allowing Ken Pitt to retain his role as David's Svengali.

At first, Ken tried to view the strident American who had stormed into his protégé's life as an asset, an ally. "I think she organized him and I should imagine she's turned out to be very good for him. He needed something like that. Her personality, and what he called her intelligence, impressed him very much," he said somewhat caustically.

However, despite the success of "Space Oddity," which Pitt had financed and supported right from the start, their business relationship had started to sour. More and more, David had proved himself to be stubborn, contrary, and unwilling to listen to Ken's advice, which had, until then, served him so well.

"When I wanted David to be extrovert he wanted to be an introvert. When I wanted him to wear beautiful clothes he wanted to wear dirty clothes," Ken complained.

Dirty clothes or not, Ken was so devoted to David that, as Michael Armstrong remembered, "Ken always did David's ironing."

The end came when David, accompanied by manager Laurence Myers, who owned Gem Productions and the record label GTO, and his partner, Tony Defries, a twenty-six-year-old former legal clerk, came to see Ken and informed him that David wanted to end their business relationship.

"Ken was absolutely shocked," Myers remembered.

Shocking as it might have been that David jettisoned his long-term, loyal, and faithful manager Ken Pitt in favor of the upstart Tony Defries, he had his reasons. For he had fallen under the spell of a consummate showman, a man who captivated anyone who crossed his path, much as David himself did.

"Tony Defries was one of the most mesmerizing people I've ever met. He was fascinatingly intelligent and could talk about everything. Everyone thought of him as if he were an ancient seer," Tony Zanetta, who would go on to become president of MainMan, said.

In April 1970, David formalized the breach between him and Ken in a letter, telling him that he no longer considered him to be his personal manager. In retrospect, a shaken Pitt said that he had thought about his relationship with David a great deal, how David saw him, what he meant to David. "I'm pretty sure it was as teacher to a pupil, which was either good or bad. Certainly I saw it that way," he said.

Down the line, David would compensate Ken for his dedication, hard work, and enduring belief in him by paying him what, in those days, was a substantial sum: £15,000. David stayed in touch with Ken through the years, and kept the lines of communication with him open to such an extent that he invited Ken to his May 1973 concert at London's Earls Court, issuing the invitation with the words "Come and see what your boy's doing."

And in 2000, he paid tribute to Ken Pitt in "Bowie Interviews Bowie," a mock interview in *the Canadian Post* in which David, age twenty-three, was "interviewed" by the then fifty-three-year-old David. In the mock interview, on the subject of Pitt, older David reminds younger David, "Don't forget that although you both had completely different ideas about what you should be doing, he stuck by you. He lent you money whenever you needed it and showed a great deal of enthusiasm for all your crazy ideas."

Now that David was signed to him, Laurence Myers renegotiated his record contracts and, until David decided that he wanted to conquer America and to eventually live there, he masterminded David's career.

"I thought David was very smart, very commercially minded, very sure of what he wanted to do and be," Laurence Myers said.

However, by the time he had spent £100,000 on David's career, when Tony Defries came to him with the suggestion that Defries open a branch of Gem in New York and run it for Myers, Laurence demurred. "I knew I would lose David if he went to America. And I also didn't want Tony to run my company because his style of business was to have a limousine on call all day, and to give an artist everything he wanted," Myers said.

Ultimately, Defries repaid Myers his £100,000 and contracted to pay him £500,000 over the next five years, leaving Tony in total control of David's career.

The son of a Spanish/Portuguese barrow-boy father and a Russian mother, Tony Defries grew up in the tough Shepherd's Bush area of London. Though he was only four years older than David, he was a bear of a man and exuded an aura of experience and gravitas. By the time he first met David, Tony had honed his Hollywood tycoon act to perfection.

"When Tony Defries took me to dinner, I got the giggles," Maggie Abbott, who was then David's movie agent said a long time afterward. "He had a very shaggy beard, and a huge coat made out of dead rabbit. In retrospect, he was like someone out of *The Producers*. Next to him, poor Ken Pitt was completely out of his depth."

It was Angie, of course, who—on the advice of record executive Oleg Wyper—had helped convince David to jettison Ken in favor of his new manager, Tony. She invited Tony and his brother, Nicholas, to Haddon Hall so she could romance them on David's behalf, and vice versa. From the first, the clues about Tony Defries's true nature and ambitions were transparent, as he was open that he modeled himself on Colonel Tom Parker, the former carnival huckster who had mas-terminded Elvis's career. A coincidence, given that David was born on Elvis's birthday, and one that Defries would work to his advantage.

"Tony was great," Angie said. "He was a thief and a gangster, but if you want something done, who do you hire?"

Despite the fact that Tony had no qualifications as a lawyer, he promised David the world. David, who had blind faith in every utter-ance that Tony made regarding his future as an international super-star, concluded that his day had finally dawned.

Singer, composer, and music journalist Jonathan King was having dinner with DJ Alan Freeman when David and Mick Ronson, David's new and gifted guitarist, walked into the restaurant. "I said hi to David, and he announced, 'I'm going to make it! I've actually cracked it!'" Jonathan recalled. "I'd been championing him for a few years, but he still hadn't made it. Now he seemed so certain, so sure. I went back to the table, to Alan, and this is what I said: 'David says he is going to make it. He was so sure. He was utterly convinced. He had no doubt whatsoever that he was going to make it really big now.' I felt as if he had sold his soul to the devil."

He was partially right. For though Tony Defries wasn't exactly the devil, in reality, David had sold himself to him, lock, stock, and barrel.

SEVEN

STARMAN

With the success of "Space Oddity" in Britain, David became more of a pampered prince than ever. Every morning, Angie would automatically run his bath, cook for him, clean for him, and generally treat him like a baby. Now and again, he was even heard to address her as "Peg," "Ma," or "Mother," and she, in turn, called him "Nama-Nama," the nickname evoking her propensity toward mothering. She opened Haddon Hall to any musicians who wanted to crash there, and served English breakfast 24/7, rather as if she was running a truck stop.

Although she later complained that half her day was spent trying to convince David to get out of bed and then persuading him to eat ("He was all coffee and cigarettes, coffee and cigarettes"), Angie succeeded in manipulating him where it was important.

"Remembering how things had to be his idea, I never actually suggested anything outright. No point giving him a chance to dig in his heels and balk the way he had with Ken Pitt," she said sagely.

Instead, she went shopping and made sure to pick out things for herself that she instinctively knew would suit David as well. "More often than not he'd take the bait, come sniffing over from his side, see the new stuff hanging there." At which point, she gleefully recalled,

David would reach into the cupboard, grab an outfit she'd ostensibly bought for herself, and "take it down, look it over, try it on, thinking he was being naughty, pulling a fast one." Meanwhile, she watched his machinations, seemingly innocent, then burst out that the look was perfect for him and that he should have the outfit.

Aside from her skill at manipulating David, Angie was loud, abrasive, annoying, and histrionic, but her artistic instincts were good.

"Angie was wonderful," said Maggie Abbott, adding, "She was so devoted to him, always pushing his career and image, had her eyes on everything, clothes, design, makeup ideas—she was brilliant with creativity."

Haddon Hall was now a hive of activity, all centering on making David into the star that Angie, Tony Defries, and David himself believed him destined to be. In the midst of it, David composed songs, watched TV, and listened to music, while Angie waited on him hand and foot.

In January 1970, drummer John Cambridge had made a trip to Hull and convinced twenty-four-year-old guitarist Mick Ronson, who was then working as a gardener for Hull City Council, to come down to London and become the guitarist in David's new band, the Hype, which consisted of Tony Visconti on bass, John Cambridge, and Mick "Woody" Woodmansey on drums.

From the first it was clear that the classically trained "Ronno," who had been playing in bands since he was seventeen, had star quality. David recalled that when he first heard him play the guitar, "I thought, 'That's my Jeff Beck! He is fantastic! This kid is great!' And so I sort of hoodwinked him into working with me. I didn't quite have to tell him that he would have to wear makeup and all that."

Mick Ronson, as Charles Shaar Murray, the journalist and seasoned Bowie watcher would point out in the documentary *David Bowie: Five Years*, was to become the only performer with whom David would ever share the stage on an equal and long-term basis. More than that, Mick immediately became a good mate, and moved into Haddon Hall, partly because he knew about Angie's uncanny ability to bring home the most free-spirited of girls who were willing to make themselves sexually available to David, Angie, and anyone else in his orbit.

As Angie told me during an interview for my book *Speaking Frankly*, part of which took place at the Oakley Street house that she then still shared with David, "I spend my happiest and best hours with my rorting team. *Rorting* means screwing chicks. There's four or five guys and me and all we do is pick up chicks and see who can poke them first.

"We've been doing this for many years: You have to pick a chick up and she has to agree to be fucked with no one leaving the room—not in private. She has to understand that from the off—it's a communal effort—like living theatre. She doesn't have to be fucked by more than the one person she fancies. What she can't do is lay down the conditions of how, when, or where. And everybody watches."

Despite all the steamy sexual goings-on at Haddon Hall, David, Mick, and bassist/producer Tony Visconti still managed to find time to rehearse David's *The Man Who Sold the World*, a hard rock and heavy metal album, there.

In the meantime, the Hype made its debut at the Roundhouse, the band dressed in comic-strip superhero silver suits, and David in silver lamé and a bluish-silver cloak, his hair dyed silver and blue—all a British prefiguring of the Village People. The audience that night (with the exception of Marc Bolan, who was practically the only person to applaud) was not prepared for David's glam/glitter rock. Undeterred, a year later, thanks to David's powers of persuasion, David and his band would all wear makeup onstage.

Telling Ronno and the other band members that they had looked a little green onstage and that maybe makeup would make them look more natural, David sealed the deal when, after the show, girls flocked to the band, obviously attracted to them by their sparkly makeup and androgynous images.

The Man Who Sold the World was recorded at Trident and Advision Studios at the end of April, with Woody Woodmansey replacing John Cambridge, and Mick Ronson's iconic guitar sound perhaps marking the birth of heavy metal. However, by now Tony Defries was calling the shots. Taking David aside, he made it clear to him that it was David Bowie he was representing, and that the band, the Hype, was irrelevant. The Hype was disbanded at the start of 1971, to be replaced by Ziggy Stardust's Spiders from Mars (bass player Trevor Bolder, Woody Woodmansey on drums, and Mick Ronson on guitar) in July of the same year.

The cover of the album of *The Man Who Sold the World* shockingly—for the times—featured David with long, flowing Pre-Raphaelite hair, reclining on a chaise longue in Haddon Hall, wearing a dress designed by London's Michael Fish. "I'm certainly not embarrassed by it or fed up with it or ashamed of it, because it [wearing a dress] was very much me," David asserted. Then, turning his thoughts to the intricacies of fashion design, he said, "The dresses were made for me. They didn't have big boobs or anything like that. They were men's dresses. Sort of a medieval type of thing. I thought they were great."

When the unsuspecting American executives at Mercury Records first set eyes on the cover, they were outraged, and immediately removed the cover picture from the sleeve of the U.S. edition of the album. Hearing the news, David erupted in anger, screaming all over Haddon Hall that the executives were philistines and fascists, to no avail.

So that while the picture of him in a dress remained on the cover of the UK album, Mercury insisted that David commission a new photograph for the American album cover. Consequently, he asked Mike Weller, an artist friend who had designed posters for the Arts Lab, to come up with an alternative cover photograph. In an eerie twist of fate, Mike's cover design featured a sketch of a cowboy standing in front of the Cane Hill asylum, in Coulsdon, Surrey—the very same asylum where David's half brother, Terry, was then locked away.

Strangely enough, Mike Weller's cover concept was born out of his visit to a friend who was in Cane Hill, and he knew nothing about David's brother being there, either. But though David might have been shocked by the coincidence, he saw that the cover reflected the somewhat dark lyrics of the album and, in particular, of the song "The Width of a Circle," and so approved the use of the Cane Hill sketch on the cover.

In January of 1971, Tony Defries brought publicist Dai Davies on board, and one of his first jobs was to travel with David to Manchester, where David was scheduled to mime "Holy Holy," a glam rock/hard rock song he'd written, on Granada TV.

"During the drive, David made it clear that he had studied what makes people stars, and that he knew all about the Hollywood star machine of the interwar years. Most people involved in the rock industry tended not to want to know all about that," Dai said. "He told me he had read that if two people walk up to a door, one of them leans forward and opens the door for the other one, but stars stall for a second or two and then the other person will open the door for them.

"He explained that if you want to be perceived as a star, you start off with little bits of behavior like that, not opening the door yourself, waiting for someone else to do that. After reading that, I doubt that David ever opened the door for himself again."

That spring, David would have the opportunity to test out his theories regarding stardom, when he made his first trip to America. At the time, *The Man Who Sold the World*, which in retrospect marks the birth of glam rock, didn't afford David the big success in Britain for which he'd been working for so long. However, when the record was released in America, Mercury deemed it important enough to fund a promotional radio tour of the country for David, thus facilitating his first visit to the United States and granting him the opportunity to conquer the land of his dreams at last.

The trip began with four days in Manhattan, where David stayed at the Holiday Inn, visited Times Square record shops searching for records that were unavailable in England, and afterward explored the Museum of Modern Art. Next, there were visits to a folk club, a short flight to Detroit, then to Chicago. Then a flight back to Detroit again, then another flight to Michigan—in those early days, David hadn't yet developed his fear of flying.

That fear has often been disparaged by a segment of the media who suspected that David's fear of flying might have been a Tony Defries production, created specifically because Elvis, too, had a fear of flying, and Tony felt that if David claimed to have the identical fear, that would enhance his mythology.

However, Woody Woodmansey, his Ziggy Stardust drummer, remembered, "We went on holiday to Cyprus and the plane got hit by lightning. He went white and fainted."

Much later on, pianist Sean Mayes, who played on the Isolar tour, witnessed David's reaction to flying and reported it in his book, *We Can Be Heroes: Life on Tour with David Bowie*. His description of David's fear of flying paints it as uncontrived and sincere.

"On the plane I sat next to David and Coco, who was clutching a huge, fluffy grey elephant. We chatted a bit and the plane didn't move. Then they announced a delay—they were running off fuel while they changed one of the engines," Sean said.

"'Oh God,' David muttered, 'that means the pilot's drunk and they're feeding him black coffee.' As we waited, he and Coco got more and more nervous. I think David was on the point of leaving the plane when they told us they were ready—'fasten seatbelts and extinguish cigarettes.'

"David was rigid, his hand whitely gripping the arms of his seat. I wanted to hold him tight for comfort, but I just put my hand on his arm and felt nearly as tense as he did as the plane threw itself into the clouds."

In the middle of February 1971, still in the throes of his radio tour of America, David flew to Houston, and from there to San Francisco, where he was met at the airport by *Rolling Stone* reporter John Mendelsohn, who had flown there to interview him.

Afterward, Mendelsohn remembered, "The vision that got off the plane bore little resemblance to the one on the album covers. This one had long flowing hair, was wearing a dress and carrying a purse. At the baggage claim, he batted his eyelashes, and I reflexively offered to carry his heavy, wheel-less trunk for him."

David had quickly realized that his Little Lord Fauntleroy charm and his pristine English manners would smooth the path for him in America, and he didn't hesitate to use them to his advantage. According to John, when David was introduced to a certain groupie, "he asked with a gleam in his eye (the blue one, as I recall, but very possibly the brown), if she fancied a guitar lesson. I found that wonderfully debonair."

And so, it would transpire, would countless other groupies, male and female, all over America. One of them, Queenie, later said of him, "David Bowie wears tons of makeup. He's got a whole suitcase full of makeup. He put some on in front of me and he even painted my toenails blue. David is the sexiest one around. Like you'll walk into a room and he'll stare right into your eyes. And he'll go, 'Hello,' and you're at his mercy. I can't help it. That's just the way he is."

By the time David landed in L.A., he was already infused by excitement regarding a character he was in the throes of creating, and brought with him some Holiday Inn stationery, on which he had begun to scribble some lyrics about a rock star named Ziggy Stardust. When Ziggy was finally unleashed on the world, David, mindful as always of the publicity value creating an aura of mystery, didn't reveal the character's genesis—it was only in 2007 that he finally did.

Claiming that he had based Ziggy on C-list rock star Vince Taylor, a failed musician who once came out onstage and swore that he was Jesus Christ, David said, "I met him a few times in the midsixties, and

I went to a few parties with him. He was out of his gourd. Totally flipped. The guy was not playing with a full deck at all."

David's impromptu account of his inspiration for Ziggy would ultimately be challenged, with biographer Peter Gillman claiming that Ziggy was either a composite of the U.S. performer the Legendary Stardust Cowboy and Iggy Pop, or, more intriguingly, that David had actually based Ziggy on himself.

"Look at how the lyrics describe him. 'Loaded,' 'Well hung,' 'God given ass.' He was talking about himself," Gillman said.

Gillman's analysis may well be the correct one. However, David did let slip that during the midsixties he had seen Vince Taylor open a map on the pavement of a street, and kneel down and examine the map with a magnifying glass so as to point out the sites where UFOs were going to land. Given that David was fascinated by UFOs at that stage in his life, and that the street that he named was close to the Roebuck pub in London's Tottenham Court Road, where he and the Lower Third regularly rehearsed, it is highly likely that he did meet him and that Vince made up a major element of the kaleidoscope that was Ziggy Stardust.

Squired around town by eccentric DJ Rodney Bingenheimer, who also worked for Mercury, David spent two days and two nights in L.A. making the rounds of radio interviews, clubs, and parties. At a party in honor of Andy Warhol superstar Ultra Violet, David, sporting a Michael Fish dress, held court. Record producer Kim Fowley, whose "Alley Oop" (which he produced while still in high school) was one of David's self-confessed favorite musical influences, observed his impact on the room.

"That night, David looked like Lauren Bacall, but with Noel Coward zest. Rudolph Valentino meets Ronald Coleman. He had humor, he had charm, and all night channeled Lionel Bart and Anthony New-

ley," Kim Fowley remembered. "And he was one of the best inter-
rogators I've ever met; he got you to talk about yourself so that you
got to say, 'I'm doing this,' 'I'm doing that,' and then he could use it
afterwards."

In the course of the conversation, David confided to Kim that he
was interested in Brian Eno of Roxy Music, and in the premise of Bryan
Ferry. Roxy Music, the band formed in 1971 by lead singer and main
songwriter Bryan Ferry, was made up of bassist Graham Simpson,
guitarist Phil Manzanera, saxophonist Andy Mackay, drummer Paul
Thomson and, of course, Eno, who played the synthesizer for the band.

That David was interested in Bryan Ferry was hardly surprising,
as, like him, Ferry was one of the few British musicians in the rock
scene who exuded the style and elegance of the past. A working-class
boy from Newcastle, in the industrial north of England, Ferry was
handsome, debonair, and, for a time, appeared to rival David in terms
of class, style, and sophistication.

Brian Eno, however, would excite David's interest even more. A
composer, producer, singer, and visual artist, Eno was at the forefront
of ambient music—a new wave of music that emphasized tone and
atmosphere over rhythm and structure. With his serious background
in art (having studied at art colleges in England), and his anarchic,
innovative approach to music, Eno was well matched to David, and
David instinctively knew it.

Flying back from L.A. to New York in March, David learned that the
Velvet Underground were doing a gig at Manhattan's Electric Circus.
He decided to go, and as only a hundred seats had been sold, he managed to get one in the front row, where he sang along to all the songs,
hoping to impress Lou Reed with his knowledge of the lyrics.

Afterward, given that the Velvet Underground were not famous
enough to command security, David was easily able to sneak back-

stage and knock on their dressing-room door, asking to speak to Lou. Within moments, Lou had slipped out, and he and David were sitting on a bench in the club, chatting. Enthralled, David informed Lou that he was his only fan in London and that he had owned a copy of the Velvet Underground record before it was even released in America. Then he plied Lou with questions about his lyrics and the rationale behind his musical choices. They chatted for more than fifteen minutes, and afterward, as David put it years later, "you float off into the night, a fan whose dream came true."

Then, the next morning, a new friend in the music business informed David that Lou hadn't been with the band for a while and that his replacement, Doug Yule, looked exactly like him. In David's own words, he was "gutted."

Home at Haddon Hall again, David began working obsessively on a new album, his fourth, *Hunky Dory*, which he would start recording in April at Trident, and which included "Changes," "Oh You Pretty Things," and "Life on Mars?" three of his most iconic compositions. With Mick Ronson, Woody Woodmansey, and Trevor Bolder, who replaced Tony Visconti on bass, *Hunky Dory* marked the first album featuring the group of musicians that would become Ziggy Stardust's Spiders from Mars.

While working on the album, David was overcome with the certainty that now, at last, he had sown the seeds of his superstardom, and although *Hunky Dory* wouldn't be released for another eight months, he already had intimations of the artistic triumph that lay ahead of him. George Underwood, his old school friend, was in the studio when David recorded "Life on Mars?" and observed afterward that when David had finished recording the song, he burst out crying.

• • •

For once, however, his career wasn't his entire focus: On May 30, 1971, his son was born at Bromley Hospital, weighing just eight pounds, eight ounces. David had always longed for a boy, and when he first set eyes on the baby, he was overwhelmed. "It was the first and only time I saw David cry," Angie remembered.

The baby was christened Duncan Zowie (after the Greek word for "life") Haywood Jones. And, as Angie later recalled, his birth marked the happiest day of her life, and of David's. However, just two weeks later, she was forced to admit that she was having trouble relating to her newborn son. "Poor little thing, he cried all the time. I had difficulty bonding. You feel your freedom has been taken away from you, totally and utterly," she said. Instead of working through her feelings, she chose to run away and, probably suffering from postpartum depression, a condition not fully understood in those days, she packed her bags and departed for a vacation in Italy with Dana Gillespie.

"David would call every day, and in the end persuaded her to come back early," Dana said, adding, "Which was unusual because he wasn't normally prone to emotion."

Dana's supposition that David was missing Angie and longed for her to be by his side, couldn't have been more wrong. Now that he was a father, he had suddenly unearthed the Victorian in himself, a deep vein of conventionality, and he was absolutely livid that Angie had abandoned his son, and, by extension, him. Their marriage would never be the same again, and, in retrospect, Angie understood that while she had gained a son, she had also lost her husband.

However, once Angie returned from Italy, neither she nor David allowed the birth of Zowie or their new roles as parents to inhibit their propensity toward sexual adventuring. When David wasn't playing a gig or working on Ziggy, he and Angie launched themselves on the Sombrero Club, a gay dance club in a basement in the Kensington area of London, and conquered as many boys and girls as possible, bringing some of them home to Haddon Hall for more fun and sex.

In particular, David and Angie were both captivated by part-time rent boy turned fashion designer Freddie Burretti, and by his coterie of fellow rent boys, call girls, and hip, cool people. One night, David became enthralled by a young Spanish boy and brought him home to Haddon Hall, where he and Angie cavorted together with the boy. But the night, and the boy, belonged more to David than to Angie, and in the morning she woke up disillusioned.

Meanwhile, Dana was on hand to take part in some of David and Angie's adventures and to record many of the proceedings on video. "I've got a short freeze-frame film sequence of things we did together in every aspect, but maybe they are not the right things to talk about," she said.

Yet as discreet about the contents of the films as Dana still is, at the same time, she still revealed that once David came home brandishing a leather mask he'd bought from a sex shop, and that she took a photograph of him wearing it, which was subsequently published in Tony Zanetta's biography of David, *Stardust*.

"He's naked, and I know it is him," she said, "His body is strangely hippy. For someone with such a thin top half, he had big hips."

Yet for all the sexual activity swirling around him, when he was working, David was capable of concentrating to the exclusion of all else.

Performing at the Hampstead Country Club one Wednesday night, David wore a big floppy hat, and theatrically twirled it around at the end of each song, while half the gay population of London, on hand to witness his performance, applauded his every move. That same night, three people who were in the audience would change the course of David's career: Leee Black Childers, Cherry Vanilla, and Jayne (Wayne) County, part of Andy Warhol's anarchic Factory in Manhattan and in London to appear in the play *Andy Warhol's Pork*.

At first, they were disappointed that David wasn't wearing a dress, but after he announced, "And the people from *Andy Warhol's Pork* are here tonight. Stand up," they were mollified. So much so that Cherry took her top off. In the midst of their outrageousness, Angie, in particular, was charmed. After David's show, the trio went backstage and invited David and Angie to see the play, which was about to open at the Roundhouse and was based on two hundred of Andy Warhol's recorded telephone conversations.

Given that David had written the song "Andy Warhol" for *Hunky Dory*, he was clearly fascinated by Andy, and it was a given that Angie and David would go to see *Pork*. Afterward, backstage, they were introduced to Tony Zanetta, who played the character based on Warhol. At first, Tony was surprised by David, as he wasn't the kind of flamboyant rock-star-in-waiting he'd been led to expect him to be.

"He wasn't very colorful. He had a little pullover on, and he was pale. It was Angie who was dynamic and vivacious. We all moved on to the Sombrero, where David just sat at a table and watched," Tony said.

The following morning, Angie and David sent a car to ferry him and the others to Haddon House, where he found that Angie and David had inexplicably switched roles.

"David was very, very engaging. Angie suddenly took a backseat and became the little wife. He and I talked about theater, fantasy, glamour, and I realized that he had been around in the music business for a long time and was no stranger to failure. He just got up and went to the next step, as he had total belief in himself and was obsessed by his work," Tony remembered, adding, "As for sex, it wasn't any big deal for him and Angie. It was like shaking hands at the end of the evening."

EIGHT

ZIGGY

In September 1971, the same month in which David started recording *The Rise and Fall of Ziggy Stardust and the Spiders from Mars* with Mick Ronson, Woody Woodmansey, and Trevor Bolder, he flew to New York (with Angie, Tony, and Mick in tow) to sign with his new record company, RCA—the record label to which Elvis was also signed. When he and Angie checked into their suite at the Plaza, they were greeted with the glitter and glory of RCA: The suite was filled with gifts—the entire Elvis catalogue, the whole RCA album catalogue for that year, and countless "Welcome to New York" gifts.

The writing was on the wall. RCA saw David as a star in the making and were treating him accordingly. Their thinking was, of course, heavily influenced by Tony Defries who, taking a leaf out of Colonel Parker's book, had been marketing David as a star long before he actually was one, providing him with bodyguards, blanketing the city with posters featuring him, and generally acting as if David's stardom was a fait accompli. Cherry Vanilla, Leee Black Childers, Jayne County, and Tony Zanetta—the Warhol people— had also contributed to convincing RCA ahead of time that David was already a star, when he wasn't.

"Tony Defries used to bring us up to RCA and we acted crazy, making demands for David, insisting that they treat him like a star. In a way, Tony used us to throw stardust in RCA'S eyes. That was part of his brilliance," Cherry Vanilla said.

During their stay in Manhattan, David and Angie made the pilgrimage to Andy Warhol's Factory, expecting that Warhol would treat David as a peer, a fellow artist. But David was completely unprepared for Warhol's way of interacting with fans, friends, and foes alike, which entailed a tongue-in-cheek, piss-taking approach. For example, when asked by this author to name his ideal woman in bed, he cracked, "Snow White." And in the same vein, Andy didn't take the earnest David seriously, not for a moment.

That day at the Factory, David was wearing size-seven-and-a-half bright yellow patent leather shoes, a gift from Marc Bolan, and Warhol—dressed in jodhpurs and high-laced boots and brandishing a riding crop—began to photograph David with his Polaroid camera. After interminable minutes, during which Warhol obsessively snapped away at David's shoes, David, close to his breaking point, cut in and told Warhol that he'd written a song about him, and proceeded to play it for him.

Warhol made no bones about the fact that he hated the track, and David was deeply hurt by his reaction. His way of demonstrating his feelings to Warhol was subtle. All of a sudden, he launched into a mime in which he pantomimed disemboweling himself, as a dig at Warhol, whose cavalier treatment of him had been tantamount to gutting him, at least in David's view.

However, despite their lackluster first meeting, Andy Warhol would pay dividends to David, if only because some of the people clustered around him eventually transferred their allegiance to David.

After signing his RCA contract, David joined Tony Defries, Tony Zanetta, Angie, music writer Lisa Robinson, and her husband for a celebratory dinner at the Ginger Man, across from Lincoln Center, where the *real* Lou Reed joined them. During dinner, while Lou talked and David listened, the basis of their friendship was formed and David did all he could to convince Reed, who was then retired, to relaunch his career—and succeeded. No minor feat, as Lou was a god among musicians, and in coaxing him out of retirement, David did a huge service to musicians and music fans.

On that same fateful night, after dinner, Lou accompanied David, Angie, Defries, and Zanetta to Max's Kansas City, the nightclub favored by both the Warhol and the music crowd, and Iggy Pop joined them there.

"David wasn't well known in America, but that night he and Lou Reed and Iggy Pop bonded," said Yvonne Sewall, who was married to the owner of Max's, Mickey Ruskin.

"There was a certain spikiness between Lou and Iggy, and they obviously didn't get on very well," David remembered.

While Iggy regaled everyone with stories about growing up in a trailer park and his forays into heroin and crystal meth, David's bond with Iggy was forged. Years later, David said, "Iggy's a lot more exuberant than I am. I tend to be quieter, more reflective. He's always a little bit on the dangerous line. I'm not particularly; I'm much more of an observer. He's more of a participant in things."

Iggy countered with, "We're so opposite. He's slick and I am what I am."

Most of the time, their friendship would be part Pygmalion, with David playing Professor Higgins to Iggy's Eliza Doolittle: musical mentor and cheerleader, but also enabler. When Iggy was in a psychiatric hospital in 1975, trying to kick his drug habit, David, with Dennis Hopper, came to visit him bearing gifts.

"We trooped into the hospital with a load of drugs for him," David admitted, long afterward. "We were out of our minds, all of us. He wasn't well: That's all we knew. We thought wc should bring him some drugs, because he probably hadn't had any for days!"

Years later, however, in Berlin, David would attempt to redeem himself by doing his utmost to save Iggy from his drug addiction, and together they would battle to kick their destructive drug habits.

Today, Tony Zanetta isn't completely sure whether what happened next happened after that first night at Max's Kansas City, or on the following night. Other than that, he is certain of all the details of what transpired. "Angie was away in Connecticut, visiting a girlfriend, and when David and I left Max's, he just gave me this look. So we went to my apartment on Fifteenth and Sixth, and we just talked and talked," Tony remembered. "It was a very exciting time for David. He had just signed a record deal and was looking forward to the future. Then we went to bed.

"David definitely was not gay, but he liked the gay world. When we were in bed together, he was more sensual and narcissistic. To him, it was about being adored. I think he was truly bisexual and I don't think sex mattered to him.

"But our night together established a kind of real kinship between us, and I felt we had something special between us. David was a real seducer. He made you feel that you are the only person who exists, the center of his universe. Then he had you in his pocket, so to speak, but after that, he would move on to the next level of the relationship," Tony said.

The next night, David continued to weave his silken web around Tony and suggested that the two of them go to bed with Angie.

"It wasn't hard-core sex, it was more romantic," Tony remembered. "It was more cuddles and a lot of cunnilingus all round. But then Angie got pouty and moody. I don't know if she was jealous or what."

"Angie talked a big game about sex and wildness," Cherry Vanilla, who became MainMan's office manager and publicist, said. "I think

David could handle the open marriage, but although Angie talked about it, I think she did that just to keep him in love with her and interested, but really wanted a more conventional thing.

"I remember once when David had an affair with Jean Millington, the singer in the band Fanny, Angie found out about it and got crazy with me because I'd mentioned it to the press," Cherry said.

After the wildness of America, David returned to England where, in September 1971, he played Aylesbury, and he wore full makeup when he performed on stage. Later in the year, though, he made a stab at playing the conventional traditional husband and accompanied Angie and Zowie to Cyprus, where they vacationed with her parents.

Angie's father, Colonel George Milton Barnett, was a fine, upstanding military man with a mustache who resembled Lawrence of Arabia. Now a successful businessman, he was canny about money, and as he attempted to advise David on how to negotiate the tricky and unscrupulous music business, David listened with respect.

Angie's mother, however, was quite another story. Only five foot two, stormy, feisty, and aggressive, Helena Marie Barnett hailed from Galicia in Eastern Europe and was such a firebrand that she actually once went as far as to hit her tall and imposing husband on the head with a frying pan. Observing the scrappy, bellicose Helena, David could not but have reminded himself that the daughter often evolves into the mother, and must have blanched at the prospect.

After *Hunky Dory* was released in December, David's stock rose considerably among the critics, who hailed the album as an artistic success. And as the ultimate accolade, popular DJ Tony Blackburn declared "Changes" to be his single of the week, January 7, 1972, and the more mainstream Peter Noone, of Herman's Hermits, recorded "Oh! You Pretty Things" with considerable success, and it hit number 12 in the UK charts.

With the dawn of 1972, everything was in place to unleash Bowie mania on the world. It all began with David's twenty-fifth birthday party at Haddon Hall on January 8, 1972, at which he made his entrance as Ziggy in the quilted multicolor jumpsuit he and Freddie Burretti, now very much on his team (and, rumor has it, one of his sometime lovers), had designed, and which seamstress Sue Frost had made for him out of thirties furniture fabric.

Lionel Bart was one of the guests, and when David played "Ziggy Stardust" for him, to his delight, Lionel pronounced it to be "a rock opera." Later that same month, David took the first step in publicly launching Ziggy Stardust on an unsuspecting world when, on January 22, under the headline "Oh, You Pretty Thing: David Bowie," Michael Watts's interview for *Melody Maker* was published.

Dubbing David "rock's swishiest outrage: a self-confessed lover of effeminate clothes" and "a swishy queen," Michael Watts described him as "a gorgeously effeminate boy," announcing, "He's as camp as a row of tents, with his limp hand and trolling vocabulary."

But it was David, himself, who delivered the coup de grâce in a line that he hadn't even discussed with Angie, but which he had secretly nursed to himself. "I'm gay and always have been, even when I was David Jones," he announced with no hesitation.

Even then, Michael Watts, who, like the rest of the world knew that David was married to Angie (but then wasn't Somerset Maugham also married, with a daughter?) and that she had borne him a child (didn't Oscar Wilde have two children and a wife?) was a little skeptical, noting, "There's a sly jollity about how he says it, a secret smile at the corners of his mouth. . . . The expression of his sexual ambivalence establishes a fascinating game: Is he or isn't he? In a period of conflicting sexual identity he shrewdly exploits the confusion surrounding the male and female roles."

Long afterward, Watts would elaborate, "I think he said it very deliberately. I brought the subject up. I think he planned at some point to say it to someone. He definitely felt it would be good copy. He was certainly aware of the impact it would make."

Chris Charlesworth, who wrote for *Melody Maker* and then went on to become a press officer for RCA, where he worked with David, said, "Personally, I think he was lying. I suspect that he is bi. I think he said it for effect as much as anything else. He is a master at misleading the press and creating headlines as a result.

"I think he learned the PR trade from Ken Pitt, who was a press officer, and in the process realized that the worst thing was to be ignored by the media. He knew what he said would cause a stir, and it coincided with the release of his *Hunky Dory* album," said Charlesworth.

"Don't you worry about me. I know what I'm doing" was David's response after Laurence Myers broached the subject of David outing himself in print.

Was David's "I'm gay" announcement a cynical ploy he resorted to to promote *Hunky Dory*, and a way of starting the process of launching Ziggy on an unsuspecting world, or was it a genuine expression of his bisexuality, his drive for sexual freedom, his battle against sexual conformity?

In a 1997 interview, *Changes: Bowie at 50,* a BBC radio program released in conjunction with his fiftieth birthday, he looked back at his revolutionary revelation that he was gay and said, "I did it more out of bravado. I wanted people to be aware of me. I didn't want to live my life behind a closed door."

Whatever the truth about the original motivation for his controversial public statement, it is incontrovertible that David was proclaiming his bisexuality when he was only sixteen years old, as Alan Dodds, formerly of the Kon-rads and now a reverend, confirmed in an interview for this book. And by later going public, he became the first mainstream star to out himself, a shocking and brave move in a country where, less than fourteen years earlier, Liberace had sued a national newspaper for insinuating he was gay and won. From that moment on, David's proclamation freed countless teenagers and young people throughout Britain (where being gay had been a crime less than a decade before) to indulge their sexual preference and even publicize it.

And that, in addition to his penchant for wearing women's clothes, sporting makeup, and flirting girlishly with the camera, served to make David a sexual revolutionary whose impact on society can never, even today, be minimized.

One morning, in March 1972, after Angie had served him orange juice and coffee in bed, as always, he announced that he wanted to dye his hair red and cut it, simply because he wanted to look different. True to form, Angie immediately swung into action and, after some thought, concluded that if she settled on one of the many hairdressers who habitually hung out at the Sombrero, to the exclusion of all others, fists would fly and tempers would fray. So instead she opted for a hairdresser nearby, Suzi Fussey, who worked at the Evelyn Paget salon on Beckenham High Street, where she also did David's mother Peggy's hair every Friday.

"Peggy was my 4:45 P.M. every Friday afternoon," Suzi, who later married Mick Ronson, remembered. "She talked about David a lot whenever she came to the salon. She was really proud of him. And when Angie asked me to go over to Haddon Hall and work on David's hair, I just thought of it as going to help the local band."

Then, as neither Angie, David, nor Suzi had a specific idea for revolutionizing David's look via his hair, they thumbed through a series of fashion magazines and eventually evolved the iconic Ziggy Stardust hairdo, which would sweep the nation and live forever.

Suddenly, there was no stopping David. Determined to smash every taboo, and to scale the heights of success and notoriety, during a June 17 show at Oxford Town Hall, he made a move that would revolutionize his image and his career, and become legendary in the history of rock. And British photographer Mick Rock, who had already photographed Syd Barrett, founder of Pink Floyd, and who would become David's official photographer, was on hand to immortalize that taboo-breaking moment.

"In the middle of the gig, David knelt down and started plucking at Mick Ronson's guitar with his teeth, and from the back, it looked like David was giving Mick head. And I got the shot," said Mick Rock.

The photograph, published on the front cover of *Melody Maker*, made David a household name.

"He loved it. He knew it would sell records," Mick Rock said.

But was it David Bowie who had simulated giving fellatio to Mick Ronson's guitar, or was Ziggy Stardust doing it? Ziggy or David? David or Ziggy? It would soon become difficult to distinguish the difference.

"David had to become what Ziggy was—he had to believe in him. Ziggy affected his personality, but he affected Ziggy's personality. They lived off each other," Mick Ronson later said.

Millions of words have been written analyzing David's creation Ziggy Stardust, and perhaps the best definition comes from David himself, who explained, "It was about putting together all the things that fascinated me culturally. Everything from Kabuki theater to Jacques Brel to drag acts. Everything about it was a hybrid of everything I liked."

And later on, he said, "I thought that was a grand kitsch painting. The whole guy. I can't say I'm sorry when I look back, because it provoked such an extraordinary set of circumstances in my life."

The day after the Oxford gig, the Ziggy Stardust juggernaut rolled on with a press conference at the Dorchester Hotel on London's Park Lane, held for American journalists flown in especially for the event. Lou Reed, whose next album, *Transformer* (which included the iconic track "Walk on the Wild Side"), David would produce, was there, as was Iggy Pop, for whom David would coproduce *Raw Power*, and later on, *The Idiot* and *Lust for Life*, and with whom he cowrote

"China Girl." (Along the way, David would also write and produce Mott the Hoople's album *All the Young Dudes*, which featured the track of the same name, not an anthem to youth, as the title intimates, but a harbinger of doom.)

Journalist Ron Ross was one of the members of the press flown over to London by RCA. He would write David's first cover story for *Phonograph Record Magazine* and later go on to become his product man at RCA. As he recalled, "David was sweet and enthusiastic. But Iggy was a snotty kid taking advantage of what was on offer to him. And Lou was rather condescending to all. I remember Lou unnecessarily talking about taking a transsexual hooker 'home' the night before, but I'm not sure I believed him. There were press in the room," Ross said.

Around the same time, musician Ron Asheton flew to London to play on Iggy Pop's album.

"The first day I was there, I met David Bowie," Ron said. "He showed up at the house, drunk, with these two Jamaican girls with identical David Bowie carrot-top haircuts, and they went down to the dining room to drink wine and stuff.

"David kind of got disoriented in the house, so I showed him to the front door, and then he grabbed me by the ass and kissed me. My arm went back to coldcock him, then I thought, *Whoa, can't do that*. I didn't hit him," Asheton said.

On a brief visit to Manhattan with Mick Ronson, (the same one during which they caught Elvis's show at Madison Square Garden), Tony Zanetta was on hand and observed a change in David, "He looked fantastic, but Ziggy neurosis had started to take over. He was a little more tense, a little more fearful," Tony said.

During that same trip, David was also reunited with Cherry Vanilla, the Factory girl who, for his own reasons, Tony Defries had co-opted into MainMan, where her duties included managing the tour, plugging David's records to DJs, and, later, ghosting a column in his name. Later on, acting in the role of his spokeswoman, Cherry confided to an L.A. radio host that David routinely made love to everyone who worked for him at least once. After that, she was deluged with people who wanted to come and work for MainMan.

Confirming the truth of Cherry's words, and consolidating his new pattern of seducing those who worked closely with him as a way of marking his territory and reinforcing his power over them, he did indeed go to bed with Cherry Vanilla.

"He was always very flirtatious. He looked you straight in the eyes, but he wasn't condescending. He treated women with the same equality as he treated men, and looked at your intelligence as well as your sexuality," Cherry remembered.

"We were in Boston, in Tony Defries's Howard Johnson hotel suite, which was on a high floor, and when I sat down in a chair, David squeezed in so I was sort of sitting on his lap. Then Tony and his girlfriend Melanie left David and me alone.

"Knowing that he had a phobia about heights, I asked him if he wanted me to close the drapes, but he told me to keep them open because he wanted to see the lights. He started taking his clothes off, and I thought he was beautiful. He reminded me of a satyr. His body was very underdeveloped in the upper regions, as he had a small upper body, arms, and chest, but his legs were very muscular. He had big hips in the thighs, almost like a Greek statue.

"I told him that I was embarrassed, because I had two big white bandages stuck on the inside of my thighs and he promised me he wouldn't laugh when he saw them.

"Of course, the moment he saw the bandages he burst out laughing," Cherry said, "And I just sat there looking down and laughing at them too, until he beckoned me, 'Come 'ere.' He was a better lover than I'd ever imagined. Not just in the physical sense. The sex was as dirty, rough, and aerobic as anyone could want, but it never felt like we were just having sex. It felt like we were really making love.

"He was amazing. He was a great kisser, and kissed me a lot, and was very tender, kissing my body all over and breathing on my neck, and although he was very butch and virile and could stay hard for a long time, for those moments, you felt as if he was making love with you," Cherry said. "He was either a fabulous actor or a man whose emotions ran deep. But if it was acting, I couldn't have cared less. It was lighthearted and hot; I was twenty-nine and I knew the score."

Meanwhile, Tony Defries took to privately referring to David as "the product," and to commissioning boxes of special MainMan matches with golden heads, to symbolize the company's opulent image. Unaware of Tony's machinations and wild extravagance, back in London, David carried on oblivious, with Tony Zanetta now working for MainMan as his road manager.

"We definitely liked each other a lot, and there was this closeness between us. One of my jobs was to get him up in the morning, but we didn't do any drugs," Tony said.

In London, after David's Sheffield gig, to which David had invited singer Lulu, he took her to bed. "Some people have beautiful hands or beautiful necks, but I discovered that night that David had beautiful thighs—the best I'd ever seen, I had my own private viewing—up close and personal," Lulu revealed in her autobiography.

On July 6, 1972, wearing a quilted multicolored jumpsuit and full makeup, complete with white varnished nails, David took the stage with Mick Ronson on the BBC's flagship music show, *Top of the Pops*, and started to sing "Starman." A few moments into the song, in the most leisurely, natural way imaginable, he slid his arm around Ronno, pulling him close to him while they sang "Starman" together, and David's status as a sexual icon was assured forever. He was now a superstar, and his image and persona would remain enshrined in the seventies: David was the miracle worker who had single-handedly triggered a cultural earthquake.

Looking back, the impact of David's cool, casual, homoerotic moment with Ronno, in full view of five million *Top of the Pops* viewers that night, and their palpable sexual chemistry, the ambiguity of their sexual orientation, with both Ronno and David exuding a macho swagger, can never be minimized. The next morning, all over Britain, David's appearance was the talk of the country. Was he a freak? Was he "a queer"? In the parlance of the day, was he a "poofter"? There was no answer, only a call to freedom of dress, freedom of image, freedom of expression.

Shocking in the extreme, especially in dreary, decaying, stifling suburban Britain, David's performance on *Top of the Pops* that July was a revelation and would transform him and his generation forever.

A major hit for David, and his first since "Space Oddity," "Starman" was to indelibly engrave David's image, his androgyny, his white-hot charisma onto the psyche of pop fans everywhere—nothing would ever be the same. His performance literally changed lives, his courage in wearing makeup on national television, whether motivated by his honest belief in sexual freedom or by PR, sparkled through, and to some, David Bowie would forever remain their shining light, their inspiration, even their spiritual guide.

The album *The Rise and Fall of Ziggy Stardust and the Spiders from Mars*, which he began recording in September 1971, which was actually released a month before David's seminal *Top of the Pops* performance of "Starman," would go on to sell 7.5 million copies. It had taken David nine grueling years of paying his artistic dues, and now, at last, he had finally arrived.

NINE

SUPERSTARMAN

In September 1972, Angie, David, and his old school friend George Underwood and George's wife, Birgit, sailed to Manhattan on the *QE2*. David dined in the ocean liner's exclusive restaurant, dressed in full Ziggy regalia, only to be shocked immeasurably when many of the passengers stared at him openmouthed. Turning to George, he said, "They were all looking at me."

"What do you expect?" George replied.

"After that, David took every meal in his cabin, alone. Another time, he came out of the bathroom and he'd shaved off his eyebrows," George recalled.

It wasn't the first time that he had done so, but here, amid the luxurious ambience of the *QE2*, it was yet another act of rebellion and self-assertion.

In America, David was scheduled to embark on a seventeen-day nationwide tour to promote Ziggy, traveling between cities via chartered Greyhound, with Angie, Birgit, and George in tow. By the start of the U.S. tour, according to Angie, she and David were more like business partners than like lovers. More to the point, she had set her sights on David's handsome green-eyed Jamaican bodyguard, Anton Jones, and had selected him as her next paramour.

And David, too, had a new passionate interest of his own, War-hol's prettiest, sexiest Factory girl, nineteen-year-old actress and model Cyrinda Foxe, who was introduced to David by Leee Black Childers at the Plaza, where Angie and David were each staying in separate suites. Cyrinda and David spent their first night together at the Plaza, and she found him tender, easy to be with, and a great lover who was happy to talk to her before, during, and after sex.

Five days later, David, Angie, Tony Zanetta, and the entire entou-rage moved on to a motel in Erie, Pennsylvania, where they were scheduled to stay the night before David played his first major Ameri-can show in Cleveland the next evening. That night, Angie was discov-ered in the hotel pool, having wild sex with Anton Jones.

"The significance of that was not that Angie was in the pool with Anton, but that this was the eve of her husband's first major show in the United States. David may have been supremely confident, but he was also nervous, and he needed her. But she wasn't there. She was in the pool, having sex with his bodyguard, Anton Jones," Tony Zanetta said.

David was hurt, but he was still determined to put on a bravura performance that night in Cleveland. Watching from the back of the theater, Cyrinda and Leee were overcome with admiration and under-stood that he was destined to become a superstar.

"Then Cyrinda said, 'Look at those pants he's wearing! Look at those earrings. They are just like mine!'" Leee Black Childers remem-bered. "Suddenly, Cyrinda realized that the pants and the earrings *were* hers! She and David were the same size, and he had decided to wear her pants and her earrings. She thought it was hilarious."

During the tour, Leee now and again found himself alone with David and was charmed. "The two of us would be together, and he would sit on the bed and almost be like a little kid. He would sit there, with his legs crossed, and giggle. Then he'd tell stories about his early years in the music business and I would tell stories about growing up in Kentucky. I remember he told me how George

Underwood damaged his eye, and as he told me, he giggled and giggled," Leee said.

At the end of the tour, on September 28, 1972, David played Carnegie Hall, to great acclaim, introducing Ziggy Stardust to the city that never sleeps. That night, backstage at Carnegie Hall, nineteen-year-old groupie Josette Caruso made a play for David. What happened next casts a light on David's life during that time, both the highs and the lows, and the nature of David himself.

"After the show, David's bodyguard approached me and invited me to a party at the Plaza. I was wearing a silver dress that reflected rather like a mirror. David took one look at me and said, 'I can see myself in you,' which was a brilliant double entendre," Josette remembered.

Then, and during their subsequent night together, David's behavior gave the lie to his open marriage with Angie.

"After he said that about seeing himself in me, he suddenly said, 'Oh dear, my wife is coming towards you and it looks as if she is going to dump a plate of pastries over you!' Sure enough, she was walking towards me with the plate and looked about to do just that, so I walked away."

Then David's bodyguard secretly handed her a card with the name of the Benjamin Franklin Hotel, Philadelphia, and a room number on it, the date of his appearance there at the end of November, and whispered to her, "David is expecting you there."

A seasoned groupie whose conquests included Jimmy Page, with whom she toured when she was only sixteen years old, Josette was determined to sample David's charms, and traveled to Philadelphia to see him, as arranged.

"When I arrived at the hotel suite, which included a living room, a piano, and two bedrooms, David was sitting on a couch, wearing a black shirt and black pants. I sat next to him. He poured me a glass of wine and started talking about *Catcher in the Rye* and he told me that he identified with the book's protagonist, Holden Caulfield," Josette remembered. "He was in a very playful mood and sang 'Walk on the Wild Side' to me. Then there was a knock on the door, and Ian Hunter and some other guys from Mott the Hoople turned up and we all chatted. Then they left, and David and I went into the bedroom together.

"In bed, he was a wonderful lover, massively endowed, but the night wasn't just about the sex act. David was very romantic, touching me, kissing me, holding me, calling me 'Josie,' whereas everyone else called me Josette. He was a wonderful lover, but it wasn't about size, but about his technique. He didn't just fuck, he made love. He was romantic, charming, but at the same time he liked to talk dirty, to ask me how much I was enjoying something, and I told him I was loving it all, which I did," Josette remembered.

"But there was nothing gay about him, nothing effeminate. I wouldn't have thought he was bisexual. He was all man. He was aggressive, took charge, knew all the moves, wasn't kinky, but really controlled me in bed. He came twice during the night. The first time, he was loud and moaning, but the second time he came in silence, and afterwards he said, 'That was a bit like Charlie Chaplin,' (meaning the silent movie star), and giggled.

"After he went to sleep, I just lay there, looking at him while he was sleeping. His skin was so white, as white as snow, and he had two moles on his neck, rather like vampire bites."

Only two things marred Josette's night with Bowie. The first was when, during the night, Suzi Fussey, then traveling with David as his personal assistant, crept into the room to get his boots and saw her in bed with him. In the morning, when Josette told him that Suzi had seen them in bed together, according to her, "David said, 'Oh, shit! She's going to tell Angie!' I wouldn't say their marriage was open at all.

"But earlier that night, I experienced the most bizarre thing that's ever happened to me in all my years as a groupie. There was a knock at the door of the suite. The bodyguard answered it and then called David.

"David was away for a few minutes, during which I could hear him very distressed and saying things like, 'Oh no, oh no! Why me? Why do they think that about me?'

"When he came back into the bedroom, I could see that he was very, very upset and that something had really happened which really horrified him. Then he told me that the person at the door had offered the bodyguard to bring him a dead, warm body for David to have sex with, as if he were into necrophilia. David was horrified."

Josette's night with David was not completely spoiled by what happened, and in the morning, they parted, never to meet again.

"But I was happy. I had been to bed with David Bowie," Josette Caruso said.

By the time David, Angie, and the entourage had flown to L.A. and checked into the Beverly Hills Hotel, along with more than forty other people who all made up the MainMan entourage, Cyrinda Foxe had become an accepted part of David's universe. One night, at the hotel, she and David and Angie had a threesome. "We all kissed and licked one another," Cyrinda remembered. "It was more interesting and curious than exciting."

However, when Angie heard Anton come into the suite, without any further preamble she announced, "Excuse me, lovies, that was just grand," and promptly departed for a night of sex with Anton. Meanwhile, David and Cyrinda carried on having sex together as if nothing had happened.

Cyrinda was now the most important woman around him, although he still availed himself of groupie after groupie. Bored beyond belief, on one occasion while having sex with a groupie, he sent for Cyrinda to entertain him.

"She was so stupid, all he wanted to do was fuck her, and he needed someone to talk to, and that was me. I'd be watching the TV and talking with David, and he'd be screwing the groupie. Very nonchalant," Cyrinda said.

David's affair with Cyrinda continued for two months. She was partly the inspiration for "The Jean Genie," although the melody came to him when he was on the Greyhound: George Underwood was strumming a John Lee Hooker riff on his guitar, and David reworked it. Cyrinda also appeared in the video for the song, but in San Francisco, after Tony Defries demanded she dye her hair red to match David's and she flatly refused, her time on tour was over, as was her time with David.

In her book, *Dream On: Livin' on the Edge with Steven Tyler and Aerosmith*, Cyrinda remembered their last night together: "I had on this long Lady Godiva wig which fell down to my knees and lots of pearls. I got into the bathtub and David was watching me. I said, 'Oh, don't touch. I want to pretend I'm floating down a river.'

"He had a robe on, and he dropped it and stood there and started to jerk off. I told him to try and come on the pearls, because I had read once that body moisture helps them retain their luster.

"It was so exciting. We were looking into each other's eyes when he came. It's cool watching a guy come. David Bowie shot all over me, all over the pearls and into the bathwater," Cyrinda said.

Meanwhile, he was exploring sex with boys, as well, and, according to Tony Zanetta, "in Pittsburgh, he had a black boy, and later on, in Japan, he had an Asian boy. He also loved those black girls, and he definitely had one night with Nina Simone. And in New York there were some well-known Puerto Rican transsexuals and David had sex with some of them."

On October 20, after appearing at the Santa Monica Civic Auditorium and winning rave reviews, David attended a party with Wolfman Jack and met Kim Fowley again. Observing that no one was talking to David, other than Mercury employee and Sunset Boulevard club owner Rodney Bingenheimer, Kim declared, "I see you are blinding the hoi polloi with your charisma."

David smiled and said, "Tomorrow they will all claim that they hung out with me all night." Then, somewhat wistfully, he added, "I'd really like to meet whoever is clever enough to get into this fucking party."

For a while, he stood on the sidelines while Kim took to the floor and danced with an extremely sexy girl. Clearly attracted to her, David "embraces me with his arm around me as if we were two gay men," Kim said.

After Kim made it clear that he wasn't interested in pursuing anything with the girl, David invited her to go into the bathroom with him. The implication that he wanted to have sex with her then and there was clear, but she didn't hesitate and walked across the lobby with him.

"They walked across the lobby, and two drag queens saw David take a real woman into the bathroom," Kim remembered. "He immediately locked the door behind him and the girl, but the drag queens took their high heels off and started banging on the bathroom door with them, shouting, 'We can suck cock better than she can!' The door remained closed. Then the drag queens started again, 'Open the door, we will take over, we can do a better job than she can,' they screamed."

But David ignored them and stayed in the bathroom with the girl for quite a while, Kim Fowley said.

David's seventeen-day tour of America had made him a star, at least to the press, if not in terms of box office receipts. He was on the cover of *Rolling Stone*. Bowie mania had begun in America in earnest, and his life would never be the same again.

David was flexing his star power now, exploring every sexual option on offer to him. However, drugs were not yet a part of his life. As he later put it, "Ziggy Stardust was actually drug-free, apart from the occasional pill: amphetamines, speed.

"When we first started doing Ziggy we were really excited and drugs weren't necessary. Then I went to America, got introduced to real drugs, and that's when it all went pear-shaped," he said.

TEN

CHANGED

David was a megastar now, and on learning that Tony Defries had registered his company name as MainMan, he naturally assumed that he was the MainMan the company's name implied.

That same year, David gave his first TV interview since his appearance on BBC TV's *Tonight* in 1964 to London Weekend Television chat show host Russell Harty. Nervous about subjecting himself to Harty's questions, David, nonetheless, had his tongue firmly in his cheek when Harty, whom everyone knew was a closet gay, asked him about his bisexuality.

"I've known quite a few men," David allowed, and when Harty probed him on the subject of male groupies, he cracked, "I've heard of them, yes. They come on like groupie chicks. And you often find out they're boys."

At the same time, when Harty did deign to ask him a serious question, he gave considered answers: "I find that I'm a person who can take on the guises of different people that I meet. I can switch accents within seconds of meeting someone and I take on their accent. I've always found that I collect. I'm a collector. I've always just seemed to collect personalities. Ideas. I have a hodgepodge philosophy, which is really very minimal," he said.

At *The Russell Harty Show*, he met American photographer Joe Stevens, whose pictures he had seen and admired in *New Musical Express*.

"He could do impersonations of me, after studying my New Yawkese," Joe remembered.

In April 1973, David released his new album, *Aladdin Sane*, which he characterized as "Ziggy Goes to America," and which immediately went gold in Britain. Afterward, although he generally wasn't happy with having Angie on the tour, he relented and invited her to join him and, with Zowie, they traveled to Japan together.

As an adult, Zowie, now Duncan, would look back and cherish his time in Japan with his mother and father. "I remember one time going to see a sumo wrestling show in Japan when I was a little kid and being amazed. There were a lot of unique things that I got to do and not a lot of people get to experience things like that. And I treasure those memories. But often I'd sit around being bored backstage at a concert," he said.

During that same trip, David and Angie also took him to Japanese temples and a model village, but his strongest memory would always be of the bustling fish market in Tokyo. It was his last trip with both of his parents, and he would remember it forever.

David had always loved Kabuki, and opted to wear the designs of Japanese designer Kansai Yamamoto. Kansai would return the compliment. "He has an unusual face, don't you think? He's neither man nor woman. . . . There's this aura of fantasy which surrounds him," he said.

In Japan, happy to be with David and with Zowie, who attracted positive attention everywhere, Angie was touched by David's reaction to being with his son, and watching him, tears welled up in her eyes. "I saw David's face shining with pride and love for his boy. . . . David could be so kind, so gentle; I loved him so much, I really did," she said.

She did indeed love David but still didn't have any intimation that her happy times with him were now all behind her. For while he had once relished her uninhibited sexuality when they were both single, childless, and flouting convention, the moment she had became the mother of his son, he instantly reverted to tradition and wanted her to stay home and play the role of wife and mother. Instead, she continued to have lovers, both male and female, and while he would, in the future, sometimes join in, he remained emotionally distant and separate from her.

Meanwhile, Bowie mania continued unabated, and when, on May 12, David performed in front of eighteen thousand fans at Earls Court, the show was halted for fifteen minutes while crazed fans who had stormed the stage battled with security.

By now Ziggy mania had reached such a crescendo that scenes like this were not uncommon, and many a time, fans would succeed in getting so close to David that they grabbed the items of clothing he waved around onstage, and literally hundreds of his shirts were torn to shreds. Even Elton John, ostensibly his rival in the music business, now appeared to be a fan, raving of David, "His stage presence was quite extraordinary. David was so beautiful, so glamorous, so androgynous, and so sexual."

Mick Jagger made the pilgrimage to David's Earls Court Show, with Bianca Jagger in tow. David had already paid Mick the compliment of name-checking him in his song "Drive-in Saturday," referring to "Jagger's eyes," and now Mick had reciprocated.

"To me, it was like the passing of the scepter," Tony Zanetta said. "David had worked for years to become a star, and to have Mick Jagger come to *his* show was an acknowledgment that he had arrived at last."

After David and the Spiders played Liverpool in June, he threw a birthday party for Trevor Bolder in the penthouse of the hotel where they were all staying. Sisters June and Jean Millington of the rock band Fanny, of which David was a great fan, were among the guests.

Although David was riding high as Ziggy, as always, his gaze was fixed on yet another horizon. "He told me he wanted to get into film. His work ethic was so strong. He had every one of his shows filmed, then watched it afterwards to evaluate his performance," June Millington said.

David began dating June's sister Jean, who played bass in Fanny and, at twenty-one, immediately fell madly in love with him. "He was magnificent," Jean said. "Before we started dating, knowing that he was married, I asked him about what was going on with him and Angie. He said, 'Angie and I have an agreement, and as long as it isn't anything that goes beyond a couple of dates . . .' But, of course, it did with us." She would remain a part of his life for the next year and a half, and would sing backing vocals on "Fame."

On July 3, at the Hammersmith Odeon show, simultaneously immortalized by the filmmaker D. A. Pennebaker in front of an audience of thirty-five hundred fans, David made the shocking announcement that "this is the last show we'll ever do."

As audience members, many of them dressed as Ziggy clones, wailed and screamed in shock, David did nothing to put them out of their misery, nothing to explain that it was *Ziggy Stardust* whom he was retiring, not David Bowie.

Angie had been filmed before the show, prattling away in an irritatingly artificial upscale British accent, and was neither shocked nor surprised by David's sudden announcement, as beforehand he had discussed with her his plan to dispense with Ziggy once and for all. However, she still remained unaware that her own departure from David's life was also imminent. For around the same time, a fan had stolen David's wedding bracelets, twins to the ones Angie wore, and their chosen substitutes for wedding rings.

"It was symbolic, I thought. Our marriage was pretty much over in all but name," David said afterward.

• • •

Apart from Mick Ronson, who had been forewarned, the Spiders from Mars, whom David had, in effect, sacked in full view of thousands, were devastated.

Bitter and angry, years later, Trevor Bolder told Dylan Jones that he had really bad memories of David "towards the end, when he changed as a person. He was ready, until then, just a regular sort of bloke, he was a nice caring bloke, but the bigger he got, the bigger his head got, and the less important you were to him."

Mick Ronson would survive the demise of the Spiders from Mars and work with David on *Aladdin Sane* and *Pin Ups*, but then they parted company. Suzi Ronson, Mick's widow, who is currently in the process of producing a documentary on Mick, said, "Mick was never bitter about David. After Mick stopped playing with him, we had a lot of times when we were stony broke. But Mick didn't care about money. It was all about the music."

As for Trevor Bolder and Woody Woodmansey, there was no time for tears or recriminations when, the following evening, MainMan threw an "end of Ziggy Stardust tour" party at London's Café Royal, which was attended by Barbra Streisand, Ringo Starr, and Mick Jagger, who greeted David by kissing him full on the lips. At that moment, as both Mick and David had intended, Mick Rock was on hand to immortalize the moment.

Like David, Mick Jagger had always known exactly how to work the press, how to excite the crowd, and how to buttress his position as Rock King of the World. Now, however, with David the freshly hatched pretender to his throne, Mick had clearly determined to keep his younger rival close. And he had every reason to feel threatened by David, for by the end of the month, five of David's albums would be in the UK top 40, and three of those in the top 20, a feat even Jagger had not been able to match.

After that night at the Café Royal, Michael Watts of *Melody Maker*, the same writer to whom David had made his famous "I'm bisexual" announcement, recalled him raving about Jagger through the entire evening, giving the impression of being utterly enamored by him.

Whether or not David acted on his emotions for Mick is a matter of conjecture. However, while Angie might have been abrasive, histrionic, and self-centered, she is not a liar, and there is a ring of truth to her allegation that she found Mick and David in bed together.

However, flamboyant Roxy Music cover model, singer, and actress Amanda Lear, who was to have an affair with David, spent time with him and Mick together. Adamant that she didn't believe that David and Mick's relationship was sexual, she later observed to Mick's biographer Laura Jackson, "I believe David was madly in love with Jagger during the time I knew him."

Yet whatever romantic emotions David might have nurtured for Mick, his ambition, as always, overrode everything.

"David particularly copied Mick a lot," Amanda Lear said. "He was jealous of Jagger's success and badly wanted to be as big. I know there was a lot of rivalry underneath their friendship as far as David was concerned."

On one notable occasion David's rivalry with Mick reared its head in an obvious fashion. While paying a visit to Mick, David discovered that Mick was hiring Belgian designer Guy Peellaert to design his next album cover. David promptly picked up the phone and hired Guy to design the cover for his own *Diamond Dogs* album, as well.

"Mick was silly," David declared afterward. "I mean, he should never have shown me anything new. He will never do that again. You've got to be a bastard in this business." He added, with a note of triumph, that Mick was now scared to walk into the same room as him with a new idea because "he knows I'll snatch it."

And Mick himself afterward allegedly even made the comment, "Be careful of the shoes you wear around David, because next time you see him, he'll be wearing them, and he'll be wearing them better than you!"

But despite the fact that Mick and David clearly had each other's numbers, through the years, they would always retain a strange sort of connection, auditioning together for the Hollywood buddy movies *Dirty Rotten Scoundrels* and *Ishtar*, neither of which they got, and even recently collaborating on a possible autobiographical TV series about two seventies rock stars, which Martin Scorsese may direct.

Away from movies and TV, however, they disagreed on the subject of music. "[Mick] believes in music as music, as a source of uplift, of enjoyment; I see it as a vehicle for ideas, as vocabulary," David said.

On a social level, they were both very different, with Mick relaxed, and David more distant and remote.

"Mick and David were both very professional. Mick would talk about sport, the current test match, but I never socialized with David," says BBC producer Jeff Griffin.

Leaving Ziggy behind him was a relief for David, who generally took five hours to apply his Ziggy Stardust makeup, and an hour each night to take it off.

In the press, there were a great many rumblings that he had been drained psychologically by playing Ziggy 24/7, but the truth was that, above all, he was a Method actor: Ziggy was performance art, and it was eminently clear to him that the time was ripe for him to move on.

Learning that Bryan Ferry was about to record a solo album of covers of oldies, *These Foolish Things*, David quickly followed suit and decided to record his own album of covers of sixties' oldies, *Pin Ups*. Reportedly, Bryan Ferry was not amused. In the future, they would share a lover, Amanda Lear (but not simultaneously), and, like David, Bryan would also grapple with cocaine. But despite their similarities, and the fact that *Pin Ups* and *These Foolish Things* would hit the charts on exactly the same day, long-term, David would outstrip Bryan Ferry.

On July 9, he traveled to the eighteenth-century Château d'Hérouville, a residential recording studio in the village of Hérouville, near Paris, set to record *Pin Ups*. Photographer Joe Stevens spent

five days there making a record of David's work in the studio for a
photo shoot commissioned by *New Musical Express*. According to Joe,
David had hired four French violinists to play on "Sorrow," and they
were ferried to the château by limousine.

The following evening, Joe noticed that David had a big bulge in
the back of the pink trousers he was wearing.

"I couldn't stop wondering what it was—couldn't stop looking at
it," Joe remembered, "They (the violinists) had been there all night
and into the day. They thought they were about to head into the studio to unpack their violins and get started, but Bowie had called the
limo service to come back, as he didn't need the violinists after all.

"He asked them how much they got paid, reached into his back
pocket, and the bulge ended up being a massive bankroll of about
150,000 francs" (the equivalent in those days of around $33,000). "He
paid 'em out and moved on," Stevens recalled.

On that same trip, as Joe remembered, "David relished getting lost
in Paris after intentionally sending away his limo, and having to fend
for himself. In his case, without euros [francs]."

After years of knowing David, Stevens observed, "David is nonr-
eminiscent. Doesn't subscribe to nostalgia, mulling over the past, yak-
king with the lads about that time in Chicago and those hot honeys.
But if he remembers you and your interests, he will come prepared
with something to chat about. The last time we met, he told me of a
film he read about that Kodak was creating in their labs, before they
did a virtual belly-up. It could show the outline of an object after it had
been removed."

David had flown Fanny band member twenty-one-year-old Jean
Millington to France to spend a few days with him at the château. "I
was there with him for two or three days," Jean remembered. "Then
Angie flew in. She came swooping into the bedroom. She was very
polite and offered me orange juice, but it was clear that was it. David
seemed very matter-of-fact about Angie finding us there together.
There was no guilt. No shame. The awkwardness was on my part. He

asked me very politely to go back to London. I did, and when he came back to England, we stayed together in various London hotels."

After the whirlwind of life between the start of his first major U.S. tour in September 1972 and the Hammersmith Odeon show, David settled down again to life in England.

"He had finally achieved his success, but now that he had retired, there was a sigh of relief. For the first time ever, he could live life in London as the superstar he had always wanted to be," Tony Zanetta said.

However, his superstardom came at a price, and he and Angie moved out of Haddon Hall, where by now crazed fans and groupies besieged him night and day, so that they were forced to transform the house into a Beckenham Fort Knox. Nonetheless, a naked girl once succeeded in breaking in and made it as far as the dining room before she was apprehended. The phone rang morning, noon, and night, and bags of fan mail flooded in every day.

Drained by life at Haddon Hall, in October 1973, the same month *Pin Ups* was released and shot straight to number one, David and Angie rented a four-bedroom, three-bathroom, two-reception-room, terraced house at 89 Oakley Street, off the King's Road, where there was very little space outside for fans to loiter or attempt to storm the house.

Once David and Angie were ensconced in the house, they set about creating a sexual cocoon for themselves, a London hybrid of Graceland and the Playboy Mansion, and the perfect environment in which to throw parties, even orgies. Consequently, as soon as she and David moved into the Oakley Street house, Angie presided over her own personal Sodom and Gomorrah, the focal point of which was 'the Pit,' a four-foot-deep fur-covered bed in the sitting room, where, in front of a series of audiences, who generally ended up participating themselves, all permutations of sexuality were explored.

Freddie Burretti and his girlfriend Daniella moved into the basement, and later, when Corinne "Coco" Schwab became David's personal assistant, she commandeered the top floor as her domain. Zowie,
of course, also lived at the house, staying up to all hours, according to
one of the Oakley Street guests. By now, David and Angie's marriage
had degenerated into verbal battles, and Zowie would cower in the
corner and burst into tears when they had one of their increasingly
frequent screaming matches.

On other nights, both Angie and David were distracted by the
sexual circus at which they were ringmistress and ringmaster, respec-
tively. One of the biggest stars of Oakley Street excesses, literally and
figuratively, was London gangster John Bindon, who had appeared
in *Performance* with Mick Jagger and who had holidayed in Mustique,
where he had taken the fancy of Britain's Princess Margaret. Above
all, Bindon was known for his overriding air of menace and his major
asset, a gargantuan endowment that he used to display with five beer
mugs hanging from it to emphasize both its length and its girth.

Bindon's girlfriend for many years, model and socialite Vicki
Hodge, said, "Angie and David used to have the most amazing orgies
at Oakley Street. Everybody fucked everybody in the Pit. Mick Jagger
used to come there and be involved with sexual things. Everybody
was so sexually liberated. John said that David was totally nice and
sweet, and very sexually aware. He told me that David watched while
he had sex with Angie."

John Bindon's biographer Wensley Clarkson confirmed Vicki's
story, writing that "Bindon was allowed by David Bowie to make love
to his wife while Mick Jagger was nearby."

Clarkson also recalled that Bindon had told him that Angie
arranged for him to have sex with five of her female friends on one
afternoon. "He became like the hired stud," a source confided to
Clarkson.

Soon after, Bindon was promoted to bodyguard for the end of the
Ziggy Stardust tour in America. But although Bindon was favored and

trusted by David, his sojourn as bodyguard on the tour didn't always run smoothly. When Bob Dylan arrived at the show, Bindon, then working security, assumed Dylan was a hobo and mistakenly tried to eject him from David's show.

Other than his brief stint as David's bodyguard, John was primarily around for fun and sexual pleasure. "John enjoyed all the perks of being a huge Cockney stud and a sexual boy toy," Vicki Hodge said, adding, "Angie and David's marriage was totally free and open, and I think that because they were doing so many drugs, they could do anything they wanted."

As far back as his Lower Third days, David had toyed with drugs, and in 1976, he confided to Cameron Crowe in a *Rolling Stone* interview, "I never got into acid either. I did it three or four times and it was colorful, but my own imagination was already richer. I never got into grass at all. Hash for a time, but never grass.

"I guess drugs have been a part of my life for the past ten years, but never anything very heavy. . . . I've had short flirtations with smack and things, but it was only for the mystery and the enigma. I like fast drugs."

He certainly did, and cocaine is clearly the fastest drug of them all, and it had begun to be a part of his life. But it was only to dominate his life utterly and completely the following year.

ELEVEN

YOUNG AMERICAN

On April 11, 1974, David disembarked from the *SS France* in Manhattan and then checked in to the Sherry-Netherland, which, courtesy of MainMan, he would make his New York base for the entire year, in between stops on the U.S. Diamond Dogs tour, a glittering theatrical extravaganza that was performed on a dizzyingly dramatic re-creation of a city, David's creation "Hunger City."

This, the next stage in David's conquest of America, was a vast enterprise, with the set weighing six tons and composed of more than twenty thousand moving parts. The U.S. Diamond Dogs tour lasted from mid-June to September, when it was simplified and renamed the Soul tour, continuing till December 1, 1974.

Meanwhile, David tasted every aspect of stardom, American-style. Dana Gillespie, whom Tony Defries signed to MainMan as well, recalled, "Tony fired David up to conquer America, and I used to be flown to America first class to join Angie and David at the Sherry-Netherland for the weekend, at MainMan's expense. David had a huge grand piano in the suite, which he played at the wrong hours, and everybody did so much coke that you fell asleep wherever you could.

"David would be strutting around on the guitar and Mick Jagger and I would be playing duets, and then he and David would be mincing about.

"Angie and David were like my family, and MainMan was massive and over-the-top and paying for us to fly wherever we wanted on first-class tickets, and I ended up staying at the Sherry-Netherland with Angie and David for six months," Dana said.

An American fashion model and singer who graced the cover of *Playboy* in 1974, Bebe Buell also hung out with Angie, David, and Mick Jagger at the Sherry-Netherland. "Mick was worried because David was doing so much cocaine that he would hallucinate," Bebe remembered. "One time we were in David's suite in the Sherry-Netherland hotel and he asked us if we could see the angels flying outside the window. He made us go and look. 'Don't you see them?' he said. 'They're flying around.'"

According to Bebe, despite David's burgeoning drug addiction, Mick still retained respect for him, "He didn't like to mock David, because he still liked to have fun with him," she said. "They used to love to pick up beautiful black girls and take them back to the hotel and have mad sex with them. . . . Mick and Bowie were mates. They would act very androgynous with each other."

While David was living a hedonistic life in Manhattan, all the time assuming that Tony Defries was footing the bills, back in London, Ken Pitt was dismayed, and later told George Tremlett, "David's made a great mistake. He's very naïve . . . and he's also trusting, innocent, and easily led. This man Defries is a shyster. He has no right to pretend to be a lawyer. . . . It's all going to end in tears."

For now, though, Defries and David were riding high. Ironically, by design, it was Defries who was riding highest of the two of them. Apart from having a penthouse on the Upper East Side, a duplex on East Fifty-eighth Street, a loft on the West Side, and an apartment at the Sherry-Netherland, he also rented a twenty-room fully staffed Greenwich, Connecticut, estate; a chauffeur-driven customized brown Cadillac with a custom cream leather interior, which had been perforated so that he wouldn't get overheated during the summer; and a fourteen-room Park Avenue office, where his staff of twenty-six worked.

In short, Tony Defries was acting as if he, not David, were the star. Moreover, every single MainMan bill was charged to the account of David Bowie, only David didn't realize it at the time.

Set on conquering America with his *Diamond Dogs* album and tour, David had also embarked on a new relationship, with Ava Cherry, a blond black singer whom, on David's suggestion, Tony had signed to MainMan. For a time, Ava, David, and Angie existed in a netherworld of ménage à trois and faux friendship. Then Angie started to crack under the pressure of sharing David with Ava on a permanent basis.

Down the line, Ava, too, would suffer virulent jealousy over David's infidelity to her. "He was fascinated by black people. Black girls, any girls he would sleep with when I was with him were black. . . . I couldn't stop him. I used to cry but he would always say 'You can't fence me in.' I was very faithful, and he wanted me to be. It was the old double standard: He didn't have to be, but I had to be. He was a male chauvinist—but I liked it," Ava said.

"Ava was a sweet girl," Tony Zanetta recalled, "but if David really fancied someone, he would send Ava back to her own room. She would go, because she was very young and she adored him."

Back in England, David and Angie's ménage à trois with Ava suddenly proved to be unworkable because of Angie's jealousy, so he arranged for Ava to live in an apartment just a few yards away from Oakley Street, and for her to have singing and dancing lessons, a new wardrobe of clothes, and a weekly allowance, all funded by MainMan, or rather—although he still didn't know it—himself.

Together, he and Ava saw Frank Sinatra perform in Las Vegas, and afterward, they waited backstage to see him, not just as fans, but because it had been bruited about that David was in the running to play Sinatra in a biopic.

David had always been fascinated by Sinatra, and in the early days of his career had written English lyrics for Claude François's song "Comme d'habitude," but was rejected, and Paul Anka went on to write the English lyrics for the song that became "My Way." But if David thought that Sinatra was interested in having him play him in a movie of his life, he was due for a disappointment. Sinatra refused to see him, sending word that "no English fag" was going to play him in a movie.

Meanwhile, disenchanted with Cherry Vanilla as his PR and office manager during the mixing of the *Diamond Dogs* album, David demanded that she be replaced. Enter Corinne Schwab, henceforth known as "Coco."

Today, Coco is as much a woman of mystery as David is a man of mystery, but in those early years, she was a shy, wide-eyed, fresh-faced ingénue, who was the daughter of Eric Schwab, a distinguished French war photographer, and his wife, whom he first met when she was working for French Allied Forces radio. Consequently, Coco's family background, as well as the fact that she'd grown up partly in Haiti, India, and Mexico because of her father's profession, lent an air of intellectual sophistication to her that must have appealed to David.

"Coco wasn't streetwise, like us. She seemed much more English and sophisticated," Cherry Vanilla observed.

After answering an advertisement in a London newspaper, without knowing the nature of the job in advance, or that she would be working indirectly for David Bowie, Coco had been hired as receptionist/secretary at MainMan's London office, where her primary job, it transpired, was to hold off MainMan's multitude of creditors.

"Tony Defries didn't pay bills, he just didn't, so the London office was left struggling with bill collectors," Tony Zanetta remembered. "But Coco became pretty stern at fending off bill collectors and was pleasant and intelligent. She didn't dress to draw attention to herself, and was plain, but not unattractive, and she was no-nonsense.

"Tony Defries decided that David should have a personal assistant, but although Suzi Fussey had played that role during the last tour, she was now involved with Mick Ronson. Suzi wasn't prepared to lay her life down for David Bowie, but Coco was, so Defries asked her to do the job instead," Zanetta said.

Coco had first met David in May 1973, at a party at Haddon Hall thrown to welcome him back from his tour of Japan. Afterward, she recalled, "My first impression was how tired and skinny he seemed! The famous red hair was a bit crumpled but his essence, the warmth and kind gentleness was there [through that worldly weariness] and he hugged Andrea [MainMan Fan Club assistant] and me and made us feel welcome."

Ava Cherry, however, would be blunter in her appraisal of the birth of the relationship between Coco and David. "She was in love with Bowie from day one," Ava said.

Angie Bowie, to her everlasting regret, was instrumental in recommending Corinne as David's personal assistant. "I thought she was my friend, but she wrecked my marriage," Angie said. "Gradually, she edged closer and closer to him—ordering the cars, ironing the shirts, making the breakfast. . . . Coco is ugly and frumpy. David doesn't want good-looking girls. He wants a mother. And Coco is a mother substitute."

Angie's words might sound bitter and vindictive, but one only has to compare photographs of Coco Schwab with those of Peggy Jones to see that there is a striking visual similarity between both women. Moreover, Coco and Peggy were both strong women, both strident, both stormy, with Coco by far the more maternal of the two, but nevertheless, more than a little parallel in nature to David's mother.

Sean Mayes gives a glimpse of Coco's brand of mothering David; part maternal, part threatening, and totally manipulative, in his book *We Can Be Heroes: Life on Tour with David Bowie,* where he writes about witnessing David's ersatz mother, Coco, in action:

"'You ought to wrap up, David,' said Coco.
'Oh, I can't do that.'"

'He's impossible,' she said. 'I've got all his woolen things packed. Oh well, I'll just have to burn his shirts with the iron!'"

The unspoken subtext, of course, is that if she deliberately singed David's shirts with an iron, he would be forced to wear his woolen sweaters after all, just as Coco had decreed, and her dominance over him in this particular context would be assured.

MainMan's Leee Black Childers gave his judgment of Coco to Kerry Juby, who interviewed him for the radio show *David Bowie: In Other Words,* which was later to become a book, and, as he did, was acutely aware of the risk he ran in talking about Coco to the media.

"A very odd woman and still, to my knowledge, has not been evil to me. But she will after she reads this. But it's the truth," Leee said. "She seemed to pick people that she didn't want to have anything to do with David, or have any influence on David, and would openly go for the throat and get rid of them.

"She was doing it even then though she had no real influence over David at all, but I think it appealed to him—that sort of approach, that sort of fierce protectiveness. He used to encourage jealousy amongst us to see who was closest to him, so I guess Corinne particularly appealed to him because she made no bones about it. She went right after it.

"So she grew in favor until she decided she was strong enough to take on Angela and she did, openly. Openly defied Angie for David's affections and David's favors," Leee said.

Later on, when David had moved to L.A., according to Tony Zanetta, Coco became very lonely, and felt that not even David appreciated her. "She wanted reassurance that she was needed and loved and was also essential to David's success," he said, adding, "It was a terrible job, but she was glad to do it because David was so wonderful, and she loved him so much. Yet he paid so little attention to her."

Coco was so successful in her single-minded campaign to become the most important woman in David's universe that soon she had usurped Angie's role as the wife/mother figure in David's life to such an extent that wherever she and David were in the world, she established a morning ritual in which she woke him with orange juice, lit his cigarette, served him coffee, and handed him the newspapers. No prince of the realm had a more devoted retainer, no son a more loving mother.

"She had a lot of backbone, a lot of spine, but she was devoted to David. Did they have an affair? Well, whoever was the last man standing got to spend the night with David, so there was a lot of opportunity there for her. It was certainly love, and definitely devotion," Tony Zanetta said.

David, of course, was intensely aware of Coco's deep emotions for him and now and again, paid tribute to her. "Coco is the one person that has been a continual friend. She's a very sweet and loving person," he once said, and credited her with saving his life during the days of his coke-fueled existence.

During that time, she worked diligently to keep him healthy, to build up his immune system, to coax him to drink extra-rich milk, which she took great pains to find for him. Above all, she kept trouble and troublemakers, scroungers, and parasites away from him, so that he could concentrate on what really mattered to him: writing and performing.

Defending her, he once said, "It's hard for her to sustain all the abuse one gets in the position of someone who's close to a 'personality' figure like myself. Unfortunately, business affairs being what they are, everything that comes out of my camp goes through Coco, so she becomes both the receiver and the transmitter of bad tidings, so if I can't be reached, then she is blamed. It's a helluva position to maintain for this many years, but she does it very successfully."

Despite David's defense of her, through the years, Coco has consistently aroused deep-seated animosity in many who crossed her path.

And she was openly dubbed by some the woman who did David's dirty work, who didn't have her own life, whose every waking hour revolved around David and no one else. Their relationship was and is unprecedented. Never married, Coco disclosed in a rare interview that she has had boyfriends, but none have ever been seen in public with her, and so they cannot be identified. Instead, she has willingly made herself available to David 24/7.

"It was as if David and she had been married for a very long time," Tony Zanetta said.

Indeed, according to Cherry Vanilla, there was definitely talk in the midseventies that David was on the verge of marrying Coco. Utterly dedicated to David, Coco appeared to live for him, and clearly she would also have killed or died for him. As his watchdog, his gate-keeper, she continued to build sky-high walls around him and alienate those who wanted to get close to him.

His agent Maggie Abbott remembered visiting David and Coco in New York at the brownstone on Twentieth Street in Manhattan where they were living around the time when MainMan was wind-ing down: "It was very bleak; they didn't have any food or money, as I think Defries had held it back, who knows? I felt sorry for her. At first she was cold and detached and I thought she was worried and anxious about David."

Aware of Coco's importance in David's life, Maggie, while she was agenting David's role in *The Man Who Fell to Earth*, made sure to include Coco in David's contract for the movie.

"At my meeting with David, thinking like an agent, I realized that he would be more attracted to doing the movie if he didn't feel alone. So I told him and Coco that I would put her into the deal officially as David's assistant, and I stuck with that all the way. So it was because of me that Coco was written into David's contract, guaranteeing her a job and a career and employment stability," Maggie said.

A few years later, Maggie attended a music festival to which she had an all-access pass, and decided to go backstage to see David. But when she got there, Coco announced, "I don't know Maggie Abbott. I've never heard of her," and refused to let her in to see David.

"That's when I saw her as a really cold bitch. Maybe it was because some people don't like to see people who know too much of them from the past. I'm sure she was in love with him. She definitely doted on him and she stayed the course," Maggie said.

In contrast, when photographer Bob Gruen was hired to photograph David during *Tin Machine* in 1991, he dealt with Coco and reported afterward, "Coco was very pleasant. She's very smart and a strong woman, a classic New York girl, very efficient and took care of business very well."

"Coco was tough. She didn't try to be personable, but just did her job and did it well," *The Man Who Fell to Earth* producer Si Litvinoff said.

"Like the Japanese, David hated to say no," Tony Zanetta commented. "So he needed Coco to be a buffer between him and the world. She has no problem getting rid of people and yet she is quite a lovely girl, and bright, with a softness about her."

Throughout her forty years with David, in keeping with her *modus operandi*, perhaps learned from David, Coco has retained an enigmatic persona, and only once emerged out of the shadows, when, in 2001, she took part in a Q&A session on David's website, and made a concerted attempt to defend herself against the barrage of criticism she had always faced. Commenting that when she began working for David she had not been prepared for the fact that she would be continually placed under a magnifying glass, she declared, "The only magnifying-glass aspect to being David's assistant that I used to find difficult was the realization that everything one did was observed. I naively never even thought of that.

"Nor did I think to watch my back. I just did what I had been asked to do and what needed to be done. I found out the hard way that just as often what I did was either misinterpreted or misrepresented or just plain old slandered.

"My effort to get the job done was sometimes seen at best as overzealous or at worst as God only (and the tabloids) knows what! However, David's friendship and understanding and the importance of what he tries to achieve helped me see fear and jealousy for what it is and not to take on other people's stuff. Today I try and do the best that I can in a day, let go of the rest and have a pretty good life!"

Although Coco did her utmost to try and temper David's drug addiction, it was an uphill struggle. Nonetheless, the *Diamond Dogs* tour would prove to be a resounding success. Chris Charlesworth, who was *Melody Maker*'s American editor at the time, saw the tour and said, "It was a completely different concept of a rock performance. David didn't acknowledge the audience and the band was on the side. He didn't introduce any songs, and the whole thing was a theatrical experience."

Chris, who went on to be an RCA press officer and had social contact with David through the years, developed the highest respect for him during that time, saying of David, "He was polite and gracious and good company and women loved him because of that. He is extremely intelligent, knows his own destiny, and is an immensely talented performer and songwriter. He is very bright. Most rock stars are philistines; all they care about is rock. They don't read or go to the theater, but David is very culturally aware."

He was all that and more. But at the same time, as he himself has admitted, he also had an addictive personality. And in his cocaine-riddled years, his addictions often meant that he suspended his intelligence and lost grip on one of the most crucial elements in his life: his finances.

"He was this hugely popular figure and didn't have the cash in the bank to show for it. I think John Lennon gave him some tips, and Mick Jagger may have put in a word, because he is a businessman," Charlesworth said.

David had met John Lennon when they were introduced in Los Angeles, at a party thrown by Elizabeth Taylor. "We went on to a great relationship over the years," David said of Lennon. "Terrific guy, very, very funny guy."

Back in Manhattan, John called David and asked if he could bring May Pang, with whom he was then having a romantic interlude, and Linda and Paul McCartney over to see David. According to Ava Cherry, who was there, the meeting between David and Linda did not go well. "I also don't think she liked David very much, and the feeling was mutual," May Pang said.

At that point, David made the unwise move of playing tracks from *Young Americans* (the soul-influenced album that he would ultimately release in 1975) to his guests, not only once, but twice, whereupon Paul McCartney asked for another album to be put on instead.

David ignored him and started to play *Young Americans* again, but John Lennon intervened and gently asked him to play another album. May Pang diplomatically did what John asked, and David left the room.

That same evening, David called John and the two of them talked for quite a while. Afterward, John confided to May that David had been really hurt when he'd asked him to change the album, but that he had managed to mollify him to such an extent that he and David had become friends.

According to Tony Visconti, David's friendship with John developed to such a degree that the three of them often spent a night on the town together. "We stayed up with John Lennon until 10:30 A.M. We did mountains of cocaine, it looked like the Matterhorn, obscenely big, and four open bottles of cognac," Tony recalled, adding of David, "During the making of *Young Americans*, he was taking so much cocaine it would have killed a horse."

John and David bonded over drugs, music, and a shared quirky British sense of humor. And when David made a speech to the Berklee College of Music's class of 1999, he told of a time when he and John were in Hong Kong together: "During one of our expeditions, on the back street a kid comes running up to him and said, 'Are you John Lennon?' And he [John] said, 'No, but I wish I had his money,'" David recalled, before going on, "Which I promptly stole for myself. [*Imitating a fan*] 'Are you David Bowie?' 'No, but I wish I had his money.' It's brilliant. It was such a wonderful thing to say. The kid said, 'Oh, sorry. Of course you aren't,' and ran off. I thought, *This is the most effective device I've heard*.

"I was back in New York a couple of months later in SoHo, downtown, and a voice pipes up in my ear, 'Are you David Bowie?' And I said, 'No, but I wish I had his money.' 'You lying bastard. You wish you had *my* money.' It was John Lennon," David said.

In contrast, however, going back to January 1975, when David cowrote and recorded "Fame" (which would be added to *Young Americans* at the eleventh hour) with John, he played the first cut for Maggie Abbott, and she remembered, "The track was really great, John and him singing. When it was released, I noticed that John's voice was less prominent in the final cut. I guess David just wanted to downplay John in favor of himself."

Nonetheless, in September 1975, "Fame" was to become David's first number one hit in the U.S.

From the time that David first met John, John warned him about Tony Defries.

Years later, looking back, David said, "I always thought there was somebody better at doing this kind of thing [managing me]. It wasn't until Lennon pointed it out to me that I realized maybe the artist is as good at managing somebody as anybody else.

"It was John that sorted me out all the way down the line. He took me to one side, sat me down, and told me what it was all about, and I realized I was very naïve. I still thought you had to have somebody who dealt with these things called contracts, but now I have a better understanding of show-business business."

Ever since he signed his deal with Tony Defries, he had refused to examine his contract closely. "None of us bothered to check our con-

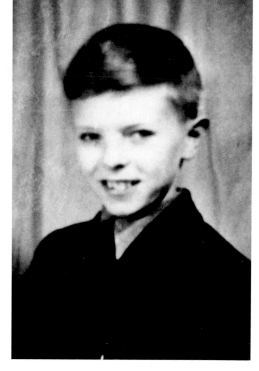

RIGHT: Star quality: Davie Jones at about seven years old. *Pictorial Press Ltd/Alamy*

BELOW: The pouty Prince Charming of Pop. *Pictorial Press Ltd/Alamy*

The newly minted David Bowie with Phil Lancaster and The Lower Third. *Pictorial Press Ltd/Alamy*

A cool looking Norman Bowie, whose last name David may well have borrowed.

Barnardo's

David and his teenage love, Dana Gillespie.

Getty Images

Angie and David at their wedding, with uninvited guest—
David's mother Peggy—1970. *Pictorial Press Ltd/Alamy*

Pretty Thing: David in a dress and posing outside his and Angie's then home, Haddon Hall. *Mirrorpix*

David (or is it Ziggy?) pays oral tribute to Mick Ronson's guitar.

Pictorial Press Ltd / Alamy

Modern family: David, Angie, and Zowie, 1974. *Pictorial Press Ltd/ Alamy*

Ziggy Stardust in all his glory. *Photofest*

Elizabeth Taylor paying court to David. *EPA/Kote Rodrigo/Alamy*

David with his fabled crown jewels accentuated in a scene from *The Man Who Fell to Earth*. *Moviestore Collection Ltd/Alamy*

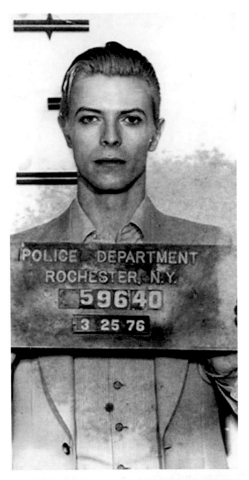

LEFT: David's mug shot after his 1976 arrest for the possession of pot, which was never his favorite drug . . . *Mug shot/Alamy*

BELOW: The Thin White Duke on the town with glamorous transsexual Romy Haag in 1976. *Getty Images*

Only *Just a Gigolo*.

Photofest

David as "The Elephant
Man," on Broadway.

Photofest

David with Elvis's ex-paramour Monique van Vooren, one of the only women who ever rejected his courtly approaches. *Photofest*

David and the former Mrs. Mick Jagger, Bianca, at the 1983 U.S. Festival. *Corbis*

David and Mick Jagger after a birthday party,
the best of friends, and—according to David—nothing else.

Mirrorpix

David in a scene from *The Hunger*
in which he plays a vampire,
with his costar Ann Magnuson.

Pictorial Press Ltd/Alamy

David stars in Jim Henson's
film *Labyrinth*. *Photofest*

David triumphs over
his old nemesis Andy
Warhol by playing him in
Basquiat. *Photofest*

David at Live Aid in 1985 with his best friend, confidant, and gatekeeper, Corinne "Coco" Schwab, his left hand and more for more than forty years. *Aidan Sullivan/Associated Ne/Rex*

David and Iman, together, now and always.

tracts in those days," Dana Gillespie confirmed, but David, of course, was less likely to do so than any of them. His father had always managed every aspect of his finances, paying his bills, his taxes, his insurance, so that David had been eager to relinquish control of his finances to another father figure, without checking his contract.

Now, though, in the midst of all his cocaine-fueled haze, toward the end of his Diamond Dogs tour David was forced to confront reality.

Continually short of money, he was now so broke that he had been forced to cancel the standing order by which the bank paid his mother £50 a month. Enraged, Peggy had called David's number one cheerleader in the British press, Charles Shaar Murray of the august *New Musical Express*, and complained bitterly about David.

Labeling him "a terrible hypocrite," Peggy lambasted David for neglecting her and the family. Outraged, David struck back and, as Peggy's sister, his aunt Pat, remembered, "he phoned her and warned, 'If you ever speak to the papers again you won't see me, your grandson, or any of my money ever again.'"

Chastened, Peggy would never talk to the press about David again, but her slurs against him left their mark. Although he would eventually reinstate her allowance, for most of the decade he restricted his contact with his mother to the minimum.

Nonetheless, after he shipped all his gold records and awards to her, Peggy erected a virtual shrine to him in her apartment in Beckenham and hoped against hope that he would contact her, but he rarely did.

By the time the Diamond Dogs tour hit Manhattan, the fact that David was truly short of money while Tony Defries was living the high life at his expense had hit him hard and he was ready to do battle with Defries.

Although Angie was spending much of her time in London with Zowie, now that she had been married to David for four years, she was intent on forging a career of her own as an actress. In quest of that, she traveled to America, where she hoped Defries would manage her to professional success. Treating her ambitions with disdain, Tony was unaware that Angie was making mental notes regarding his lavish lifestyle, in contrast to hers and David's.

"I think Angie saw that Tony had a penthouse, a mansion in Connecticut, yet he was always on at her about spending too much, and I think she put a bug in David's ear regarding Tony," Cherry Vanilla said.

After Defries made the fatal mistake of berating Angie about the $100,000 she'd spent on airfare in the past year, David, ever the chivalrous husband when the crunch came, sprang to her defense, and on the second night of the Diamond Dogs show at Madison Square Garden summoned MainMan president Tony Zanetta to the Sherry-Netherland for a meeting. There, he proceeded to interrogate Zanetta about the terms of the contract, which he, David, had signed with Defries. Over and over, he insisted to Zanetta that he owned 50 percent of MainMan, and Zanetta over and over recited the litany: "You are to receive fifty percent of the profits *after* your expenses are deducted, of the monies generated by you and you alone. You own no portion of MainMan. MainMan belongs exclusively to Tony."

In his drug-infused miasma of shock, David flatly refused to believe Zanetta. As if they were a mantra, he repeated the words "I own fifty percent of MainMan."

But money wasn't the sole bugbear between David and Tony Defries. "David felt Defries had abandoned him," Tony Zanetta said, "They had been very close, but once Defries set foot in America he started to move on with me and Cherry. It became Defries's world, and it no longer orbited around David so much anymore.

"David had only been a vehicle for Defries to get where he wanted to go. And that was to become head of a studio and rich. That's what Tony wanted, but David expected him to revolve around him a hundred percent, like it had been in the beginning. But now he was no longer the most important client in Tony's life and we were no longer a family."

Finally, when dawn broke over Manhattan and David began to think more clearly, he was compelled to confront reality: Tony Defries, the man in whom he had put all his trust, at whose disposal he had put all his talents, had used and abused him, and, ultimately, had played Tom Parker to his Elvis Presley. It was too much for David to bear.

However, although he would spend the next few months attempting to extract himself from Defries's web, he refused to be diverted from the only things that truly mattered to him: his music, his career, and his future.

TWELVE

FALLING

Throughout 1974, as David spent much of his time ensconced at the Sherry-Netherland in Manhattan, he encountered many of his rock contemporaries—not always with the best of results.

Author Steven Gaines, then ghosting Alice Cooper's autobiography, remembers visiting David at the hotel: "David was kind of weird, reserved, and I couldn't tell if he was stoned or not. He certainly wasn't especially clean.

"He had a color Xerox machine in his suite, which, in those days hadn't been around long, and he made each of us put our face forward onto the Xerox machine and told us to keep our eyes open while he made portraits of us. He did that to anybody who came up to the suite," Steven said.

"I don't think he and Alice really hit it off. Alice was really drunk at the time. I think Bowie was more into drugs. It was really odd."

On December 12, 1974, David, Bob Dylan, Bette Midler, Coco, and the group Manhattan Transfer went to Reno Sweeney's to see Dana

Gillespie perform, and at one point in the evening, were joined by twenty-seven-year-old Wilhelmina model Winona Williams. Winona, who had already met David at a Melba Moore show at the Café Carlyle, invited him and the entire table to her Ninth Street house, where she lived with Shep Gordon, Alice Cooper's manager, who was then out of town.

"David seemed very impressed by Dylan, and put on *Young Americans*, looking for some sort of endorsement from him, but Dylan wasn't complimentary at all," Winona remembered. "David was visibly upset, and I took him to my bedroom to try and calm him down. He put his head in my lap, rather like a child.

"When he started feeling better, he tried to get a little sensual, and his hands started moving. I told him that no, that was not going to happen, as this was my man's house and doing anything with him there was out of the question, and David said, 'Nobody's ever had that much respect for me.' "

After he failed to persuade Winona to let him stay the night with her, he went back to the Sherry-Netherland, still devastated about Dylan, and later said, "I think he hates me."

The following morning, he dispatched a limo to take Winona and her nine-year-old daughter, Mia, to him at the Sherry-Netherland.

"When I got there, Coco opened the door to the living room, where Zowie was alone, playing, and Mia joined him. Then Coco said, 'David is in the bedroom,' and led me in there. It was almost as if she were procuring me for him. She knew that he was interested in me, and she was fulfilling his need. So she left me alone with him in the bedroom.

"He was naked in bed, with newspapers and magazines all around him. He was drinking fresh-squeezed orange juice, and had some of his white powder around. I stayed talking to him for a couple of hours, and although the sexual desire was there, I was involved with Shep Gordon and was trying to be good," Winona said.

"David and I saw each other a few more times, and although I knew he was seeing other women, when I was with him, everything was rumor and he made me feel as if I were the only woman in the world. He showed me the artwork for the *Diamond Dogs* album, which I thought was very bizarre, and also showed me a deck of tarot cards which he was designing."

David had always been riveted by the tarot, by astrology and psychic phenomena. According to Bowie biographer Christopher Sandford, author of *Bowie: Loving the Alien*, "Bowie's mother had taught him to be passionate about memory, and he shared with her the ability to experience various fragmentary moments of mental telepathy."

So convinced was David of his own telepathic abilities that he once challenged a friend to concentrate on a five-figure number, which David would then repeat to him.

"After ten minutes, just when his friend suspected an anarchic hoax, Bowie opened his eyes and spoke in a high, reedy voice. Four of the sequence of five were correct," Sandford said.

While he was in Manhattan at the Sherry-Netherland, David made an attempt to forge a professional relationship with teen idol and *Partridge Family* star David Cassidy. He called him, suggesting that he produce an album for him, that he and various other people would write. Consequently Cassidy flew to Manhattan and met with David at his suite.

In his memoirs, Cassidy remembered of David Bowie, "I found that he lived in a very subterranean New York, an avant-garde kind of world of transsexuals and transvestites. It was like a carnival at his place. There were some people in other rooms doing mime. He had a whole bunch of people around him who, I guess, made life interesting for him, including some whom I couldn't tell the gender of—and perhaps they weren't sure either. Bowie just enjoyed feeling part of this very hip, inside, New York, artistic scene. To me it held no fascination at all. It felt false and posed.

"We were different ends of the spectrum, two guys sitting by history—one's success in the pop music field largely behind him, the other's largely in front of him. He was very enthusiastic over the next album he had coming out [*Diamond Dogs*] and all of the touring he would be doing to promote it."

To Cassidy, the idea of touring was anathema, and there was no way he was about to make the album that David had suggested and then promote it on tour. But according to Cassidy, David felt very differently. "He really craved all of the mass adulation that I'd had enough of. My own take on him was: I don't want to be where you're headed. Been there. Done it. Thanks.

"He played me a couple of songs that he'd written, and that Lou Reed had written, for the album he wanted me to do. I just didn't think they were interesting enough," Cassidy said.

That same year, David's movie agent, Maggie Abbott, flew to Manhattan to talk to him about a film project she had found for him, *The Man Who Fell to Earth*. Her suggestion that he star in a movie was not the first he'd received. He had set his sights on Hollywood, but had nonetheless turned down Elizabeth Taylor's offer for him to appear in her movie *The Blue Bird*.

"She said, 'Read this and make it with me. Be my leading man,'" David remembered. "I was so excited when she handed it to me and I go through it and it was absolutely awful."

"She was a nice woman and all, even if I didn't get much of a chance to get to know her. She did tell me I reminded her of James Dean—that endeared me to her—but her script was so . . . boring," David said to Cameron Crowe afterward.

Fortunately, Elizabeth didn't take offense at his refusal, as they had already begun what the French would call *unc amitié amoureuse,* an amorous friendship.

Photographer Terry O'Neill, who knew Elizabeth well, had originally made the introduction at her request, and a meeting between her and David was set up at the Beverly Hills home of director George Cukor.

"Elizabeth had a reputation for being late, but it was Bowie who arrived three and a half hours after the agreed time. It was the height of his cocaine addiction. Elizabeth was so angry she almost left," O'Neill remembered.

But, by some miracle, she did not, and during David's few weeks in Los Angeles, he and Elizabeth became instant friends, and each morning when she woke up, she invariably called David at his hotel, the Beverly Wilshire, just to chat about makeup, hair, Hollywood, her marriages, her illnesses, while he usually listened in silence, rather like a geisha.

At one point, he went up to her house. "Everything there was fake, and when he opened the bathroom door, the handle came off in his hand," Tony Zanetta remembered.

Back at the hotel, David still managed to evade Ava Cherry and sample a selection of the crowds of groupies who invariably stalked him wherever he went. Groupie Lori Lightning lost her virginity to David and told the tale to Pamela des Barres, who reported it in her book *I'm With The Band.*

"He escorts me into the bathroom and takes off his kimono, gets into the bathtub, and sits there staring at me with those different colored eyes. You have to understand—he's so gorgeous, his skin is so white and flawless," Lori said.

Ever the gentleman, and aware that this was Lori's first time, David invited her to wash his back. After that, he was gentle with her, but she felt guilty about her friend, Sable, who was in the next room crying because she wanted so badly to have sex with David. Feeling sorry for her, David asked Sable to join him and Lori in bed, and she did.

He took his pleasure wherever, whenever, and with whoever it was offered, and at the after-show party held at the Plaza in honor of his Madison Square Garden show, he disappeared into a closet with Bette Midler and Mick Jagger for an inordinate amount of time, leaving the hapless Ava Cherry sobbing in the next room.

"The three of them were in the closet and spent the whole party in there, doing coke," Tony Zanetta said, adding, "And I'd be very surprised if he didn't have Bette Midler then or at one time or another."

That many of David's sexual adventures were fueled by drugs was patently obvious. Hardly sleeping, he was ingesting massive amounts of cocaine, the quality of which was far stronger in America than it had been in England. His energy was at an all-time high, with groupies, fans, and roadies all ready and willing to supply him with endless grams of coke. Taking the drug became so habitual for him that he didn't even balk at snorting it in full view of Ava Cherry's parents when they invited him to dinner.

Jean Millington of Fanny, still in love with him, saw him in L.A. and remembered of that time, "When I was first around David, we were offered drugs all the time, but he always said no. But now he'd gotten heavily into cocaine. He was producing a demo for Iggy Pop, on which I was playing bass, and we were recording it in a small L.A. studio. I stayed up for two days, but David was maybe up for five whole days. I thought to myself, 'I can't do this. He's not in his right mind.'" Their relationship ended, and Jean went on to write "Butter Boy," ostensibly about David.

His drug addiction had ended his relationship with Jean, which, given his admiration of her work and that of the band, which he dubbed "one of the finest rock bands of their time—they were extraordinary," he may well have regretted.

Years later, looking back on that era of his life, he said, "I was undergoing serious mental problems . . . a young man with too much time on his hands and too many grams of amphetamine or PCP or cocaine, and maybe all three, in his system. It's a blur, topped off with chronic anxiety, bordering on paranoia. However, I made some good music."

In another interview with Paul Du Noyer, David confessed, "I have an addictive personality. I'm quite clear on that now."

On the subject of cocaine, in the same interview, he went on: "And it was easily obtainable and it kept me working, 'cause I didn't use it for . . . I wasn't really a recreational guy, I wasn't really an out-on-the-town guy. I was much more, 'Okay, let's write ten different projects this week and make four or five sculptures.'

"And I'd just stay up twenty-four hours a day until most of that was completed. I just liked doing stuff. I loved being involved in that creative moment. And I'd found a soul mate in this drug, which helped perpetuate that creative moment."

Asked by Du Noyer if he meant cocaine, David said, "Yes, cocaine. Well, speed as well, actually."

His old bandmate Keith Christmas, who played acoustic guitar on the *Space Oddity* album, remembered hanging out with him in Manhattan and seeing him "doing amyl nitrate all the time," and that "David took me to the loo, whipped out a double-sided razor, and slashed into a huge chunk of coke."

That same summer, for a brief spell, twenty-year-old British rock star Glenn Hughes of Deep Purple was afforded entrance into David's drug-infested, star-crossed universe, and, in the process, gained insight into the man himself. He and David first met at the Wilshire, where they were both staying, and they spent a week together shooting the breeze, mulling over the business and black music, all the while drinking and taking drugs. They became good friends and began to talk on the phone on a weekly basis.

In October, when David was playing Radio City Music Hall in New York, he and Glenn met again and their friendship intensified.

"David never came on to me, but I always used to question what was really going on between us. He and Angie had a very open marriage and were staying at the Pierre, and I was staying at the Plaza," Glenn Hughes said. "Suddenly David suggested that I should go back to the Plaza with Angie. I wasn't sure if he wanted to be there while Angie and I were having sex, or if he even cared. But Angie and I were getting close; she was very attractive and very intimidating and we went back to my hotel together.

"One thing led to another, and next thing she's on top of me, and I'm just taking it, feeling pretty sad and morose and almost in tears, because although David wanted what was happening to happen, I felt bad that I was cheating on him."

After his night with Angie, Glenn nonetheless spent time with David and did cocaine with him.

"He could handle cocaine better than I could," Glenn said. "He could think and go on and on about the Nazis and that. But he also had his eye on my girlfriend and then on my wife. I don't know if anything happened, but it was built around cocaine."

Around the same time, David took to hanging out with Cherry Vanilla, who was performing in cabaret and was no longer with Main-Man. Reassured regarding her loyalty to him, he spent hours with her in her Chelsea loft.

"I loved him when he was on cocaine. He was really interesting. He would tell stories about magic and fantasy, and come out with conspiracy stories and crazy theories that Tony Defries was Hitler reincarnated and Lou Reed was the devil, and that together, they were out to get him," Cherry Vanilla said. "We had sex a couple more times, but most of the time we stayed up all night talking. He brought Jean Millington over to my place once, to fuck, and also Claudia Lennear, but I didn't mind.

"Mick Jagger came over to my place, and one time he was in the living room listening to music while David and I had sex in the bedroom. I think at that time in his life, David needed a lot of business and financial advice, and I think a lot of his talks with Mick were to do with that," Cherry said.

The extent of David's drug use was evident in the December 1974 television interview he did with Dick Cavett. For although his charm was on display, he was clearly higher than the highest kite. That impression was intensified when Alan Yentob's landmark documentary, *Cracked Actor*, aired the following January on the BBC, featuring David, clearly drugged up, clearly on the edge.

With him during a limousine ride captured on film was a pretty girl in a white gypsy dress, gold chains dangling around her neck, her hair in curls—none other than Coco, looking for all the world like a hippie chick, head bobbing along to the music, eyes shining, and—for that moment, at least—playing the part of classic rock star girlfriend. There is also a stray shot of Tony Defries in a yellow suit, all shaggy hair and paunch, clutching a purse.

Most of all, of course, there is David, painfully thin, with knife-blade-sharp cheekbones and jaw, emaciated, strung out, and still sniffling from his most recent line of coke.

THIRTEEN

CRACKING ACTOR

In a 1997 BBC Radio interview, David admitted that the documentary *Cracked Actor* "is very painful for me to watch." He later went on, "My drug intake was absolutely phenomenal. I was addicted."

Although *Cracked Actor* exposed his addiction to the world, the documentary would also serve another purpose: It would win him the role of *The Man Who Fell to Earth*. Maggie Abbott, who also represented Peter O'Toole, Sean Connery, Peter Sellers, Liza Minnelli, and Mick Jagger, among others, had known David since 1973, and had gone to all his concerts.

"I went to Oakley Street a few times; we'd sit around in the conversation pit for long evenings, and people came by. The child [known then as Zowie] always stayed up very late," she remembered.

One of her clients, Donald Cammell, owned the rights to *The Man Who Fell to Earth*, and the director, Nicolas Roeg, and producer, Si Litvinoff, were determined that Peter O'Toole play the role of Thomas Jerome Newton, the Man of the title. When Maggie informed them that Peter was committed to another movie, the name Mick Jagger was bandied about for a moment until Nic Roeg judged that he was too strong.

"Nic said that 'we want somebody who is rather weak or slender or pale. He has to look as if he has no bones,'" Maggie remembered him saying before she chipped in with the name David Bowie. Si Litvinoff immediately knew who she was talking about and said afterward, "I thought it was brilliant, as I was a fan of Bowie's and thought it would be great to get the film score from him to help promote the film and I believed that his fan base was ideal for this film. I was so happy that I could not stop singing 'Space Oddity.'"

But neither Nic nor Donald knew who David Bowie was, so Maggie suggested she first talk to Angie. With great foresight, Maggie also convinced a friend to sneak the video of *Cracked Actor* (which hadn't, at that point, been broadcast) out of the BBC so that she could screen it for Donald and Nic. The moment they saw it, Donald and Nic immediately recognized that they'd found their Thomas Jerome Newton, their man who fell to earth, and Maggie was enlisted to help make the deal.

On good terms with Angie, Maggie went to see her. "Angie really wanted David to have a successful career and do movies. She's been totally underrated and undervalued. I remember us sitting round thinking what movies we could get for him, and Angie said, '*Spider-Man!*'" Maggie said.

At Angie's behest, Maggie had a conversation with David, who was interested in making *The Man Who Fell to Earth* and pleased that his contract with Defries did not stipulate that MainMan receive any commission for any work he might do in movies.

Next, Maggie arranged to fly to New York with Litvinoff and Roeg to meet David at the brownstone he was then renting on West Twentieth Street. There, as Si remembered, "The door was opened by Ava Cherry, a striking black girl with orange hair wearing a *Clockwork Orange* sweater, which I considered a good omen, as I had optioned the book. And David was very gracious and seemed enthusiastic about starring in the movie."

Soon after, David, preparing to make the break with Defries, hired attorney Michael Lippman to represent him. By now, David had come to terms with the fiasco that had been MainMan. Confiding to Michael Watts during a *Melody Maker* interview, he said, "I'll never condone completely what went on. I don't know whether I was absolutely manipulated but I believe all my business was manipulated. I believe that a lot of what were very good ideas were cheapened for the sake of getting things out economically rather than going the whole hog and doing things properly.

"Stage shows were never what they were supposed to be because suddenly the money was not there to pay for what I wanted initially. Things would always be done shoestring and I could never understand why, because apparently we were very, very popular and . . . where's the money?"

Asked whether he would ever consider going back to Defries, David erupted, "Oh, Lord no! That's absolutely . . . It couldn't be further from my mind. I have literally no idea of what he does, where he is, and what kinds of things he does anymore. It was an astonishing chaotic period."

Now that David was represented by Lippman and not Defries, Maggie Abbott found her role as David's agent for *The Man Who Fell to Earth* being eradicated. "Lippman started to put a barrier between us, and asked for more money," Maggie, who had negotiated a $75,000 deal for David to star in the film, plus another $75,000 to write the score, said.

Finally, despite the fact that she had put the entire movie deal together, Maggie received a cease-and-desist letter from Lippman cutting her out of the project, and making it clear that she was not allowed to set foot on the movie location. And although she finally did get paid a $7,500 commission, that was the end of her involvement with the movie.

"I felt quite bitter and annoyed at being banned from the set of a movie I'd made happen for the star," Maggie Abbott said, adding, "David knew how to let go of people he didn't want. He let go of me because he didn't need me anymore. Overall, I felt terribly insulted by David's behavior. He didn't acknowledge what I had done for him, how it changed his career and really launched him in movies."

Meanwhile, back in Los Angeles, plans for the movie proceeded apace, and David invited Si for lunch at an elegant French restaurant in West Hollywood.

"It was clear that he was knowledgeable about French cuisine, and I believed he felt comfortable with me," Si said.

While he was preparing for the movie, David stayed at Glenn Hughes's mansion behind the Beverly Hills Hotel, though Glenn, who was touring with Deep Purple, wasn't there at the time.

"I was calling the house every day and my house guy, Phil, said there was all kinds of birds up there, black girls, white girls. They were coming and going, and I think soul singer Claudia Lennear and Slash's mother, Ola Hudson, were some of them," Glenn said.

"When I got back, I felt so close to David as a friend. He was in my closet; he threw away all my shoes and told me, 'You have got to change forever.' He was a great influence on me. But it was still all about drugs for him.

"He had hidden all the knives under the bed, telling me that the Manson family was around. He was paranoid. Super intelligent. But super paranoid. He was moody, as you are on drugs, and I never saw him sleep. He was in a coke storm. We would both be up three or four days at a time. We were both addicted to cocaine but didn't realize how addicting it was.

"Later on, he moved to a house and Coco was with him. It seemed to me that she was constantly tending to him, giving him milk, trying to get him to sleep. I'm not sure if he would still be here if it wasn't for her. She absolutely loved him," Glenn said.

Glenn was also around when David made the album *Station to Station*. "Even though he didn't let anybody in there, I was allowed in a few times, and he was as high as a kite," he said.

Glenn and David were to meet again the following year, when David played Wembley Stadium. "I went down in my Rolls-Royce, which David hated. He was like, 'What are you doing in this machine? You should be driving a caravan!' He was being funny. He would joke and people would laugh with him and it was all becoming old for me.

"There was nothing emotional or sexual between us. He drew me and signed it 'Ol Big Head.' He would call me that, but I don't know why. It sent me into a bit of a state because I had been so nice to the guy," Glenn said.

"When we last met, I took him to the Elbow Room, a nightclub, and we brought two birds back to the hotel, and we might have been drunk, but we weren't on drugs. I thought we would talk, but he was more interested in getting these two birds in the sack. So it all ended between us, and I felt used."

Now that David was living in L.A., Winona Williams was back in his life again. After spending a great deal of time with David in Manhattan, she had decided to commit to Shep Gordon, after all, and had moved out to Los Angeles to live with him in Bel-Air. Despite that, David wasn't prepared to let her go.

"He would get Coco to call me and tell me that if I didn't come to see him immediately, he was coming up to the house," Winona remembered.

"He asked me to go house hunting with him, and although I was trying to get away from him, he ended up renting a house on Stone Canyon Drive in Bel-Air, right down the road from where I was living. That's when things began between us. I realized then that he was brilliant, a very sensitive man with a tortured soul. I went up to UCLA with him where he was learning about Kirlian photography," Winona said, adding, "He has a very curious mind and he was exploring all things mystical and occult as well as scientific breakthroughs in the uncharted functions of the brain."

. . .

Filming of *The Man Who Fell to Earth* began in Lake Fenton, New Mexico, in July 1975, and over the six weeks of filming, David, who had refused the offer of a hotel room during the shoot, lived in a Winnebago trailer. He was still frighteningly thin, and it was obvious that he was still snorting cocaine on a large scale.

From the first, David and Nic Roeg got on extremely well, and afterward David said, "I'm ever so slow in forming human relationships. I don't really have a circle of friends unless you consider Nic a circle."

Nic was extremely impressed by David's performance. "What's extraordinary about David, as an artist he can't be classified," Nic said. "He can't be singled out, 'Ah that is Bowie,' because that's the way he always does that. He never appears the same way twice.

"And he's got fantastic concentration and he's also got an amazing kind of self-discipline. He seemed the perfect person for this."

Nic, who had directed Mick Jagger in *Performance*, later compared him to David, saying that they were "very similar, very different . . . but they're very similar in terms of their absolute concentration on the character they're playing. They're not just a singer with a band. Their whole magnetism comes out in acting."

David's female costar, Candy Clark, was initially apprehensive about working with him, but was relieved to find that he wasn't spoiled and that he was totally involved in the movie. Unfortunately for Angie, although Candy was Nic Roeg's unofficial girlfriend at the time, she seemed to be making a play for David, as well.

Initially, Angie had invited Candy and Nic to dinner at the home she and David were renting in L.A. so that they could read through the script with him.

"While I was playing housekeeper and serving wine, she [Candy] attacked my husband in my own house and was mauling him like a tiger," Angie said, mindful that David would also be filming love scenes with Candy.

And although Candy was to enthuse of David, "His skin does reflect the light so beautifully. He does look like he's from another planet," producer Si Litvinoff was adamant that there was no romance between her and David. "She was always disappearing with Nic Roeg and didn't spend any offscreen time with David," recalled Si.

At the same time, on one occasion when David was too sick to film, Candy stepped in, and, wearing a big hat that overshadowed her face, played his part instead. May Routh, who designed the costumes for the movie, said that David was so thin that in some scenes he had to wear boys' clothes.

"He usually stayed up very late at night composing the score," Si said, although ultimately that score never survived, other than the track 'Subterranean,'" which David released on his subsequent album, *Low*. "He was wonderful in the part. He told me he wasn't going to do any drugs.

"There was one incident on the set when Rip Torn came in to do a shoot with David. Rip was very wound up. So I had to get some tequila for Rip and I got some NoDoz energy pills for David and, as he didn't like to take pills, I ground them up and he snorted the powder," Si said. "I saw David a lot when he wasn't shooting. I had custody of my two young sons for the summer and he had Zowie with him. Zowie was adorable, with very long hair."

At one point on location, David decided that he wanted to do some sculptures, and within a day, Coco had assembled all the necessary materials for him. "He was happy as a bunny," May Routh remembered.

David also spent much of his time between takes reading the biography of silent screen star Buster Keaton, whom he was considering playing in a biopic. Around the same time, he was also having an affair with beautiful black costume designer and model Ola Hudson, whose son, Saul, would grow up to become Slash of Guns N' Roses.

Slash was eight years old when he walked into a room in his home, only to find David there with his mother, stark naked. "He was always over. They had a lot of stuff going on, but my perspective was limited. Then it turned into some sort of mysterious romance that went on for a while after that," Slash remembered, adding, "Looking back at it now, it might not have been that big of a deal, but at the time, it was like watching an alien land in your backyard."

During his affair with Ola, David would often come by her house, bringing Angie and Zowie with him, as well.

"It seemed entirely natural for Bowie to bring his wife and son to the home of his lover so that we might all hang out. At the time, my mother practiced the same form of Transcendental Meditation that David did. They chanted before the shrine she maintained in the bedroom," Saul said.

Aware that, far from wanting to mother Zowie, Angie was much more intent on her own ambitions and her lovers, including bass player Scott Richardson, who was into drugs, and, afterward, actor Roy Martin, David hadn't really played a part in Zowie's life until then. "I was around so infrequently I can't imagine what an abyss that has caused," he said later, admitting, "My son's seen me through some of the most awful depressing times when I was really in absolute abject agony over my emotional state, the heights of my drinking and drug-doing. He's seen the lot."

Fortunately, the boy had primarily been in the care of Scottish nanny, Marion Skene, and, as Angie later admitted, "David and I were away doing drugs, at first together and then later apart. Marion effectively became Zowie's mother."

"I've always considered her as my mum," Zowie said years later, adding, "so I never felt I was missing out in any way."

. . .

Still dedicated to having sex with as many partners as possible, David compelled Ava to endure his multiple affairs, and even to listen when he rated the prowess of his sexual partners. Worse still, he even went so far as to give her details about his fling with one of The Three Degrees.

After the shoot was over, David came out to Si Litvinoff's house in Malibu a couple of times. "He played music, we had dinner, and he didn't drink anything. He was always with a beautiful black girl, but not Ava Cherry anymore," Si noted.

During filming, Angie had paid a short visit to the location, but she left swiftly as it was finally clear to her their marriage had disintegrated almost beyond repair. And the writing was even more firmly on the wall, when, the following year, David squired Bianca Jagger (now separated from Mick) to a birthday party at the Manhattan disco Hurrah and photographers snapped them together, whereupon all hell broke loose with Angie.

David, of course, was well aware that by taking Bianca to such a public venue, it was inevitable that they would be photographed together. Beforehand, in a rare manifestation of conscience regarding his double-dealing with women, David made somewhat of a show of worrying about the feelings of the other women in his life, former girlfriends though they might be, and, for once, demonstrated a modicum of concern that they might suffer pangs of jealousy upon seeing him with Bianca.

On the night of the party, as Coco confided to Sean Mayes, "He was rather shy about coming here tonight as several of his ex-girlfriends were here. But you should have seen their faces when we walked in!" she went on with some relish.

"David had walked in with Mrs. Jagger. And we missed it!" Mayes added.

For Angie, the blow of learning that David was dating Bianca was mortal, although he had also had a brief dalliance with Marianne Faithfull. He and Marianne had first met in 1964, during the Manish Boys' tour, when they had performed on the same bill. Nothing had happened between them then, primarily because Marianne was enthralled with Gene Pitney, who was on the same tour with her.

Later on, David hired Marianne to sing on his *1980 Floor Show*, which, confusingly enough, was actually recorded in October 1973, for the NBC TV show *The Midnight Special*, and invited her to the Rolling Stones' Wembley concert. But conscious that being seen in public with David would give the impression that they were having an affair (which they weren't at the time), she went to the concert with his entourage and not with him.

However, with her boyfriend, antiques dealer Oliver Musker, Marianne eventually began to spend a lot of time with Angie and David and was drawn into their sexual web.

In her memoirs, she recalled, "One night, we were all a bit drunk at David's house and David began coming on to me. We went into the corridor. I unzipped his trousers. I was trying to give him a blow job, but David was scared to death of Oliver. Oliver does have this Gestapo officer vibe to him. Absolutely terrified of Oliver David was, and so he couldn't keep it up."

Angie, however, told another story and in her second autobiography, *Backstage Passes*, wrote of Marianne at Oakley Street "playing naughty with David, Ava, or Amanda or some combination thereof."

Marianne was wild and untrammeled, and later on seduced Angie, but in Angie's eyes that very wildness made Marianne less of a threat to her. But Bianca Jagger, however, cold, remote, elegant, was Mrs. Mick Jagger and to Angie appeared to be a much more serious threat to her marriage.

Worse still for Angie, after Cannes, Bianca and David, who had Zowie with him at the time, vacationed together on the Spanish Riviera and afterward were the guests of Prince Hohenlohe at his exclusive Marbella Club. Angie did her utmost to ignore David's burgeoning romance with Bianca and instead carried on carousing at Oakley Street, taking drugs.

At the time, David was in the throes of acting out his roles as the Thin White Duke, his final stage persona after Ziggy Stardust, and that of Aladdin Insane, a strange hybrid of a thirties cabaret star and a Rat Packer, which was clearly born out of David's cocaine paranoia. Suitably pale and emaciated, in his guise of Thin White Duke, David would perform in a foppish white shirt, black waistcoat, and trousers, and exude a combination of icy malaise and lounge-lizard cynicism. With a high degree of self-hatred not unrelated to his mega–drug use, he would label his Thin White Duke "a very Aryan fascist type. A would-be romantic with no emotions at all."

David had a brief fling with Ronnie Spector of the Ronettes, whose description of her moments with David in her book, *Be My Baby*, paints a snapshot of his life in Manhattan during his Thin White Duke years. At a reception after the Isolar tour (aka the Thin White Duke tour, which was in support of the album *Station to Station*, which began in February 1976 and ended in May of the same year) at Madison Square Garden, with a show that Ronnie attended with May Pang, David sent one of his gofers to invite Ronnie to join him at dinner. Afterward, he invited her back to his suite at the Plaza. There, Ronnie was faced with a room full of people, and a coffee table covered in cocaine. Within minutes, she was summoned into David's vast bedroom, where she found him sitting on the floor, naked, and surrounded by music cassettes.

"One look at this guy and I could see how excited he was to see me. Very . . . Sure enough, we made love right there on the floor, and we didn't even bother to kick the cassettes out of the way," Ronnie said.

Afterward, they lay in bed drinking cognac, but the noise from outside the suite was so loud that Ronnie put on her clothes and informed David that she was going home. "Then he asked if he could come along. He said he could do with a little peace and quiet himself, but I got the feeling that wasn't all he wanted," Ronnie said.

After David's limousine ferried them to her apartment on York Avenue, they had just started making love when they heard water running in the kitchen. In shock, Ronnie realized that it was her mother, who had the key to the apartment and must have come by unexpectedly.

"'Your mother?' Bowie asked. He looked at me like I was joking. But when he saw that I wasn't, he started laughing out loud. 'Your mother?' he said, still chuckling. 'Oh, Ronnie. That's so quaint,'" Ronnie remembered him saying.

His dalliance with Ronnie was lighthearted, but away from that, his drug taking had increased and his grip on his own sanity was clearly weakening considerably. Looking back, he admitted, "I never fully kicked until the mid-eighties. I've an addictive personality, and it took hold of my life. I'm ambivalent about it today. It was an extraordinary thing to have to go through. I certainly wouldn't want to go through it again, but I'm sort of glad I did."

Rolling Stone's Cameron Crowe interviewed him at various stages at the height of his addiction and described the scene: "[David] pulled down the shades at one point to reveal strange symbols on the curtains of his bedroom and, for a time, he saved his urine in bottles.

"There was an odd belief system at play—a kind of white magic he was exploring," Crowe wrote.

When David attempted to read Crowe's article thirty years later, he found that he couldn't finish it. "It was probably one of the worst periods of my life," he said. "I was undergoing serious mental problems."

At the time, his libido was set aflame by his excessive cocaine use, David continued to indulge every aspect of his sexuality. When he played Vancouver in February 1976, he conducted an orgy with four women and orchestrated the entire evening, positioning the women, including cocktail waitress Cheryl Hise, almost as if he were art-directing a movie.

Now giving every appearance of being resolutely heterosexual, the following month, David was interviewed by Chris Charlesworth for *Melody Maker*, who ended the interview by asking him about his bisexuality.

"Momentary shock. Oh Lord, no. Positively not. That was just a lie," David said, and disingenuously went on: "They gave me that image so I stuck to it pretty well for a few years. I never adopted that stance. It was given to me. I've never done a bisexual action in my life, onstage, record, or anywhere else. I don't think I even had a gay following much. A few glitter queens, maybe," he said to Charlesworth, having suddenly morphed into a Dr. Goebbels of pop propaganda.

Clearly unnerved by David's blatant dissimulation, Chris said nothing. He was past being surprised. David had begun the interview—which he was giving in a suite at Detroit's Hotel Pontchartrain, where he was dressed in a designer suit, while in the street outside, a Mercedes was on constant call for him—with the words "I'm just doing this tour for the money. I never earned any money before, but this time I'm going to make some. I think I deserve it, don't you?"

Chris remembered, "He clearly wasn't broke, but he knew that if he said he was broke it would be the headline of my story. And it was a good headline. David was very wise about how to manipulate the press and create a headline."

However, his next headline—the one that hit the newspapers on March 22, 1976: "How Bowie Copped It at Pop Rave-Up," for once, was not engineered by him. As the newspaper reported, he and Iggy Pop and two friends had picked up two women in the bar of the Flag-ship Americana hotel, where they were staying in Rochester, New York, little knowing that both women were undercover cops.

After David invited them up to his seventh-floor suite, one of the women made a call to waiting police, who raided the room and found half a pound of pot there. David and Iggy and their friends were all arrested and locked up in a jail for the night. In the morning, David posted bail for all of them.

Nothing else came of the incident—an irony, as everyone who knew David at the time agreed: He generally used harder drugs than pot.

"He called me after he was booked and was freaking out. He used to hate pot, so I don't know why he got booked for using it," Glenn Hughes said.

After David sailed through the drug bust, untouched by the bad publicity, on May 2 of the same year, he ignited a controversy that finally did tarnish his image, almost irrevocably. Arriving in London on the Orient Express, he was met at Victoria Station by a chauffeur driving his newly acquired black convertible Mercedes, which Coco had only lately purchased on his behalf from the estate of an Iranian prince who had been assassinated.

Fans and photographers crowded the station, desperate for a glimpse of David. After he finally emerged from the train, wearing a black shirt, which, to some, recalled the attire of Oswald Mosley's followers, once so admired by David's mother, he proceeded to stand up in the open-topped Mercedes, raise his arm, and make what to some looked like the Nazi salute. Afterward, he flatly denied that he had made it, and insisted that he was merely waving to the crowds.

However, *New Musical Express* ran the photograph under the headline "Heil and Farewell"—and, given that David had once said of Hitler: "His overall objective was very good, and he was a marvelous morale booster. I mean, he was a perfect figurehead." Although Bryan Ferry, who had always exhibited similarities to David in terms of his style and image, in 2007 also made the mistake of expressing the sentiment that "the way the Nazis staged themselves and presented themselves, my Lord! I'm talking about the films of Leni Riefenstahl and the buildings of Albert Speer and the mass marches and the flags," the outcry against him didn't match that against David. Although David went on to qualify his remarks regarding Hitler with, "He was a nut and everybody knew he was a nut," in some quarters, he was damned as a Nazi supporter.

All of which was ironic, given that his best friend, Coco Schwab, was of Jewish origin: Her father had been a legendary photographer of the concentration camps and had liberated his own mother from one of them.

After the Victoria Station debacle, David did all he could to mitigate the damage to his image, and, in an interview with Allan Jones of *Melody Maker*, he swore, "That didn't happen. THAT DID NOT HAPPEN. I waved. I just *waved*. Believe me. On the life of my child, I waved. And the bastard caught me. In MID-WAVE, man. . . . As if I'd be foolish enough to pull a stunt like that. I died when I saw that photograph."

David may have sounded devastated by the dent in his image, but not so much so that he allowed his plans to be derailed: He spent the next year or more living in relative seclusion in Berlin.

Long afterward, he defined his motives for moving there: "I needed to completely change my environment and the people I knew. I had a small handful of what one might call normal friends. The rest were dealers. It was extremely unhealthy. Stereotypical rock-and-roll behavior," he said.

Meanwhile, seven years into her marriage to David, Angie was unaware of his plans. Desperate to save the marriage, she had pinned her hopes on starting a new life with David in Switzerland, where she had gone to school. Using his tax problems as an excuse (and the truth was that had he remained in California, where he was then based, his tax bill would have been sky-high), she procured a seven-bedroom chalet near Blonay, overlooking Lake Geneva, where their nearest neighbors in Vevey were Charlie Chaplin, his wife, Oona, and their brood of eight children. But though the house, named Clos de

Mésanges, was idyllic, and though Angie set about furnishing it exquisitely, David hated it on sight.

Nonetheless, still with Coco, his ever-present companion/nanny, constantly by his side, he spent some time there, while Angie, dispirited, went back to London, where she carried on her whirlwind drug-driven party existence without him, becoming more strung out.

Zowie, meanwhile, was primarily brought up by his nanny, Marion Skene, who was more of a parent to Zowie than David and Angie were. David did attempt to father Zowie in the best way in which he knew how, instilling in him a love of movies. When Zowie was seven, David would screen *The Seahawk*, a pirate movie starring Errol Flynn, for him. And when the boy was eight, David showed him a video of *A Clockwork Orange*, the movie that had played such a seminal part in his own career, influencing as it had, his creation Ziggy Stardust.

"I remember he was sitting with me on the sofa with his arm around me, explaining everything," Zowie said, recalling with warmth and nostalgia the closeness he and his father had.

Stifled by the arid beauty of Switzerland, David, though he loved walking by Lake Geneva, painting, reading, and working on sculptures, found both the countryside and the house too serene to hold his attention. Berlin beckoned him partly because he had read Christopher Isherwood's *Goodbye to Berlin* (which was adapted into the movie *Cabaret*); it was set in the Weimar Republic years running up to World War II, featuring louche songbird Sally Bowles. Isherwood had painted the Berlin of those years as a decadent, lush city, which Toulouse-Lautrec might well have immortalized, just as he did Paris. Unhappily for David, though, as Isherwood informed him face-to-face when they finally met: "Young Bowie, people forget that I'm a very good fiction writer."

The truth was that Berlin in the late seventies, far from being glamorous and debauched as depicted by Isherwood in his novel, was a grim, impoverished city, torn asunder in the Second World War, and dominated by the Wall and the heavy Russian presence ruling over half of it.

But David didn't care. "I went to Berlin to find an environment unlike California, that dreadful, parasitic mire. It seemed foreign and alien to anything I'd been through. Rough and tough, not a sweet life.

"I was just doing things like shopping and walking around. Anything that had to do with survival and nothing to do with rock and roll."

FOURTEEN

BERLIN

Coco was with David in Berlin, and so was Iggy, ostensibly playing Sancho Panza to his Don Quixote, Jeeves to his Wooster. But in actual fact, David's oft-stated mission in inviting Iggy to come to Berlin to live with him was to help Iggy kick his drug habit. Along the way, of course, he also hoped to cure his own.

"David said he came to Berlin to get over drugs, but that was silly, as Berlin was a drug town," fashion designer Claudia Skoda, who was a close friend to David during his time in Berlin, said afterward.

David acknowledged the truth years later. "I didn't have any idea till I got there that Berlin was the smack capital of Europe," he said wryly.

Nonetheless, he started to create a home for himself and Zowie there, spending more time with him and giving him some of the attention that Angie seemed unable to provide, as she was now deeply involved with actor Ray Martin and had traveled to Morocco to be with him.

Meanwhile, David did his utmost to transmit his own enthusiasms to Zowie and, as soon as he was old enough, gave him an 8mm camera. "He taught me, in a lovely way, the basics of making a movie," Zowie remembered. After David taught him how to do storyboards, write scripts, and do the lighting, Zowie made animated movies featuring his Smurfs, and took to carrying his storyboards and scripts around with him in a blue box when he traveled to concerts with his father, playing with them backstage while David performed.

In February 1977, David was back in England, where Iggy gave his first solo concert at Friars Aylesbury. Though David played the keyboards and sang backup, "the Duke remained out of the stage spotlight and had certainly dressed down for the occasion," journalist Nick Kent noted. "In an anorak and flat cap, he looked more like a registered taxi driver than a rock star."

Despite David's attempts to underplay himself, it was clear that he was now in charge of Iggy's professional destiny—and some hardcore punk fans were not amused, with Johnny Thunders snarling, "Jim's just Bowie's bitch now."

In March 1977, David went back to America with Iggy for his twenty-nine-performance Idiot tour, in which David would play keyboards in his backing band. Along the way, he invited Debbie Harry of Blondie to join them on the tour.

"Bowie and I both tried to hit on her backstage," Iggy said. "We didn't get anywhere, but she was always very smooth about it. It was always, 'Hey, well, maybe another time when Chris [Stein] isn't around,' always very cool about it."

Despite refusing both Iggy and David so very elegantly, Debbie was flattered to be hit on by them: "Of course," she said, "it was a lot of fun. They're two really great stars, musicians, and writers that I've always admired. The whole thing was mind-blowing to be on tour with them in the first place. And to have flirtations with guys like that was just the icing on the cake."

Meanwhile, Angie Bowie still hoped to win David back. But during the few times she braved the journey to Berlin, he was drunk and stressed and once even had a panic attack—thinking that he was in the throes of heart failure, he was rushed to the British Military Hospital, where he had a full checkup and was given the all-clear.

But as rock-and-roll as his drink and drug intake still appeared to be, he had designed his Berlin existence to be as low-key and mundane as possible. After a short spell in a hotel, he rented an apartment at Hauptstraße 155, Schöneberg—the same part of Berlin where screen icon Marlene Dietrich (whose image and persona as a glamorous bisexual siren had influenced the style of his cover photograph on the *Hunky Dory* album) grew up. Far from the glamour of the Sherry-Netherland and Plaza suites to which he was accustomed, Hauptstraße 155 was a decaying five-story building painted a faded yellow, and David's three-bedroom apartment was shabby, almost derelict, with rain leaking into it during stormy weather.

Nevertheless, he was content there, and established a daily ritual of starting the day with coffee and cigarettes at the nearby Nemesis café, where pictures of James Dean decorated the walls. Then there was Joe's Beer House, on Berlin's main drag, the Kurfürstendamm, and the Empire Bar—both places where he would drink vast quantities of his favorite beer, König Pilsener. Apart from these locales, he haunted neighborhood art galleries and bookstores, and anyplace where he could listen to the music of Kraftwerk. Wearing a flat cap and worker's clothes he bought in a local Kreuzberg store, he was rarely recognized by fans.

However, despite David's sincere attempt to get back on the straight and narrow again—and to help Iggy do the same—Iggy once confided to *Rolling Stone* that over the space of a week, he and David spent two days intoxicated, two days recovering, and three days sober. Describing their daily routine, Iggy said, "Get up in the morning on bread and cheese and eat. Then walk over the city, which hasn't changed since 1910: organ grinders who still had monkeys, quality transvestite shows. A different world.

"By evening, I'd go have dinner with Bowie, see a film, or watch *Starsky and Hutch*—that was our big thing. If there wasn't enough to do, I knew some bad people, and I'd get stoned and drunk. Sometimes I'd do the bad stuff with Bowie and the good stuff with bad people."

For a more objective view of David and Iggy's life in Berlin, and of David and Iggy themselves, Claudia Skoda, who ran a Berlin artist's commune, the Factory, remembered, "The first time David came to the Factory, a big loft on the sixth floor, which you reached via lift, David walked up all six flights with Coco and Iggy. He was thin and he had a beard, which I didn't expect. He was much more underplayed than Iggy, who was cheeky and funny and immediately drew you to him.

"I was married at the time to an artist, Jurgen Skoda, a very handsome man, and we had an open marriage. David liked Jurgen because he was an artist. He loved painters, and saw musicians differently. His admiration was always for painters.

"He had come to Berlin for a new identity. He had been doing glam rock, but he was so intelligent that he knew he had to do something else. He and Iggy were friends and nothing else. He was also on drugs, but he wanted to help Iggy. Iggy was wild. David was a Thin White Duke and Iggy was a Rude Wild Guy.

"David was curious about Berlin. We used to hang out together in a group, and he never acted like a star. He was very friendly, but when he was drinking, he became sexually aggressive. He didn't see straight then. He was okay when Coco was with him, but if he went out on his own, he got drunk and definitely had a groupie.

"He was a complete womanizer, and he always liked big, black, sexy, strong, dominant women. But after a one-night stand, which he usually had when he was drunk, the next morning he didn't recognize the woman anymore.

"Once I was out at a club with him and a lesbian friend of mine, who had a female skinhead with her. David came on to the skinhead, all goo-goo eyes. She said, in a Berlin type of way, 'What are you staring at me for?'

"He said, 'You look like a female Marlon Brando.' It was true, but she didn't know what he was talking about. He wanted to go with her, but she didn't want it. He said, 'Come with me, I like you.' He wanted to have her, but she told him she wasn't interested. But he was a gentleman."

Amid all the drugs and the womanizing, David did try and make an attempt to forge a more solid relationship with a woman. That woman was Winona Williams, who flew to Berlin at his invitation and spent time with him there.

"I went because I was trying to make up my mind about whether I wanted to commit to him, and he wanted me to see how I felt living with him there, as well," Williams said. "While I was there, he painted a great deal, and also had all this Nazi memorabilia around him, including German propaganda minister Dr. Goebbels's old desk, which he had in his apartment. It didn't mean that he had any Nazi inclinations, or was anti-Semitic—just that he was interested in Nazi history and style," she said.

One night, David took Winona to a small nightclub where they saw Romy Haag, a beautiful, intensely feminine-looking transvestite, still biologically a man (though she would eventually have a sex-change operation years later.) That night at the club with Winona was not the first time David had met Romy. They had met when she had been in the first row of his Thin White Duke show in Berlin in April 1976; their eyes met and "it was clear to both of us that we would spend time together," Romy said afterward.

After that, they met again, at the Alcazar in Paris, and their relationship began. At the time of their first meeting, outwardly, Romy was a perfect woman—and a glamorous one, at that. However, David was captivated not only by Romy's appearance, but by her artistry, as she mimed to songs at her own club in Berlin. There, she ended her act by brutally tearing off her wig and then smearing her lipstick straight across her face, so that it looked as if someone had slashed it. The theater was reminiscent of something Lindsay Kemp might have done and so irresistible to David that he used exactly the same theatrical effect at the end of the video of "Boys Keep Swinging."

"Romy is very, very, feminine, and she was very much in fashion at the time when David met her. I can understand what he saw in her," Claudia Skoda said.

David spent a great deal of his time in Berlin at Romy's club. "He loved the energy of the club and was always sitting in the corner and watching everything. He was a little boy. A lovely boy, and I was twenty-three years old and I fell in love with his eyes," Haag said. "He loved to be in the dressing room of my club, trying the clothes on, and we had a love affair.

"He was doing coke at the time, not lines of coke but bowls of it, and I had to put up with that. It got on my nerves sometimes. It was much too much.

"But to know the real David Bowie, you can't do anything but love him. I have never considered myself to be a man; neither did David. God, how I love him," she said.

As for David, according to Winona Williams: "David would have found Romy fascinating and, being the experimental person that he is, I think he would have had a relationship with her."

His relationship with Romy endured until the evening of his thirtieth birthday, which he and Romy spent together at a nightclub. A paparazzo jumped out of the shadows and snapped a photograph of them together. Infuriated and believing that Romy had tipped off the paparazzi that he'd be at the club that night, David turned on her and blamed her for trying to exploit her relationship with him, and then and there ended it. Afterward, his anger continued to mount, and he accused her of "fucking up" his birthday for her own reasons. When she wasn't around, he complained continually about her, accusing her of using their affair to boost her career.

And, much as she might have denied it, the events that transpired afterward seem to prove him right. Despite knowing how much he valued his privacy, Romy gave an interview about him to the prestigious *Berliner Morgenpost* and also revealed intimate details of their affair on TV talk shows. Even today, her nightclub act includes her bravura performance of David's iconic song "Heroes." Thirty-eight years since their relationship ended, the chief currency of Romy Haag's career seems to be her past romance with David.

On a more personal level, when Claudia Skoda visited Romy's apartment, David's presence there remained palpable. "Romy had a nice photograph of them kissing on display," Claudia remembered. "I asked her about it and she said, 'Yes, we had an extraordinary relationship.'"

As for David, he has never talked about his relationship with Romy or how it ended. Nor has he been specific about his mental state in Berlin, although it was clear to those encountering him during that period that he was enamored with the myths surrounding the city, with the art, the history, the ghosts haunting the streets, the echoes of the past. And although he was at low ebb emotionally and physically, he used his time in Berlin to recharge his creativity and, perhaps most important of all, to forge an existence with Zowie and to distance himself yet further from Angie.

Negative stories filtered back to him from London, where she was attempting to make her mark as a cabaret artist, model, and actress, sometimes under the sobriquet Jip Jones. Along the way, she auditioned for the TV series of *Wonder Woman*, but, forever her own worst enemy, categorically refused to wear a bra and, as a result, didn't get the part.

David was beset by the twin specters of Romy in Berlin, who had turned out to be a publicity-obsessed opportunist, and Angie in London, who demonstrated scant interest in mothering their son, Zowie, but was hell-bent on becoming a star in her own right. Additionally, he was living in a divided city populated by the survivors of Nazi Germany, escapees from East Germany, those separated from their loved ones. All this would incite a case of weltschmerz in all but the most stable, so it was hardly surprising that in Berlin, David drew close to the edge. More deliberately self-destructive than he had ever been, after having had a row with "somebody," he took his car out of the garage and drove it around and around an underground parking lot, driving increasingly faster, secretly hoping against hope that he might hit a pillar and end his life that way.

"As I was getting up to forty and fifty, going round the corners, I remember looking at the dash, thinking, *Jesus! Aren't I going to crash soon?*" he said. Remembering James Dean and his tragic early death in a car crash, he said to himself, "I'll put a twist on it—I'll just crash into a pillar in this underground car park in Berlin."

Fortunately, his death wish went unfulfilled, and he survived. But the temptation he felt at that moment spoke volumes about his passionate nature, and the suicidal tendencies still simmered very close to the surface of his nature, particularly here, in Berlin, the city of the Götterdämmerung of the Third Reich, the era that fascinated him so.

At the same time, thanks to living in Berlin, where he continually listened to the techno-rock of Kraftwerk, his creativity was set aflame, just as he knew it would be when he first moved there. As a result, the city ignited his God-given gift for turning a negative into a positive and milking his own life and experience and transmuting them into lyrics. Consequently, when it came to writing his next album, *Low*, he confessed, "The first of *Low* was all about me. Always crashing in the same car and all that self-pitying crap. Isn't it great to be on your own? Let's just pull down the blinds and fuck 'em all."

Low proved to be a dramatic move for David, given how close he moved to Kraftwerk and away from the glam rock of Ziggy, Aladdin, and the Duke. Working with writer-producer Brian Eno on *Low*, he attributed the considerable volte-face in his music to Berlin itself. "I can't write without conflict. That's one reason I liked Berlin so much, because there's so much friction there," he said afterward, adding, "I found it the most convincing place to write. I could never write in a comfortable atmosphere. It would be ludicrous."

Brian Eno would prove to be one of the most important of David's collaborators ever. Until 1976, they had only met sporadically. Roxy

Music had appeared with Ziggy and the Spiders from Mars at their show at the Rainbow, but David and Eno only really bonded after one of the *Station to Station* shows at London's Wembley Stadium, when they talked for hours and conceived the idea of Eno working on Iggy's first solo album, *The Idiot*.

Though that project didn't come to fruition for Eno, his *Discreet Music* album of ambient music made a great impression on David. He and Eno had always experienced a strange brand of synchronicity. During David's Ziggy Stardust days, Eno had also been an adherent of glam rock and had dressed accordingly. But then, like David, also influenced by Kraftwerk and Tangerine Dream, he decided to look to Berlin to reinvent himself.

Before recording *Low* at Château d'Hérouville, David and Brian spent hours brainstorming together. Iggy was also around, and would sing on one of the album's tracks, "What in the World." The lines were drawn clearly between David's work and Eno's, in that David would sing the vocals on the album and Eno would sing backup on some tracks, and direct and compose most of the second side of the album.

Zowie was now primarily living with David in Berlin and going to school there. He had made friends with the other children, and seemed to be happy. David did his best as a father, but often was inadequate in communicating with him, and on those occasions, according to an eyewitness, they would sit together in awkward silence. The tension escalated when Angie arrived in Berlin for a visit and, in the heat of the moment, she and David had sex for the first time in a long time. But if Angie believed that this heralded a reconciliation, she was wrong. And, as always, Coco proved to be a stumbling block.

Over and over, Angie demanded that David fire Coco, cut her out of his life, but he refused—and with a combination of naïveté and incredulity insisted, "Angie, how can you ask that? You know how much I rely on her. She's part of the organization. She knows everything about my business. Who else could run it the way she could?"

Angie volunteered that *she* could, but David ignored her. When he discovered that Coco had fled the apartment, where she had her own room, he became extremely concerned and searched Berlin for her, desperate. However, having witnessed the level of his concern for Coco, Angie knew she had been vanquished.

Before she left Berlin, Angie executed one last dramatic move: She threw all of Coco's things out of the window, then left the apartment forever.

By now, eight years after Angie and David gotten married, she had a new boyfriend, Keeth Paul, sound engineer for pop group the Heartbreakers, who was living with her in Switzerland, where she was funded by the $35,000 annual allowance David was paying her, in addition to her rent, travel and almost all her other expenses, which he paid.

London *Sunday Mirror* journalist Tony Robinson traveled to Switzerland, where Angie and Keeth were staying in a nine-bedroom rented chalet near David's home in Blonay. Just back from a trip to America, Angie had arranged for six-year-old Zowie to spend time with David in Berlin, but was now hell-bent on getting full-time custody of him.

When Robinson arrived at the chalet, he found Angie in a dreadful state. "She was nearly senseless," he recalled. "A few hours later, at about 4 A.M., she got out of bed and locked herself in one of the chalet's nine bathrooms, and took sleeping tablets and tranquillizers.

"Then, before they took effect, she went on the rampage around the house, breaking ornaments and glassware—particularly in the room used by Zowie's Scots nanny."

After Keeth Paul tried to calm her down, "she hit him a crippling blow on the kneecap with a heavy rolling pin. In the kitchen she picked up a steel carving knife and tried to summon the courage to fall on it," Robinson said.

Tony and Keeth managed to coax her into getting some sleep, but the following morning, Angie "got out of bed, smashed the glass shade of a standard lamp outside her bedroom, and threw herself down stairs to the basement.

"We found her in a crumpled heap with her face swollen and covered in blood," Robinson said.

"I just couldn't take anymore . . . I wanted to top myself . . . I thought, *What the hell*," Angie said afterward.

Soon after, David asked Angie for a divorce, and she agreed, granting him custody of Zowie, claiming that she knew she would not have been awarded custody, as David had Polaroids of her having sex with a woman. As a settlement, David paid her $750,000 in 1980, while she agreed to a ten-year gag order forbidding her to talk to the media about him and their marriage. But apart from a brief meeting with David in Lausanne, where he signed their divorce papers, she never saw him again.

Afterward, Angie would claim that she had wanted to put up a fight and claim custody of Zowie, but that attorneys dissuaded her. "David had money. Zowie was with him. I thought Zowie was better off with David than with me, initially," was one of her rationales.

The union of Angie and David Bowie, once mirror images of each other—both young and ambitious, androgynous and anarchic, each completely in tune with the other—had come to an end with a bang, followed by a lifetime of whimpers from Angie. Only a year after accepting David's $750,000 and agreeing not to talk to the press about him, Angie promptly broke the gag order and published her first autobiography, *Free Spirit*, written with show business journalist

Don Short, who flew to Los Angeles and interviewed her in depth about her life and about David.

"She was bitter, and felt that she had been short-changed and that what she had done for him professionally hadn't been recognized; but she still said that she admired him," Short said.

And even at the end of her second memoir, *Backstage Passes*, Angie looked back at her life with David with a degree of positivity and paid him this tribute: "Regardless of his performance with me, David did do a wonderful job of broadcasting sexual freedom and personal liberation. He shone his light into a lot of dark places in people and helped them see themselves, and maybe love themselves a little better."

David, however, was not so sanguine about Angie. Describing "the maternal side" of Zowie's life as tragic, he went on to crack of her, "It was like living with a blow-torch," and, "She has as much insight into the human condition as a walnut and a self-interest that would make Narcissus green with envy."

In Berlin, with Coco by his side, David did his utmost to build a home for Zowie, and did all he could to make up for the lost years. By the time Zowie was ten, David had, for the most part, kicked drink and drugs and had morphed into a relatively conventional father, taking Zowie to the movies, and on tour with him, where the boy was watched over by the roadies when David was performing.

Finally, in an attempt, perhaps, to restore some routine to Zowie's life, David went so far as to send Zowie (who went on to change his name to Joey when he was twelve, simply because he wanted to be known by a regular name at last), to the spartan Scottish boarding school Gordonstoun, which Prince Charles had attended.

And while Joey, who quickly revised his nickname to Joe, submitted to the harsh regime at Gordonstoun, he wasn't particularly happy there, and as an adult described himself as "a sensitive child," who needed "a few more hugs."

For though Angie did telephone him repeatedly at Gordonstoun, she was off on her own adventures and wasn't around to give her son love and tenderness. In July 1980, with her then lover, punk musician Andrew Lipka, who performed under the name Drew Blood, she had a daughter, Stacia. After Angie's father helped wean her off drugs, he and her mother both died in 1983, leaving Angie bereft and living in reduced circumstances in Greenwich Village. Joe did visit her there when he was thirteen years old, but after he commented on how she was living, she rounded on him and yelled that he was "bourgeois."

From that time on, Angie's letters to Joe at Gordonstoun (where he would remain for five years) remained unopened, and Joe never saw Angie again. "She's a woman who didn't have a very positive effect on my upbringing, so I think it was the right move," Zowie, now calling himself Duncan, asserted to Caroline Graham of the *Mail on Sunday* in August 2009.

For the past twenty years, Angie Bowie has been living with electrical engineer Michael Gassett, who is nearly two decades her junior.

In contrast to Angie's track record as a parent, from the time when David assumed full custody of Joe, he transformed himself into a committed and strict father, a dramatic change—but then, change has always been the essence of David Bowie.

Ironically, in keeping with a natural fatherly desire to protect his son from the pitfalls he'd faced along the way in the ultimate expression of "do as I say, not as I do," David took Joey to see Johnny Rotten, then on tour in Switzerland—and afterward, Joe dyed his hair alternately silver, red, and blue. When David saw him, he erupted with, "Joey, you don't think I'm going to go out with you looking like—"

Whereupon Joe just looked at David and said, "Dad. . . ."

"And it suddenly hit me," David confessed, adding, "It was momentarily hard to deal with."

In 1993, during an interview in *Arena* with Tony Parsons, David looked back at his relationship with his son and confessed, "I didn't give him enough time until 1975. Then I took over from that point as father and parent. Up until that point his nanny had been his mother. His real mother was in and out of his life. And it was a pretty rotten childhood, I think. Probably one of the most major regrets of my life is that I didn't spend enough time with him when he was really young."

In contrast, Joe—who began going by Duncan when he was eighteen years old—seems to bear no resentment toward David for his early neglect of him. Although he claims to have been grumpy, confused, and upset in his twenties, after being asked to leave Gordonstoun at the age of eighteen because he fell asleep in an examination, he studied philosophy, then went to the London Film School and worked his way up to becoming a director, winning multiple awards for his film, *Moon*.

Supportive of David and full of love for him, Duncan doesn't harbor a shred of bitterness towards his father for the past, "'He's just a wonderful guy and father and I think he understands that I'm a creative person in my own right. He gave me the time and the support to find my feet and the confidence to do what I do," he said.

On September 16, 1977, David suffered the end of one of his oldest relationships when Marc Bolan was killed in a car crash at the age of twenty-nine. A month earlier, David had performed on Marc's TV show, and he was devastated by his friend's untimely death. At his funeral, he sat behind Dana Gillespie and cried.

Marc Bolan died just before his son Rolan's birthday. And because Marc wasn't married to Rolan's mother, the boy was left in dire circumstances. David, who was Marc's godfather, paid for his education and other expenses.

"David's generosity helped my mother and me to survive," Rolan Bolan said. "It wasn't just the financial help, but the time and kindness. He kept in regular touch by phone, and his first and last words every time were: 'Don't hesitate to tell me if there is anything I can do.' He'd shrug off our thanks, saying it was the least he could do for the family of a good friend."

. . .

In September 1977, David managed to pry himself away from Berlin and fly to London, where he cut two of the most successful Christmas duets ever recorded—"The Little Drummer Boy" and "Peace on Earth" with Bing Crosby. Bing was in London at the time, touring, and David—along with Twiggy—guested on Bing's Christmas special, which aired on November 30, 1977. The gig was a radical departure for David, who, when he arrived at the studio, announced that he hated "The Little Drummer Boy," and asked if he could sing something else—hence he also sang "Peace on Earth" on the special.

David was thirty years old to Bing's seventy-three, and fans and critics alike were surprised that David had appeared on the show. Somewhat ingeniously, he explained his duet with Crosby away by saying that he'd decided to appear in the show "only because my mum liked him." Given that he and Peggy had been at loggerheads for years, his explanation sounds hollow, to say the least. Living in the Beckenham apartment that David had purchased for her, with only his gold records and awards to remind her of his fame and fortune, Peggy was bitter and alone. Guilty that she had allowed her son Terry to be committed to a state asylum, Cane Hill, in nearby Coulsden after the family curse of schizophrenia had struck him, Peggy left much of his care to her younger sister, Pat. As for David, Peggy was heard to snap, "He owes me," and she accepted his monthly allowance without a great deal of gratitude.

Back in Berlin, David was rattled when an art dealer approached him and, clearly assuming that he was a Hitler fan, tried to sell him a bust of Hitler. David was outraged, and even more so when, one day, walking past the Wall in West Berlin, he came upon graffiti depicting his name entwined with a swastika. Whether or not he had become associated with Hitler because of the notorious photograph of him giving the Hitler salute, or because he had purchased Goebbels's desk and had mentioned that he wanted to make a biopic of Goebbels's life, is not on record. But as famous as he was, and always would be, it remained virtually impossible for him to erase the ripple effect of the negative press coverage of his salute from the Mercedes.

Berlin's history, past and present, continued to play on his mind. And on the anniversary of the Wall's erection, he happened to be at a punk club, where a birthday cake replica of the Wall was on display. "And as midnight struck, all these punks just started lunging into the cake, rooting pieces out of it. I wished I had a camera. I had never seen anything like it," he said afterward.

David had recorded "Heroes" at Hansa Studio, just five hundred yards from the Wall, in full view of armed guards and barbed wire. Afterwards, Tony Visconti, who produced the track, joked, "The band played it with so much energy, I think they [the band] wanted to go home, actually."

But while David and Eno's rousing anthem "Heroes" was purported to be about two lovers separated from one another because of the Berlin Wall, the truth happened to be that David chanced to see Visconti and singer Antonia Maass walking hand in hand in the shadow of the Wall. When Tony and Antonia got back to the studio in the midst of recording, David and Coco told them that they had seen them walking by the Wall, and, inspired by that vision, then and there, David sat down and wrote the lyrics to "Heroes."

"I am totally a creature of environment," he once said. "My albums are expressions of, reflections of, that environment. 'Heroes' certainly is, and you have to understand that to understand the album and the music at all."

FIFTEEN

JUST A GIGOLO

On the evening of July 1, 1978, in the Royal Box of London's Earls Court auditorium, Peggy Jones was thumbing through the program for David's *Isolar II* world tour when the door of the private box opened, and there was David.

He'd stayed away from her for so long, had been so out of touch that, for a moment, the voluble Peggy was tongue-tied.

"You didn't have to come up here to see me," she said, finally.

"You're my mum," he said, without any hesitation.

That he had invited her to the show was naturally a given, but that he had taken the trouble to greet her himself was quite another story. He had proffered his mother an olive branch from afar. Now, however, he had upped the ante by making the effort to come to see her face-to-face, taking a tentative first step toward the kind of acceptance that only age and experience seem to draw out of families. The reunion, however, did not herald a new closeness between David and Peggy, but it was a start.

British TV personality Janet Street-Porter was on hand at Earls Court that night to interview David. He had invited her because he was impressed by her brassy burgundy hair. Beforehand, he stipulated that the interview be filmed while they walked from his dressing room to the stage, so that the screaming fans would be seen in the background.

"Bowie was charming, softly spoken, and completely captivating, although he said absolutely nothing of note," Street-Porter said years later, highlighting the fact that despite the intervening years, David, the son of public relations maven John Jones, still remained the boy who had studied the craft of PR at Ken Pitt's feet. With his slick, polished British manners, and perhaps partly aping the tactics of Dr. Goebbels, whose desk he owned, David effortlessly retained every iota of control possible over his own image.

Still living in Berlin and completely out of touch with London life, David continued to cleave to his new existence in Germany.

"I ended up in Berlin. It makes it a very good place for someone like me to live, because I can be incredibly anonymous. They don't seem particularly joyful about seeing a famous face," he said.

He still retained his Swiss home outside Geneva, and it was there that actor-turned-director of *Blow-Up*, David Hemmings, went to visit him in the hopes of persuading him to play the part of a young, jaded Prussian officer who comes back to Berlin after the First World War, finds himself alienated from everything around him, and, in despair, resorts to becoming a gigolo, working for a sinister baroness, who the producers hoped would be played by none other than Marlene Dietrich, one of David's idols, a cabaret star par excellence, a Hollywood siren and, perhaps equally important, a woman who had pioneered both bisexuality and open marriage in her own private life.

When Hemmings flew to Switzerland to meet with David, Hemmings was instantly captivated by him. As he wrote in his autobiography, "He was, as I had expected, hugely stimulating to deal with—clever, funny, original, and with a very special natural elegance. . . . Bowie, thank God, was fascinated by the character he had to play. He was anxious to delve into the persona of the gigolo, the male heterosexual hooker—a type he had always found somewhat inscrutable and difficult to get to know. And the role allowed him to show the sensual side of his nature, which hadn't been possible in his last film, *The Man Who Fell to Earth*, where his character didn't have any genitals!"

Relatively charmed by Hemmings—but even more so by the fact that, as he later said, "Marlene was dangled in front of me"—David decided to negotiate his own contract. But when he arrived at Hemmings's office, according to coexecutive producer Joshua Sinclair, who told the story to Charlotte Chandler for her biography of Marlene, David slammed his hand on the table and declared that he wanted $250,000 to play the part, plus 5 percent of the French box office earnings.

Stunned, Joshua agreed on the spot, and David said, "Good. Write up the contract," and walked out.

After a great deal of negotiation, Marlene, too, agreed to play the role of "the Baroness" in *Just a Gigolo*.

The sole reason why Marlene, then in her late seventies and, since the death of her husband, Rudolf Sieber, living in Paris as a recluse, decided to accept the part of the baroness in *Just a Gigolo* was the $250,000 fee for just two days' work. Nonetheless, Dietrich, cannily playing to David's youthful fan base, declared, "I'm happy David Bowie is in the movie. It's interesting for me because he wrote the song 'Kreuzberg.'" Kreuzberg is a district of Berlin, the town where Dietrich was born, and with which her name was synonymous.

David's contract to appear in the movie had been long since signed when he learned that Marlene categorically refused to come to Berlin to shoot the movie with him. Instead, she demanded that her scenes with him be shot in Berlin from his perspective, and that the same scene then be shot from Marlene's perspective—separately, in Paris,

ensuring that the two of them would never appear together in any of
the scenes.

Marlene's refusal to leave her apartment at 12, avenue Montaigne,
Paris, close to the Arc de Triomphe and the House of Dior, where she
had often purchased the couture clothes she wore with such panache,
shouldn't have been a surprise to Hemmings, or even to David himself. Her iconic glittering beauty now a faded memory, her legendary
legs—which had once been insured for one million dollars—swollen,
her balance precarious, Marlene, who had dedicated her life to per-
fecting the legend of Dietrich, was not about to allow her cherished
image to be exposed to the harsh light of day.

Moreover, she was also aware that her appearance in Berlin, once
the heart of Hitler's Germany, the country she had abandoned when
he came to power, could give rise to violent demonstrations against
her, particularly as she had moved to the United States and devoted
herself to entertaining the Allied troops during the war. Not only that,
but sixteen years before, she had made her last movie, Stanley Kram-
er's *Judgment at Nuremberg*, starring as the widow of a German general,
and a woman virulently opposed to Nazism.

For Marlene it was clear that traveling to Berlin to film *Just a Gigolo*
was out of the question—the filming must come to her, she decided,
and her scenes must be filmed in Paris, without her performing with
David, face-to-face. Naturally, David had been intent on meeting the
legendary Marlene Dietrich, the ultimate symbol of sexual androgyny, a woman whose lovers were as varied as his own (ranging, as they
did, from John Wayne to Edith Piaf), and a fellow Capricorn, the sign
under which he was proud of being born. When he learned that she
would not be filming with him in Berlin, he was gutted.

After filming began, initially unaware of David's disappointment
at not meeting Marlene, David Hemmings was unendingly enthusiastic about his performance. "He had a face that always looked beautiful on camera: he didn't have any bad angles, which, as it happened,
posed a problem on this film," Hemmings remembered. "We went to

a lot of trouble to make him look filthy and down-and-out, buying the scruffiest clothes we could find, but as soon as he put them on, they became an elegant new look.

"We laughed about it a lot—the 'Gardening Look' in wellies, baggy old cords, tatty sweaty, and a cloth cap. When I wore it, I looked like a gardener: when Bowie wore it, he looked like the front cover of *Vogue*," Hemmings said.

Kim Novak was David's other costar in the movie, and he would dance a steamy tango with her.

"A splendid woman. She oozes femininity, doesn't she? Happily married, though," he said of Kim, and, instead, turned his attentions to Sydne Rome, a diminutive American blond actress he'd first met the year before, in Paris, where they had discussed her appearing in his proposed movie on the Austrian artist Egon Schiele.

Beguiled by Sydne, David invited her to accompany him to the French premiere of *The Man Who Fell to Earth*, and for a time, they were inseparable. However, Sydne's blond beauty wasn't her only attraction for David. Then one of Europe's rising stars, a rival to Maria Schneider of *Last Tango in Paris* fame, Sydne also must have appealed to the synthesizer of contacts in David. As a twenty-one-year-old aspiring actress from Sandusky, Ohio, she was discovered by director Roman Polanski, who cast her in his movie *What?* and promoted her as a latter-day cinematic Cinderella.

What? featured Sydne in a daring seminude scene, and after working with the prestigious Polanski, she topped that by making a movie directed by the distinguished Réne Clément. In short, Sydne was a conduit to Polanski and Clément, if only by association, and thus was irresistible to David.

Nonetheless, he wasn't about to restrict himself to one woman. At his invitation, Winona Williams flew to Berlin to be with him during the making of *Just a Gigolo* and remembered, "David and I had dinner with Sydne Rome. She was a little bitch and tried to goad me into some intellectual tête-a-tête, trying to show me up."

Coco, too, was hostile to Winona. "Although she brought me coffee and orange juice in bed, she also sat at the kitchen table and told me how I wasn't right for David, and that Bianca Jagger was more suited to him," Winona said. "But I never took her seriously because she was definitely in love with him and manipulated situations to get women out of his life."

However, Coco didn't succeed in banishing Winona from David's life. As Winona remembered, "I loved David very much, and he prided himself on mentoring me, and left little notes around for me to ponder, like 'Never handle more power than you are capable of controlling.' For my birthday, he brought me a limited edition of the occultist Austin Osman Spare's book *The Book of Pleasure (Self Love): The Psychology of Ecstasy* and inscribed it with, 'Winona Happy Birthday 1999 love from me.' I really did love David very much, but being with him was very draining. He seems to be able to extract energy from people, and whenever I was around him for more than a few days, I would feel so drained. I don't know how he did it, but I would literally have to leave to refuel my own fire. He managed to touch and take from every fiber of my being," Winona said, explaining why she left Berlin and ended her relationship with David.

Despite the fact that Marlene wouldn't shoot any scenes with him, David was still determined to meet her, so he announced to coexecutive producer Joshua Sinclair that when Marlene was scheduled to shoot her scenes in Paris, he intended to fly there, along with a photographer, and pose for photographs with her anyway. Floored for a moment, Joshua rallied, and, aware that David was due to perform at a major rock concert in Australia on April 4, maneuvered it so that the Marlene shoot would be switched to exactly that date.

"Three, four o'clock in the morning, David Hemmings and David Bowie come storming into my hotel in Berlin," Joshua Sinclair recalled. "They had been drinking and were very angry. I thought they had come to kill me."

According to Joshua, David Bowie was boiling over with rage and demanded, "Who do you think you are? You think you can just come and tell us when you shoot? You forced the film to be shot on the fourth . . . You made a deal behind our backs."

Although his plans had been thwarted, David wasn't about to be vanquished just yet. "Because Bowie, of course, being a pop star, hadn't given up on anything," Sinclair said.

Set on having stills taken of him, in his gigolo suit, with Marlene beside him, David flew to Paris to see her. But charming, handsome, and brilliant as David is, and as clever as he has always been at getting his way, Marlene, his fellow Capricorn, had been charming the world and successfully imposing her will wherever and on whomsoever she wanted for far, far longer. Point-blank refusing to pose for any photographs whatsoever, with David or without, Marlene flatly turned him down.

"She said no," Joshua recalled, "and, according to him, she said it adamantly: 'I did the movie. I think you're a great singer, but no.' I think David Bowie was at the height of his career, or close to it, but he couldn't get Marlene Dietrich to do some stills with him."

David's dreams of working with Marlene, or, at the very least, of being photographed with her, were dashed, but that wasn't even the worst disappointment of his experience on the film. He had fervently hoped that this role would win him accolades as a serious actor, something that, despite his good reviews for *The Man Who Fell to Earth*, he hadn't yet been accorded. But when the movie premiered at the 1978 Cannes Film Festival, it was derided as "an unadulterated flop" and an "international misadventure"—the reviews were so dire that David Hemmings went back and reedited the movie.

The new version of *Just a Gigolo* premiered in Berlin in November 1978. Fortunately for David, he was on tour and not in the movie theater, as the audience fell about laughing at the inanity of the plot and the movie as a whole. Finally, the film was recut, and premiered in London in February 1979, again to terrible reviews. Whereupon David made the immortal comment, "*Just a Gigolo* was my thirty-two Presley movies rolled into one."

Returning to music, he recorded *Lodger* in France. Refusing to be cowed by the failure of *Just a Gigolo*, he determined to take on another theatrical challenge, one instigated by the new love in his life. . . .

Her name was Oona O'Neill Chaplin, and she was the still-beautiful daughter of legendary American playwright Eugene O'Neill, and the widow of Charlie Chaplin. (At fifty-five, she was twenty-two years David's senior.) After Charlie Chaplin's death in 1977, she had remained at their white colonial-style mansion, le Manoir de Ban, Vevey, on the shores of Lake Geneva, just over three miles from David's home in Blonay.

Oona's first meeting with David was facilitated by her youngest son, Eugene, who worked as assistant engineer at Mountain Recording Studios in Montreux, Lake Geneva, where "Heroes" was mixed.

"I was a big fan of David's and the only fan club I ever joined in my life was his," Eugene Chaplin remembered, adding, "When I met him, he was very kind and we became friends."

David met Oona for the first time when Eugene invited him to dinner at le Manoir de Ban and was immediately taken with her. Her pedigree as the daughter of a celebrated American playwright and widow of the one and only Charlie Chaplin added luster to her in David's eyes.

Growing up in Kennington, which was adjacent to Stockwell, where David first went to school, Charlie Chaplin was not only a fellow South Londoner but a great mime artist, a latter-day Pierrot, a dancer, an actor, a gifted writer, and a great romantic who had composed "Smile," the classic performer's anthem.

There was another eerie similarity between David and Chaplin: Chaplin's mother, Hannah, had been incarcerated in Cane Hill asylum, just as David's half brother, Terry, now was.

Then there was the fact that Chaplin, notorious for having married a girl who was sixteen to his thirty-five, thus opening himself to charges of statutory rape, was also a sexual outlaw, a pioneer, a sexual revolutionary of a kind, just as David was. A contemporary of Buster Keaton, the silent comedian whom David once wanted to play in a biopic of his life, Charlie Chaplin was a movie immortal, and in dating Oona, his widow, a legendary doe-eyed dark-haired beauty, who had married him when she was eighteen and Chaplin fifty-four, David may well have felt close to Chaplin and his genius, as if he could imbibe some of the latter simply by osmosis.

David had once said that in another life, he might have wanted to be a journalist, and his curiosity, the way in which he fired questions at the more interesting of those whom he encountered, virtually interviewing them, soaking them dry of opinions and information, treating them as intellectual and emotional sources, was not far removed from the modus operandi of the best journalists.

A more negative interpretation, perhaps, could be that David consistently exhibited a slight sociopathic streak whereby human beings were only valued for what they could offer him, teach him, spark off in him, and that other people were merely grist for his creativity. True or not, it was indisputable that in dating Oona Chaplin, David had access to the great love of one of the world's most legendary geniuses and from her, could glean a great deal about Chaplin.

None of which is to denigrate Oona's tremendous charm and beauty, as observed by this author during her friendship with one of Oona's eight children, Vicki, with whom she spent time and stayed with at Oona's home in Switzerland.

Truman Capote cited Oona as one of his inspirations for the character of Holly Golightly, the heroine of his *Breakfast at Tiffany's*. Both Oona's brother and her half brother committed suicide. No stranger to tragedy, and finely attuned to sensitive, creative geniuses, in many ways Oona was perfect for David. But although they were photographed together in Manhattan by the paparazzi, she persisted in denying that her relationship with him was anything other than purely platonic.

"I'm crazy about David," she said at the time. "This very charming, very intelligent, very sensitive fellow, who came from the same part of London as Charlie, walked in and wanted to talk. It was as simple as that. I really am very fond of him."

Nonetheless, although Eugene Chaplin says today that he didn't know that there was a romance between his mother and David, one of his siblings reportedly suspected that wedding bells were about to chime for the pair, but then joked that it would be more like "a merger than a marriage."

Oblivious of anyone else's opinions of their relationship, Oona became so close to David that she felt free enough to throw down a gauntlet: She challenged David, saying that she would accept a part in a movie offered to her by young producer Keith Rothman, provided that David agree to accept the part in a play he'd lately been offered.

In the end, Oona chickened out and declined the role offered to her, but David rose to the challenge anyway and accepted the part of John Merrick in *The Elephant Man*.

The play had first been produced in London, with illustrious actors such as David Schofield playing the leading role of John Merrick, the tragically grotesque "Elephant Man." But after seeing Bowie in *The Man Who Fell to Earth*, director Jack Hofsiss was convinced that David could master the part.

"I thought he was wonderful," Hofsiss said. "The character he played had an isolation similar to the Elephant Man's. His perceptions about the part and his interest were all so good that we decided to investigate the possibility of doing it."

Before he accepted the part, David visited the Royal London Hospital Museum, where he saw plaster casts of Merrick, who had spent his early life in a workhouse, then became a carnival freak, and spent the last four years of his life sheltered by the London Hospital. After visiting the museum, David said, "It made me aware for the first time how grotesque he was—the plaster sculptures are quite stunningly grotesque. And the cap itself is so sad, with the mask down the front. It must have been a terrible burden."

David joined the *Elephant Man* company in San Francisco and made his debut at the end of July in Denver, after only two and a half weeks of rehearsal. Before his first performance, he confided to rock journalist Lisa Robinson, who had met him when he first came to America: "It's the most terrifying position I've ever put myself in, ever. I've had no legitimate theater training whatsoever. I've just had a mime thing, which is very different. I went in with a very naïve conception of how one acts."

He had seen the play before and was aware of the rigors of the part, so he exercised preshow and postshow, and also was treated by a chiropractor at the end of every performance. After he opened in Denver, his reviews were uniformly positive, with one critic raving, "Bowie seems to have been sculpted to play the role."

The next stop was Chicago, where he also garnered superlative reviews for his performance. During his run there, rather unwillingly, he agreed with RCA that two British newspapers could send a reporter to interview him about his role in the play. So Chris Charlesworth, then RCA press officer, flew out with a reporter from the London *Sunday Times* and another from *New Musical Express,* on the condition, set down by David's handlers, that each one of them would be granted just an hour of his time.

"They had to fly all the way from London to Chicago and back, just to spend one hour with David, and no more, and the *New Musical Express* man was appalled," Charlesworth remembered. "So I took him aside and said to him, 'Look, it's up to you. If you are interesting, if you ask the right questions, you might persuade David to overrule his minders and give you more time.'

"Fortunately, the *New Musical Express* man was an intelligent bloke. He and David got on so well that David gave him two hours that day, and an hour and a half the next. David's minders were angry about this because they had to change his schedule, but I told them it wasn't my fault, it was David's. He had decided he was the boss.

"As a result of David giving the *New Musical Express* man three and a half hours instead of one in which to interview him, *NME* gave him six pages and the cover, and the bosses were pleased. David knew better than his minders what would help promote his career," Charlesworth said.

After his interview in Chicago with *New Musical Express*'s Angus MacKinnon, David opened on Broadway as the Elephant Man. And although Oona Chaplin had characterized her relationship with David as being "strange," she praised his "quiet, serious side," and was there in the audience at the Broadway opening of *The Elephant Man*. She said afterward, "He was breathtakingly good at expressing physical agony." David and Oona became so close that during his Broadway run, she went so far as to buy an apartment in Manhattan, and over the next three months, she and David spent most of their time together.

"They are an unlikely pair, but David Bowie and Oona Chaplin are in love," one source close to them claimed, while another said, "Age doesn't seem to matter to them. If you didn't know them you would think they were truly an odd couple. But underneath, they are really perfect for each other."

Perfect or not, David was also wooing other women apart from Oona and turned his attention to socialite and former Warhol star Belgian-born Monique van Vooren, who had, years before, dated none other than Elvis, with whom he had been fascinated since childhood, and with whom he shared a January 8 birthday. Just as dating Oona Chaplin had brought David close to Charlie Chaplin, by association, dating Monique would have the same effect vis-à-vis Elvis.

Initially, Monique had been his escort to the Manhattan premiere of *Close Encounters of the Third Kind* in November 1977. Three years later, when David was in Manhattan rehearsing for *The Elephant Man*, a friend of Monique's invited her to a party where he was also a guest.

"David wanted to take me out, but I was interested in someone else at the time," Monique recalled. "But he still came over to my house on Sixty-Sixth Street for dinner, and he learned his lines for the play with me and rehearsed the various scenes with me, as well.

"I thought he had great style, but it wasn't a romance, although he wanted it to be. He kept calling me, kept sending me little gifts—a blue-and-white floral silk scarf, a copy of *The Prophet* by Kahlil Gibran—and sent me flowers, as well.

"Someone calls you, invites you out, sends you gifts, invites you here and there, and then you know he is interested in you, but that was that. We kissed, and it was marvelous. But I was committed elsewhere and couldn't take it further. David was a bit surprised when I turned him down, because I suppose everyone fell for him. But I didn't," Monique said.

During *The Elephant Man*'s Broadway run, David played to packed houses every night, and although he was exhausted after every performance, he said, "I'm enjoying it thoroughly. I never believed that old axiom about being able to find a different part of a character playing it every night, but it turns out that it's quite true. With this play, the terrifying discipline is the entire thing. There isn't any room for outward physical spontaneity. It's blocked all the way through: very different from rock and roll."

Audiences from Elizabeth Taylor to Andy Warhol, David Hockney, and Christopher Isherwood were all won over by David's bravura performance. John Lennon, too, had hoped to see the play with David in it, but that was not to be. David was immeasurably shocked by Lennon's December 8, 1980, assassination, and his immediate reaction was recorded by May Pang, who relayed it to Paul Trynka, author of *Starman*.

According to May, David, like her, experienced great difficulty in accepting John's assassination. She remembered him screaming, "What the hell, what the fuck is going on with this world!" not just once, but many, many times.

After John's murder, David increased his own security, and, in a quirkier coincidence, he rekindled his relationship with his mother once more. After flying her to America, he invited Peggy to *The Elephant Man*, where he personally introduced her to every single member of the cast. Afterward he and Zowie had dinner with her. But although Peggy's stay in Manhattan heralded a more positive understanding between her and David, their relationship would never be particularly warm or close. For while there were those who had speculated that after the murder of John, David had reignited his relationship with his mother primarily because he was worried about who would care for Zowie, if David, like John, died before his time, they probably had no idea about exactly what kind of mother Peggy had been to David as a child. Nor did they know that even though he had now finally brought her back into his life, he would still never be able to erase the past and forget.

Toward the end of the year, still rattled to the core by John Lennon's murder, David retreated to Switzerland, where he spent Christmas with Oona Chaplin and her children, the eldest of whom, actress Geraldine, raved of him, "He's simply charming."

Meanwhile, Oona continued to deny that she was having a relationship with him. "He sometimes comes over for a meal. He's very nice, sweet, intelligent, and talented. I find him stimulating and fun. But there is no romance at all. There have even been reports that I may marry him. It is absolutely not true, though my children were very amused by the idea," she said.

While he was appearing in *The Elephant Man*, David also took time to play himself in the German movie *Christiane F.*, and his sequences were shot at Manhattan's Hurrah club. His willingness to make a cameo in the movie was motivated by an extremely personal reason: *Christiane F.* was based on the 1979 book *Christiane F.: Autobiography of a Girl of the Streets and a Heroin Addict*, the story of a teenage heroin addict. Apart from being an exposé of Berlin's drug culture during the seventies, the book was based on the real-life Christiane F.'s flirtation with heroin, which, shockingly, first began when she attended a Bowie concert.

David's agreeing to appear in a low-budget foreign movie, and the fact that he also wrote the songs and the music for it, was a clear testament to his belief in karma. In recent years, astrology, too, had become an important part of his life. Before he agreed to be interviewed by a particular journalist, he always insisted that the reporter submit his or her exact time and place of birth to him, so that he could draw up the person's chart and employ the tarot in order to decide whether or not to grant that journalist an interview.

The world press continued to treat David with a combination of respect and fascination. And while there were those who felt that David had strayed far from the musical mainstream with his Berlin Trilogy, starting with *Low*, they were mollified when, in 1981, he released the far more commercial album *Scary Monsters*, which stormed to number one in the UK. Recorded without the participation of Brian Eno, *Scary Monsters* would give rise to two of David's most iconic hit singles, "Fashion" and the track "Ashes to Ashes," in which he made the shocking assertion, "Major Tom's a junkie," thus despoiling the image of the hero of "Space Oddity"—a classic Bowie move, remolding, recasting, then destroying his own creation, rather as he once did with Ziggy.

With Queen, at Mountain Studios, Montreux, he also wrote and recorded "Under Pressure," which later appeared on Queen's album *Hot Space*, and went on to reach number one on the charts. David's unique connection with Queen's Freddie Mercury dated back twelve years, to when—soon after the release and success of "Space Oddity"—he dropped by London's Kensington Market to see Scottish rocker Alan Mair, a bassist he'd worked with who now ran a stall at the market selling handmade boots. It turned out that the stall was managed by Freddie Mercury.

Mair remembered, "I asked David if he wanted a pair of boots and he said no, that he didn't have any money and had just come to say hello. I said, 'But you've had a hit record.' But in those days hit records didn't mean a lot financially, initially, anyway.

"I said he could pay me whenever, and Freddie fitted him for a pair of boots. I introduced them. Freddie's career hadn't taken off at this point. I wish I had taken a picture of Freddie on his knees fitting David's boots," Alan said.

David and Freddie also had a high degree of professional mutuality. A brilliant songwriter, Freddie had not only written the eclectic classic "Bohemian Rhapsody" but also "We Are the Champions," a song which, like "Heroes," would become a sporting anthem. And as David himself phrased it, "Of all the more theatrical rock performers, Freddie took it further than the rest."

After Freddie's tragic death from AIDS, at the age of only forty-five, in 1992, David took part in the Freddie Mercury Tribute Concert for AIDS Awareness in Freddie's honor, and in full view of the seventy-two-thousand-strong audience at Wembley Stadium, and the global audience of nearly one billion watching a live feed of the show, fell to his knees and recited the Lord's Prayer for an (unnamed) friend of his then suffering the ravages of AIDS.

More than anything else, in the 1980s, David's focus was on acting. In March 1982, he appeared in a BBC TV production of Brecht's *Baal*, for which he received the standard fee of £1,000. Critics were underwhelmed by his performance. The same year, decades before *Twilight*, David had the foresight to play a vampire—John Blaylock in *The Hunger*, in which he costarred with Catherine Deneuve and Susan Sarandon. While shooting in London, David wore prosthetic makeup that aged him three hundred years; he was completely unrecognizable. On the set to visit his father, Zowie, at the time eleven years old, was so shocked by the sight of David that he burst into tears.

Ironically, David, who in his bid for stardom had worn makeup in order to attract attention, ended up employing it for the reverse reason now that he was a star.

"He enjoyed wearing the old-age makeup because he could nip out to the pub and no one would recognize him. I know he did that more than once," Nick Dudman, assistant makeup artist on *The Hunger*, remembered.

During the making of the movie, David embarked on a relationship with Susan Sarandon, which was hardly surprising, given her street cred and rock-chick aura. Susan, who was from a Catholic family, had grown up in New Jersey where, in high school, she was arrested for civil rights protests. Sensual, sexy, and unconventional, and a startlingly beautiful woman, Susan Sarandon was, in many ways, yet another perfect woman for David. Calling her "pure dynamite," he enthused, "Working with Susan was terrific." (Tellingly, he didn't mention Catherine Deneuve, who played his vampire wife in the movie.) At the time, Susan was seeing, and partly living with, Italian director Franco Amurri, and they had a child together. A free spirit, after filming ended, she carried on a three-year affair with David.

Both *The Hunger* and David's next movie, *Merry Christmas, Mr. Lawrence*, were unveiled at the Thirty-Sixth Cannes Film Festival, where he was mobbed by thousands of fans, and riot police had to be called in to quell the crowd. Nonetheless, the movie was booed by the festival audience and received a pasting from the critics, with Rex Reed calling it "turgid pretentious kitsch."

The Hunger premiered within two weeks of the premiere of *Merry Christmas, Mr. Lawrence*, in which David played Major Jack Celliers, a prisoner in a Japanese POW camp.

"David Bowie plays a born leader in Nagisa Oshima's *Merry Christmas Mr. Lawrence*, and he plays him like a born film star," Janet Maslin wrote glowingly in the *New York Times*, further enthusing, "Mr. Bowie's screen presence here is mercurial and arresting and he seems to do something slyly different in every scene."

David did indeed have star quality, and by rights he should have been a far bigger movie star than he ended up being. Part of the reason may have been his tendency to ricochet from genre to genre, and to play dramatically different characters, thus confusing Hollywood's more unimaginative powers-that-be. His divergent movies and the disparate parts he played had always been filled with as many contradictions as David himself is. Perhaps aware of the conundrum of his own making, he eventually attempted to cast light on his choices to make movies as varied as *Just a Gigolo*, and now *Merry Christmas, Mr. Lawrence*.

"I've never chosen films for roles. I've always chosen for the director who's involved or for somebody in the cast. I'm in a privileged position, in that people are willing to take a chance on me," he said.

While promoting *Merry Christmas, Mr. Lawrence* in Cannes, David had an uncharacteristically open conversation with British journalist Hilary Bonner. "I feel tremendous guilt because I grew so apart from my family," he said. "I hardly ever see my mother and I have a step-brother [sic] I don't see anymore. It was my fault we grew apart and it is painful—but somehow there's no going back."

Isolated from his family, yet content in his isolation, David continued to concentrate on his career to the exclusion of all else. In 1983, he made his highest-selling album ever, *Let's Dance*, produced by Nile Rodgers and appealing to a new generation of fans who had never heard of Ziggy Stardust. The first single from the album, "Let's Dance," went on to become David's first record to reach number one in both the British and the American charts.

The success of *Let's Dance* came out of the blue for David—he had assumed that his biggest hit, "Fame," was behind him. "I was quite comfortable in that position," he said, "I thought, well, I've had my big deal, this is where I am. . . . Then the explosion happened when that song was a hit, and that really threw me for a few months. It just snowballed, it was unbelievable."

To top that, "China Girl," on the same album (which had been written by Iggy Pop and featured on his 1977 album, *The Idiot*) was a big hit—although, down the line, David would become disenchanted with it. When Rosie O'Donnell, a friend of his and Iman's, who was obsessed with "China Girl," interviewed him for her show in March 1997, she cracked, "I always ask him to sing that and he's like, 'I hate that bloody song. Shut up about it.' And then Iman's like, 'I want to go to dinner but please don't bring up 'China Girl,' Rosie, no.' "

Though David intimated that he was tired of doing songs from the eighties, nevertheless, "China Girl" did carry a personal resonance for him: When he was shooting the video in Sydney, he embarked on an affair with his twenty-three-year-old costar, Geeling Ng, and invited her to Europe, where they had a two-week affair. She was sweet and exuded normalcy, but in the end she was totally overwhelmed by all the trappings of his rock-star lifestyle and left the tour to return home to New Zealand with no hard feelings on either side.

All through the summer and fall of 1983, David performed his Serious Moonlight tour in sixteen countries, in which more than two and a half million fans attended ninety-six performances. Singer-composer Jonathan King, whom David had known in London at the start of his career and who had been one of his earliest and biggest champions in the music press, was now hosting a TV show in Britain. After a great deal of negotiating with David's management, King arranged to fly to California to interview him at Anaheim Stadium, where he was performing on the tour.

Jonathan remembered, "I hadn't seen David for fifteen years and I said to the crew, 'This is going to be great!' We set up in a dressing room, and David had loads of staff there, but we didn't see him.

"Outside, there was a crowd, and then all of a sudden, a massive buzz, and sure enough, it was David, come to be interviewed. He comes in with ten other people. I say, 'Hi, David.' He sits down, looks at me, says, 'You are a fat shit,' and walks out again with his entourage.

"So we packed up and left the dressing room, but on the way out, we saw David's guitarist, Peter Frampton. He and his girlfriend Mary used to stay with me quite often, so I said, 'Peter, what the hell is going on?'

"And he said, 'Well, I think there's a bit of a problem.' He tipped me a wink and didn't say anything, but I put two and two together and the words 'white powder' came up in my head."

After the Serious Moonlight tour, David followed up with the album *Tonight*, which featured the single "Loving the Alien." In quick succession, he appeared as Jareth, the Goblin King in Jim Henson's $20 million tour de force *Labyrinth*, with Jennifer Connolly, and dedicated the movie to Zowie, in very much the same way as in 1978 he had recorded *Peter and the Wolf* with the Philadelphia Orchestra for his son as a gift.

While shooting *Labyrinth*, David was lighthearted, and during the scene with "Toby," Jennifer Connolly's younger brother, played by Toby Froud, thought nothing of acting on camera while all the time putting on a puppet show off camera to distract little Toby and stop him from crying.

As always when David made movies, Zowie, then twelve, was on the set. As a result, through contacts he met there, he would ultimately get his first job working for Muppets creator Jim Henson.

Although *Labyrinth* was to become a cult classic, David turned down the opportunity to play the part of the villain Zorin in the Bond film *A View to a Kill*.

"It simply was a terrible script," he said, forthrightly. "I saw little reason for spending so long on something that bad . . . And I told them so. I don't think anyone had turned down a 'major' role in a Bond before. It really didn't go down too well at all. They were very tetchy about it."

However, later on he added, "To be honest, I haven't watched a James Bond film since Sean Connery was in them. I don't really like them."

On the other hand, he did agree to appear as himself in Ben Stiller's *Zoolander*, judging the script, "too funny a script to walk past. An absolute hoot," and also did a cameo playing a hit man, complete with mustache, who jams his gun into Jeff Goldblum's mouth in John Landis's *Into the Night*. That same year, he played Vendice Partners, an adman, in *Absolute Beginners*, modeling his transatlantic twang on that of his boss at Nevin D. Hirst during his advertising agency years. "I enjoyed playing him. He's such a bastard," David said.

The movie's director, Julien Temple, had worked with him before on a video and was extremely impressed by him. "Bowie's not only very interested in film, but he has a lot of knowledge about it," he said. "I get a lot of input from him, which is very different from working with the Stones, who always want you to do everything yourself."

Appearing in *Absolute Beginners*, in the part of Flora, was Mandy Rice-Davies, who hadn't seen David since their lunch together at La Gioconda, almost twenty years before. "We didn't have a scene together, but David came round to my dressing room and said, 'Do you remember me? Do you remember the Gioconda?'" Mandy said. "He hadn't changed at all. I went on the set and watched him. He was still a very self-confident young man."

Patsy Kensit, the female star of the movie, was eighteen years old and utterly unraveled at the prospect of working with David. "I was beyond excited about that and expected him to instantly fall in love with me the moment he laid eyes on me (as you do when you're eighteen)," she remembered. "There's a brilliant scene in the film where David dances on top of a globe, and on the day it was being shot, the soundstage at Shepperton was packed because everyone wanted to watch him perform. We were all in awe of him, and he was amazing," Patsy said.

He was a big star now, both of movies and of music, but somewhere inside, he still remained the romantic sixteen-year-old boy who had once wooed a fourteen-year-old girl, Dana Gillespie. Through the intervening years, he never forgot the secret of his success.

"One day, I was sitting in the makeup chair. And he walked over to me, picked up a hairbrush, and started brushing my hair. He didn't utter a single word, just put down the brush after he'd finished and left the room," Patsy Kensit said.

SIXTEEN

ASHES

On January 16, 1985, David's forty-seven-year-old half brother, Terry Burns, lay down on the railroad tracks, just yards in front of an oncoming express train then traveling at a speed of seventy miles an hour toward Coulsdon South station. It was too late for the engineer to brake, and all ten carriages rolled over Terry's body and crushed him to death.

For Terry's funeral, David, who had stayed away, ostensibly because he was afraid of all the press who might stampede the funeral, sent a basket of yellow and pink chrysanthemums along with a card that read "You've seen more things than we could imagine but all these moments will be lost, like tears washed away by the rain. God bless you. —David."

During David's childhood and teens, Terry had exposed him to jazz, to coffee bars, to Soho, to subversive literature, and—as Terry was prone to smashing seats in the Astoria Brixton—to bad-boy rock-star behavior, as well. However, any nascent violence in Terry was not due to willfulness or a desire to rebel for rebellion's sake, but to his mental and emotional instability. Back in December 1966, David and Terry had gone to a Cream concert at the Bromel Club together, and there, David witnessed his brother's paranoid schizophrenia in full flower.

"I know that he was getting to a pretty tranced-out state watching Cream, because I don't think he had ever been to something as loud as that in his life. I remember having to take him home because it was really affecting him," David said in a 1993 interview on BBC Radio One.

He had always been concerned about Terry, cared about him, and had even taken Dana Gillespie with him to visit Terry at Cane Hill. But it was Angie who had shown Terry unlimited kindness, and who, in 1971, invited him to stay at Haddon Hall with her and David, leaving David perplexed.

"I'm not sure whether he's kinda run away or what. The majority of the people in my family have been in some kind of mental institution. As for my brother, he doesn't want to leave. He likes it very much," David said at the time.

Terry's idyllic sojourn at Haddon Hall was not destined to last long, and before, during, and after, as Angie revealed in her memoirs, David continued to be terrified that he might follow in Terry's footsteps. Incarcerated in Cane Hill asylum, Coulsdon, Surrey, where his mother, Peggy, had committed him, in 1982, Terry tried to commit suicide by throwing himself out of the window. He survived with a broken arm and leg and ended up in Mayday Hospital, Croydon, just seven miles away from Beckenham.

Hearing the news, David made a surprise visit to Terry, bringing with him gifts of a radio/cassette player, some books, and cigarettes. More important, he promised to get Terry released from Cane Hill. But no matter what David may or may not have attempted to do for Terry behind the scenes, Terry remained where he was. Around the same time, outraged by what she perceived to be David's neglect of Terry, whom she loved as if he were her own son, David's aunt Pat gave a series of interviews to Leni and Peter Gillman, then writing their biography *Alias David Bowie.*

"Pat talked to us because she was angry at David and wanted to get his attention. Terry was passionate about David, and David used to worship Terry, but when he became famous, it appeared to Pat that he wanted to put his relationship with his brother behind him," Leni Gillman said. "Pat felt that Terry was being harmed by David's neglect, and she hoped that by talking to us and giving the family perspective, it might cause David to put it right.

"Terry would say that 'David said he was going to come and see me,' 'David said he was going to do this or that,' but then nothing happened. David did write Terry some letters, but Peggy had probably told Terry that David was going to do this or that. She was giving Terry false hope, but I imagine she did it in good faith and she thought that David would do those things," Leni said.

In December 1984, Terry made a second suicide attempt by throwing himself in the path of an oncoming express train. But just as the train roared closer and closer, he jumped out of the way. Then, before anyone could stop him, he grabbed a massive number of sleeping pills out of his pocket and swallowed them.

That suicide attempt failed. But on his next attempt, made just three weeks afterward, Terry succeeded in killing himself.

"Terry had such a bright mind and it was just awful that he would deteriorate like that," David said afterward, and went on to muse as to whether or not he would one day suffer the same fate, relating his drug use to "attempting to be my brother." It was an easy rationale, one that sat well with the press and didn't give a glimmer of what David, who grew up worshiping Terry, really felt about his half brother's suicide.

However, his aunt Pat would never forgive him for Terry's incarceration and untimely death. As she confided in journalist Amanda Cable seven years after Terry's suicide, David's neglect of Terry had run so deep that even though she had repeatedly written to him to beg for cash so that Terry could be transferred from the grim Cane Hill asylum to a gentler, more luxurious private clinic, David did not.

"He left Terry for nineteen years in a mental home without sending a penny for private treatment," Pat said. Then, in a moment of insight, she added, "Terry was handsome, charming, and intelligent. But when he fell ill David didn't want to know, because it was a reminder that the same thing could happen to him because it ran in the family."

In 1985, David performed at Live Aid, for which he initially intended to do a transatlantic duet with Mick Jagger. However, after deciding that the logistics were against them, David proposed that they do a duet with one of them singing from inside a space shuttle and the other one singing down on earth. Unsurprisingly, NASA was not prepared to lend them a space shuttle, so Mick and David recorded "Dancing in the Street" together. Originally, their duet was supposed to be live, with one of them in Philadelphia and the other in London, but the idea was scuppered owing to technical problems.

Consequently, the duet was recorded in London's Docklands, with just Mick and David, alone, and there was a strong homoerotic vibe to the taping. Although David was happy with the first take, Mick was not. Throughout the whole process, David was friendly to the musicians and anyone else on set, but Mick was not. Nonetheless, David and Mick's rendition of "Dancing in the Street" hit number one on the UK charts and stayed there for four weeks.

Kevin Armstrong, who put together David's Live Aid band, felt extremely positive about David and observed, "I don't think he's quite so Machiavellian as people make out, or so calculating. . . . He has quite a sort of boyish enthusiasm for something and he'll just follow it."

David ended his Live Aid performance by introducing "Heroes" and dedicating it "to my son, to all our children, and to the children of the world," and was met with tumultuous applause.

To some outsiders, it might have seemed as if David and Mick's rivalry was still in full flower, but they had shared so much, even the same women, and by now were friends—so much so that Mick and Jerry invited David and Coco to spend Christmas with them at their Mustique estate. Captivated by the beauty of the island, and by the privacy, David immediately bought a plot of land close by and set about commissioning architects and designers to work on building his Caribbean paradise.

Apart from being a bastion of billionaires, blue bloods, and superstars, Mustique is also dominated by classic Caribbean architecture, and although David did follow in Mick's footsteps by purchasing a property there, as much a nonconformist as ever, he said, "I wanted something as unlike the Caribbean as possible," and designed and commissioned an Indonesian-style estate, high on a hill, with lush Japanese gardens dominated by koi ponds, a swimming pool cut into the hill, and romantically beautiful Balinese pavilions. When work on the estate was completed, David was so happy with the result that he declared in an interview with *Architectural Digest*, "My ambition is to make music so incredibly uncompromised that I will have absolutely no audience left whatsoever. Then I'll be able to spend the entire year on the island of Mustique."

Whenever Joe spent his vacations in Mustique with his father, it was akin to paradise. "I'd go to Basil's Bar, eat some banana bread, eat some lobster, watch films, have a swim. The whole Jagger clan would be down there," he recalled.

During much of the eighties, David and Joe shared their spells on Mustique with the new love in David's life, the beautiful Melissa Hurley, who is twenty years his junior. They first met when David's Glass Spider tour hit L.A., and Melissa was one of the dancers in the show.

Born in Vermont, Melissa, then twenty to David's forty, was a statuesque, elegant ballet dancer, a soloist with the Los Angeles Chamber Ballet. Beautiful, with long legs and a talent for doing the splits effortlessly, she had show business in her blood. Not only did she dance the tango in the movie *Rent*, but later on, in 1990, she also costarred with Steve Martin in *My Blue Heaven*.

With Melissa, an all-American girl with style, class, and good manners, David experienced a relatively conventional relationship. And although he had been dallying with Hawaiian model Marie Helvin and English aristocrat Sabrina Guinness (whom he invited to Wimbledon, and to Mick Jagger's birthday party for his then girlfriend, Jerry Hall), he gradually settled into a more regular way of life with Melissa. Careful not to expose her to too much publicity, he made sure that they never arrived at or left a restaurant together. Consequently, they were very rarely photographed in tandem.

A shadow fell over their relationship early on during the Glass Spider tour, when he was charged with raping a thirty-year-old makeup artist named Wanda Lee Nichols at Dallas's Mansion on Turtle Creek Hotel, where he was staying. After two years, the claim was dismissed when Wanda failed a lie detector test and it was also proved that she'd met David at a party at 2 A.M., spent the night with him, and then sent him a thank-you note in the morning. However, when he refused to see her the following evening, she pressed charges against him.

With the charges dropped, happy with Melissa, and at the top of his game professionally, around the same time David enthused, "I'm more like I was in 1967 now, say, than I was in 1977. I feel like I am, anyway. I feel as bright and cheerful and as optimistic as I was then—as opposed to feeling as depressed and sort of nihilistic, as I was in the seventies. I feel like I've come full circle in that particular way," he said.

After proposing to Melissa during a romantic trip to Venice, in January 1990 David went so far as to confirm in the press that they were getting married: "I have absolutely no idea when exactly the wedding will be, but we're engaged, and a wedding is what that usually leads to."

However, soon after, their relationship ended amid speculation that Melissa hadn't been strong enough for David, and that in the end, the age difference between them had contributed to the rift. Later, David characterized their relationship as "one of those older men, younger girl situations where I had the joy of taking her around the world and showing her things. But it became obvious to me that it just wasn't going to work out as a relationship, and for that she would thank me one of these days."

Melissa went on to marry David Cassidy's half brother Patrick.

In the wake of David's relationship with Melissa, it seemed as though their time together had taught him to value peace and happiness. Now in his forties—and perhaps in part thanks to the perspective that the age difference between him and Melissa had afforded him—David was finally primed to embark on an intimate, lasting relationship with a woman. During the Sound+Vision tour (having overcome his fear of flying somewhat), he took a flight from Madrid. On the plane, guitarist Adrian Belew noticed David leaf through a magazine, then stop at one particular page and comment, "This girl's interesting."

Her name was Iman.

But before he met her and his life became utterly transformed, he made a stab at returning to his roots, by becoming one fourth of a band called Tin Machine. And although drummer Hunt Sales cracked, "The thing that makes us different from other bands is that the lead singer's a millionaire," David did his utmost to be one of the boys, even insisting that no journalist interview him without the rest of the band present. Far more of a team player now than he had ever been in the early days with the King Bees, the Kon-rads, or any of his other bands, he was now happy to share the spotlight because he no longer had anything to prove.

When Tin Machine played the Brixton Academy in November 1991, in an exercise in nostalgia, David asked the tour's bus driver to make a detour on the way to the venue and drive down Stansfield Road, Brixton. According to Tin Machine guitarist Eric Schermerhorn, who confided this to biographer Paul Trynka, David began crying and through his tears said, "It's a miracle. I probably should have been an accountant. I don't know how this all happened."

His spectacular rise to fame and fortune might have been a mystery to him (although it is highly likely that, if pressed, he would have come up with a vast number of valid reasons for his success), but nothing could have prepared him for the romantic fairy tale in which he was about to be cast in the leading role. In retrospect he was to say, "Over the years I've become a very buoyant, happy character; 1989 was the period I realized for the first time in my life that I was an exceptionally lucky man. Many things, such as meeting my wife, made me realize that I should bless every damn moment I am alive because I was having, and have, an extraordinary life."

As it happened, the deus ex machina who set David's fairy-tale ending in motion was a Los Angeles hairdresser named Teddy Antolin. The date was October 14, 1990; the occasion, a birthday party for Teddy, at which David and Iman were both guests. Later, they would classify their first meeting as a blind date, but there was nothing prosaic about David's first reaction to Iman.

"I was naming the children the night we met. I knew that she was for me; it was absolutely immediate. I just fell under her spell," David said, then elaborated, "It was so lucky that we were to meet at that time in our lives, when we were both yearning for each other."

The very next day, Iman flew out of L.A. bound for a fashion shoot, but when she arrived back, David was on the tarmac, waiting for her. The bisexual, promiscuous, try-anything sex addict who'd go to bed with anyone had miraculously evolved into a romantic, love-struck swain.

David proposed to Iman on October 14, the following year, on a boat floating up the Seine, while in the background, a pianist he had hired just for the evening played romantic standards as David serenaded her with "April in Paris," the song that would one day be played at their wedding. Iman's engagement ring dated back to eighteenth-century Florence, and, on a more modern level, as part of consummating their relationship, each of them would submit to having a tattoo. Iman had a Bowie knife tattooed above her ankle, with the word *David* written on the handle and his name in Arabic lettering tattooed around her belly button. David got a tattoo of a man riding a dolphin on his left calf. A frog rests on the man's left hand, and there is a Japanese translation of the Serenity Prayer superimposed on both the man and the dolphin. Afterward, David proudly explained that he had the tattoo done "as a confirmation of the love I feel for my wife and my knowledge of the power of life itself."

And when Iman expressed her feelings about David, they were interchangeable with his for her. "I have found my soul mate with whom sexual compatibility is just the tip of the iceberg. We have so much in common and are totally alike in a lot of things," she said. Moreover, as she put it, "David has his feminine side. I have a masculine side."

If her remark is slightly reminiscent of the days when David and Angie swapped gender roles on a regular basis, his marriage and his life with Iman were destined to be diametrically opposed to the marriage and life he had once led with Angie. At separate times, journalist Noreen Taylor Greenslade interviewed Angie and Iman. "Iman and Angie are both strong women. The two women represent both ends of his life: Angie the drug-fueled sixties and seventies, and Iman the New York life," Taylor Greenslade said.

"Angie was full of angst and bitterness, the woman cast aside. I know that she claims she was seminal in creating him, but I didn't see anything in her to inspire him. If she had some talent, it would have come out since they divorced, but it hasn't. Angie is a very destructive part of his life.

"Iman is an intelligent woman, a businesswoman, she's got a great sense of humor, she's very wry, and she has irony. She exudes calm," Taylor Greenslade said.

Poised, self-sufficient, highly intelligent, and startlingly beautiful, Iman was the exact antithesis of Angie. In fact, Angie was a million miles removed from Iman, the second Mrs. Bowie, just as David was now a million miles removed from his other self, David Jones.

SEVENTEEN

HEROINE FOR MORE THAN JUST ONE DAY

Iman Mohamed Abdulmajid was born in Mogadishu, Somalia, the product of a great romance between her mother, Marian, and her father, Mohamed. At fourteen, Marian was destined for an arranged marriage with an older man. Instead, she fell madly in love with a seventeen-year-old Arabic teacher from Ethiopia, Mohamed, and together they eloped.

Iman, born in 1955, was originally named Zahara, but her grandfather renamed her Iman, which is a man's name, and which, Iman believes, makes her the only girl in Somalia named Iman. Being given a man's name, she says, has had a very specific impact on her life and her psyche. "I am very in touch with my masculine side. I am as independent as Somalia," she has said, proudly.

After spending the first three years of her life living with her grandmother, she returned home only to find that her mother was jealous of her grandmother, who quickly moved away. From that time on, Iman's relationship with her mother was fraught. "I have had an adversarial relationship with my mother," she has said, admitting, "She is powerful and I am, too, and we have locked horns like bulls all my life."

However, in contrast, she adored her father, who became a diplomat, and who loved to read to her, just as David always has. "He reads to me all the time," Iman has said of David, "When he reads, he plays all the characters and uses different voices for each one. When he reads to me, it's like being a little girl again."

In 1969, when Iman was fourteen and living in Saudi Arabia with her parents, the president of Somalia was assassinated, and Iman and her family fled on foot to Kenya.

Her parents sent her to boarding school, which she hated, and she swore to herself that if she ever had children, she would never subject them to a similar fate. She had been brought up as a Muslim and, when she was very young, had been taken to Mecca. When she grew older, although she no longer prayed, she fasted at Ramadan.

After serving in the Somalian military for two years, she studied political science at the University of Nairobi, spoke five languages, and in between classes waitressed and worked as a translator. When distinguished writer-photographer Peter Beard approached her in the streets of Nairobi in 1975 and asked her if she had ever been photographed, she was outraged.

"I thought, *Oh God, here goes another white man who thinks we've never seen a camera,*" she said. On the other hand, as Beard remembered, "Iman was dead anxious to get out of Africa."

No matter how much she wanted to leave Africa, though, she still drove a hard bargain and would only allow Beard to photograph her if he paid $8,000 for her college tuition—which he did. In Manhattan, he took her to Wilhelmina, one of the top modeling agencies of the day, famous for representing Lauren Hutton and Anjelica Huston, and then called a press conference to introduce her to the fashion establishment. With an eye to media coverage and building Iman's mythology, Beard claimed that he had met her in the bush, giving enough detail for *Newsweek* to take the ball, run with it, and elaborate by describing her as "a Somali tribeswoman," and for other publications to go further and describe her as a "nomad."

Eugenia Sheppard, distinguished fashion columnist for the *New York Post*, heralded Iman's arrival in America, writing on July 22, 1975, "New York will soon be bowled over by the arrival of a fashion model from Nairobi who will appear wearing an elephant-fetish jacket and a dozen or so gold band necklaces. She is five foot ten and a half, one foot of which, from her photographs, seems to be a miraculous neck."

Headlines described her as a "Cattle Girl," and the subtext was that here was a noble savage and that hers was a latter-day Cinderella story. "It was all a fabrication," Iman admitted afterward. "But I am definitely not the victim of it: I was an accomplice. I knew exactly what was going on."

All in all, just like David at the start of his career, at the start of hers, Iman was unafraid to spin a good story in order to use the media to promote her. And in Peter Beard she had found a masterly accomplice. "Okay, so we did set up the legend, but it got completely out of hand. The press ended up calling her a goat herder, which was a complete insult. We said she was herding cattle: there's a big difference," he said.

In Manhattan, she was immediately photographed by Arthur Elgort for *Vogue*, but as she had never seen the magazine in her life, she was completely unaware as to the significance of the shoot. Moreover, she had never worn makeup or even a pair of high heels before. "Suddenly I was wearing both and standing alone in front of a camera and a barrage of people," she remembered. "I was like a deer caught in the lights of a car. Afterwards, when I looked at the pictures it didn't look like me. I saw no trace of the Iman I was."

"She wasn't very good in her first show," Betty Ann Grund, then fashion editor at *Harper's Bazaar*, remembered. "But she learned very quickly. She had an elegance and was like a gazelle."

When Iman's parents discovered that she was in Manhattan and that she was modeling, they were far from delighted. In particular, her father, who had dreamed of her becoming a politician, was deeply disappointed. And from then on, both parents "spent years asking me when I was going to get a proper job," Iman said.

At first, though, she had great difficulty in adjusting to America. As she told photographer Scavullo, she had been offered American food but was scared to eat it owing to the artificial flavoring, and consequently quickly dropped seven pounds. And however much she tried to enjoy New York, she found the city and the business so hardscrabble that she sometimes felt as if her neck would break from all the tension. She was still accustomed to a more peaceful life in Africa, and the noise of the city invariably woke her at around five every morning.

From the first, she had hated modeling. "I've been trying to quit since the day I started," she said. "In the beginning, I thought that modeling was only a job for people who didn't have any other way to go. I had a lot to me, you know. In my schooling, in my mentality, I think I had quite a lot. But the job proved to me otherwise."

But despite her disdain for modeling, or perhaps because of it, she was showered with praise for her performance on the catwalk. Karl Lagerfeld called her "one of the greatest models in the world." Saint Laurent dubbed her "flawless," and Scavullo termed her "a great beauty." Bill Blass said, "I used her from the start. The truth is, she's a great actress. She's always still Iman, but her ability to transfer her attitude from one house to another is incredible. She used her body like an instrument, and I'm not talking about her sensuality." By wordlessly conveying emotion, or lack of it, Iman was, in her own way, somewhat of a talented mime, just like David.

Summing up the secret of her appeal, she said, in a quote that could have come straight from David, "You have to give people fantasies. You have to create illusions all the time."

In the midst of all the adulation of Iman, the projection of her as a black Cinderella who had become queen of the catwalk, a Somalian named Hassan Gedi, who was then working at the Kenya Hilton, came forward claiming that he had married her, that she was his wife and had lived with him in Kenya for the past two and a half years, and that he still loved her. With no alternative other than to admit the truth, Iman said, "I was married—not an arranged marriage—it was my choice. My parents were totally against it and within months I found that I had made a huge mistake."

Like David, it transpired that Iman possessed the facility never to be truly tarnished by scandal, to emerge with her aura of innocence and her image intact, and the sudden revelation that she was married did not damage her reputation one iota. By now, she was a superstar in the world of modeling and, unlike most models, even did her own makeup and styling.

Betty Ann Grund remembered, "She is wonderful, warm, and very intelligent. She was quite different looking from other black models." Bill Blass would sum up the essence of her modeling success: "She's the High Priestess—we call her that [*Iman* means "priest" in Arabic]. Of course she's dramatic, but behind the slightly grand attitude she's very professional. Never lets you down. And whatever happens, if there's a problem, she'll handle it: make them laugh, keep them in awe, whatever is needed to cover a disaster. But beyond the fact that she's famous, Iman is the perfect model, she gives expression to the clothes."

In 1978, she met basketball great Spencer Haywood, who played for the Knicks, then for the Lakers, on a blind lunch date in Manhattan. Afterward, she and two of her friends went back to Spencer's apartment, where Iman was impressed by his African art collection and his knowledge of African culture and history. For his part, Spencer said, "I was completely fascinated to be talking to this incredibly lovely and innocent woman who was from the very part of the world that so intrigued me, the homeland I wanted to know everything about. I wanted to listen to Iman and look at her forever."

After that, their romance skyrocketed, as hand in hand they took strolls in Central Park together and went jogging. She happily watched him play basketball at Madison Square Garden. And when, five months after their relationship began, Iman got pregnant, naturally Spencer immediately married her, partly because of the baby, and partly because she didn't have a green card—a strange coincidence, given that David had married Angie so that she would get British residency. And then there is the fact that Spencer's last name is Haywood—the same as David's father's unusual middle name and the middle name that David also gave his son.

On July 5, 1978, Iman gave birth to Zulekha, her daughter with Spencer. Soon after, the famously difficult and demanding producer Otto Preminger discovered her and cast her in *The Human Factor*. Afterward she reported, "If filming hadn't ended when it did one of us would have killed the other. We had terrible differences." In contrast, Preminger's production manager, Val Robins, insisted that the director "was very gentle with Iman . . . he worked with her and tried to get it out of her."

In her private life, conflict erupted between Iman and Spencer when it became clear that he was against her posing nude for *Vogue* and for *Playboy*, and escalated yet further when she had breast enlargement surgery in advance of her nude centerfold being shot. When Spencer was traded to the Lakers, he, Iman, and Zulekha moved to Los Angeles. He was still in love with her, but their marriage went into decline when he began taking drugs and then was arrested for beating Iman, a charge he still denies.

Finally, as he wrote in his memoirs during a ball in Paris, "Iman hooked up with Grace Jones. Some of the Frenchmen kissed Iman's hand, as is their custom, but they went well beyond the hand. They put their tongues in Iman's mouth and were grinding her. With me standing right there. The whole scene was too weird for me," he said. "I was horrified. But Iman told me I was being ignorant. 'These people are all gay and they are all my friends,' she said. 'This is how it is in

Paris.' What happened to that conservative African girl I met in New York all those years ago?" Spencer Haywood asked himself.

" 'It's not a big deal,' she told me. But it was a big deal. They were mocking me and her. Iman didn't understand that. Then Iman and Grace Jones were dancing together, another strange scene, grinding each other with everyone else standing around watching them like they were the floor show," he said.

However, Spencer was far from squeaky-clean himself. Almost as an aside, in the book, he lets slip that he fathered a child by another woman while still married to Iman. Ultimately, they divorced and a bitter custody battle between them ensued, at the end of which Iman won legal custody of Zulekha.

In 1983, Iman suffered a near-fatal accident when the taxi in which she was a passenger was hit by a car driven by a drunk driver who had run a light. She was instantly thrown forward. Her face went through the glass, and she broke her cheekbones, collarbone, and three ribs, and dislocated her shoulder. Her arm was in a sling. She fractured a bone in her ear, and afterward had five hours of reconstructive facial surgery but remembered nothing of the accident because, immediately afterward, she fainted.

But no matter how much pain she had suffered, and how deep her injuries, Iman soldiered on. She was now the first black model to front big advertising contracts, and to command fees of $30,000 a day or more. But although she was now at the peak of her modeling career, she still held fast to her ethics and refused to take jobs specifically for black models.

By now, she was living in a duplex with a boyfriend, stockbroker William Regan, and in 1989 she retired at the very top of the modeling profession. Along the way, she also helped other models to achieve their potential.

"She's really like a mother figure to me, and she's taught me so much. She taught me how to walk and how to take my jacket off in a show. She's helpful to everybody. Not just black models, white models, too," supermodel Naomi Campbell said.

As an actress, while she was breathtakingly beautiful, by the beginning of the 1990s, she had not met with great success on-screen. By then, though, she had found happiness in quite another arena: She had met David Bowie.

Iman has said, "What I love about David is that he's a true gentleman, very old fashioned and English. He never lets me walk on the outside of the pavement, opens doors for me, and because we met on the fourteenth, he sends me flowers on the fourteenth of every month. He's a scholar too—he reads a lot, writes, does sculpture and paints, so I've learned so much from him."

Unlike David, she always had the example of her parents' happy marriage to inspire her. "They're still in love and always have been; they hold hands all the time. If it weren't for them I'd have given up the whole idea of romance and love. Their marriage is unique," she said.

Nowadays she says, "This is the happiest time of my life, because this is the first time that I am happy with my life exactly as it is. I'm totally at ease with him—totally myself. I don't have the feeling that if I reveal something about myself, that something is going to happen to the relationship. I know that whatever he knows of me, he will always be with me."

In return, David has said of her, "She is an excellent person and a wonderful mother and she has such a wonderful, well grounded sense of independence about the way things are, about her career, and what she wants to do. She has changed my life. I give far more over to her than before. So it takes a wedge out of what I would be throwing into my work. But it doesn't seem to have caused me many problems."

David couldn't bear to be parted from Iman for long, and, during the early years of their marriage, decided not to tour because, as he put it, "I think getting married and then running away for ten months would be an absolute disaster."

Putting his rampant sexual past behind him, he revealed, "I have no temptations whatsoever. I have so been there and done that. I cannot tell you what I've done. You cannot show me anything new. None of it holds water for me anymore. There are no temptations—coffee, maybe."

Both of them had left their pasts behind, and, as Iman said, they had "both lived a bit on the wild side, and we're both, deep down, homebodies."

He has said of Iman, "My wife has a strong sense of who she is. And that's what I need in my life—someone who doesn't have a fractured personality, very down to earth, not flippant. I no longer need attention. I wanted the adoration of the masses, the audience, because I was incapable of one-to-one communication. I used to feel nothing without my work.

"Now I no longer feel guilty if I'm not working. My idea of an experience is a yacht cruise with Iman. I want to be with her. She is my soul mate. I can't believe that a relationship like this has been so smooth sailing. There really have been no difficulties. We don't try to put up hurdles for each other."

Traveling the world became their biggest joint pleasure. They spent their six-week honeymoon in Bali. And closer to David's roots in the UK, together they explored Cornwall, and, in particular, the putative haunts of the mythical King Arthur and Camelot, his court. And, according to journalist, Billy Sloane, the night before David played Glasgow on his Earthling tour, he and Iman went for a walk around the west end of the city, studying all the architecture, "and then they went to the Botanic Gardens and bought an ice cream and just walked, with no security, no nothing."

Since his marriage to Iman, David had become far more open and gregarious than he had ever been before, and in February 1992, despite the attendant publicity, he and Iman went to Elizabeth Taylor's sixtieth birthday party at Disneyland. A few years later, they befriended Princess Diana and Dodi Fayed, and when they were killed in Paris, Iman and David went into shock. "It's such a loss," Iman said. "The last time I saw her it was July on her birthday at the Tate Centenary. We laughed and joked. It still hasn't sunk in."

On a more positive note, in 1997, after Iman and David met British prime minister Tony Blair and his wife, Cherie, when they attended one of David's concerts, Tony Blair enthused that Iman was "stunningly beautiful," and she reciprocated with, "It was very sweet of him. I think he's a very good looking man, too!"

Of David, she said, "There is that comfort of thinking that you have known this person all your life, but still the freshness. My heart flutters whenever he walks into the room." One Christmas she made him slippers, getting up every morning at five to work on them and to embroider his initials on them before he got up at 6 A.M.

Before she and David married, Iman asked her family what they thought of him, whereupon her father announced that he would have preferred her to marry a Somali or a Muslim, or, at the very least, someone black. And her aunts and uncles even insisted that he convert to Islam. "Can you imagine David Bowie converting to Islam?" she said. But her parents were quickly captivated by David. "They love him, and what they love is that I love him," Iman said.

The union of David and Iman had caught the imagination of the world, and together they made a dream couple. But, not content to rest on their romantic laurels, they both continued to pursue their separate career destinies. Always a businesswoman, just as David was always essentially a businessman, Iman said proudly, "I was always careful to save, to spend wisely, to build my business sensibly."

Rather than focus on acting, in 1994, Iman launched her own cosmetic company and proved to be a consummate businesswoman. "From day one I wanted to create makeup for all women of color, not just black women. Grouped separately we are a minority, but if all women of color pull together we are a majority," she said.

Offering specific shades of foundation formulated for African-American, Asian, Latina, and other women of varying ethnicities, Iman's company was such a runaway success that in 2010 it was a $25 million business. Moreover, in 2007, Home Shopping Network invited Iman to create her own clothing line, which she later expanded with accessories, all with great success, winning her fans and customers among women of all ages.

EIGHTEEN

GOLDEN YEARS

David was happy and content with Iman, and although he had stepped down his work considerably, he still pursued an eclectic array of artistic projects. In an utterly radical departure from his image and from the world of rock music, in April 1995 he made a deal with the flowery British fabric and fashion company Laura Ashley to design a range of wallpaper.

As he explained, "I chose wallpaper because of its status as something extremely incongruous, particularly in the world of art. I haven't completely lost my sense of irony, you know!"

The wallpaper was only on sale in a limited edition at the London gallery where a retrospective of his paintings was on exhibition. In the midst of it all, he nevertheless retained a sense of humor: "Hanging wallpaper isn't my kind of thing, but I could definitely art direct, and I could light it beautifully. I could tell other people how to hang it, believe you me," he said.

Meanwhile, in September 1995, Brian Eno produced David's *Outside* album, on which David sang in a series of different voices. That same month, he co-headlined an American tour with Nine Inch Nails called the Outside tour, which bred a million-dollar-selling album and won him the Lifetime Achievement award at the Brits, which was presented to him by then prime minister Tony Blair.

Morrissey briefly toured with Bowie, but their relationship had never been smooth or trouble-free. In his autobiography, Morrissey remembered meeting David for breakfast at a Beverly Hills restaurant and being horrified that David was about to eat some cold cuts. Whereupon, he asked, "'David, you're not actually going to eat that stuff, are you?' Rumbled, he snaps, 'Oh you must be HELL to live with.' 'Yes, I am,' I say proudly, as David changes course and sidles off towards the fruit salad and another soul is saved from the burning fires of self-imposed eternal damnation."

On a different note, Morrissey revealed, "David quietly tells me, 'You know, I've had so much sex and drugs that I can't believe I'm still alive.'" Down the line, according to Morrissey, David telephoned and asked him to cover "Mr. Ed," a recent song of his. According to Morrissey, "He stresses that if I don't do the cover, 'I will never speak to you again, haha,' which is hardly much of a loss since David doesn't ever speak to me.

"A few months later I am at my mother's house when the telephone rings. My mother hands me the 1940s shellac antique. 'It's for you—it's David Bowie,' and boyhood's fire is all aglow again, although I cannot understand how David found my mother's number.

"He explains that he would like to send me something through the post. 'Do you have an address?' I ask. 'Oh, just write to me care of the management,' he replies. 'No, I meant do YOU have an address for ME?' I say."

Iman did not always travel with David, or see his shows, simply because, as she put it, "How many times can you hear the same songs?" Alone on the *Outside* tour, David telephoned Iman regularly and also stayed in touch with friends and fellow musicians.

During the Outside tour, as Eno remembered in his diary, "Bowie called me from a distant American hotel room to relay the O. J. Simpson verdict to me as it was delivered, describing the scene in court, etc.

Then it was on our TV too, so we were watching it together. I don't know what city he was in—Detroit, I think."

David was deeply unnerved by the trial verdict. Eno quoted him as saying, "It's all down to investigative journalism now."

On the movie front, David agreed to appear in Julian Schnabel's *Basquiat*, playing the part of Andy Warhol. When they had first met, Andy had failed to take him seriously, had rejected him, and David couldn't have failed to note the irony. "God knows what he would have thought of me actually playing him in a film all those years later. We never particularly got on," he said, later adding, "I'm not sure that there's such a thing as a fond memory of Andy Warhol. He was a strange fish. Even people who say they knew him well, I don't think they did. I certainly didn't know him well."

Intent on portraying Andy in every aspect, he borrowed his clothes, including Andy's handbag and its contents, from the Warhol Museum in Pittsburgh. When the film was released in August 1996, he received positive reviews, with no less a luminary than Janet Maslin of the *New York Times* praising his performance with, "Andy Warhol . . . is brilliantly caricatured by David Bowie as an art world Wizard of Oz."

Julian Schnabel observed, "I thought it was like a doppelgänger thing, where I have a pop icon play a pop icon. So you know you're watching David Bowie in a sense, but it's almost like, 'Is Andy Warhol playing David Bowie, or is David Bowie playing Andy Warhol?'"

There was, of course, a third possibility: Perhaps David Bowie was playing David Bowie playing Andy Warhol.

In 1998, again in stark Bowie contrast, David played a gang leader in *Everybody Loves Sunshine*, simply because Goldie, whose script it was, had asked him.

In 1997, David made a return to solo albums with *Black Tie White Noise*, which included "The Wedding," inspired by Iman, and "Feel Free," on which he reunited with Mick Ronson after twenty years. Just a short time after they recorded the song, Mick died of liver cancer at the age of just forty-six. Afterward, David would say, "Of all the early-seventies guitarists, Mick was probably one of the most influential and profound and I miss him a lot."

In 1997, now without Mick, he released his new album, *Earthling*, posing on the cover in a tattered Union Jack Coat, which he codesigned with Alexander McQueen. That same year, in a strikingly innovative move, one that was quintessentially David, mixing the visionary with the mercenary as it did, he issued $55 million of Bowie bonds, selling shares in back royalties of his twenty-five albums recorded before 1990, in return for an up-front payment. Investors would then be able to buy and sell "Bowie Bonds" which promised an annual 7.9 percent return.

"I just wanted the money. I couldn't give a damn who bought them," said David, then revealed that all the bonds had been purchased by Prudential Insurance. "I am very proud of what I've written and I've created. And I'm quite happy to earn my living by it. The money doesn't present me with any embarrassment. Basically, I do the art and sell it," he said. "I have a lot of money coming in over the next ten years from my back catalogue, but I'd rather have the cash now and not have to wait."

Similarly, on the real estate front, in January 1996, primarily because Iman was never happy in the rarefied atmosphere of Mustique, David sold his estate there to businessman Felix Dennis for $400,000 less than the $4 million at which he originally put it on the market.

As always, uncannily forward thinking, intellectually searching, and continually alert for the next trend, the next world-shaking innovation, even at the early stage in the general use of the Internet, David was already ahead of the curve. He plunged in heart and soul, carried a portable computer everywhere, and, a full two years before e-mail became a popular form of communication, used it as much as possible. An e-mail addict at a time when only a small number of Americans had it, he enthused, "I'd be completely lost without it! I always like to e-mail quick messages to Iman if I know she is out for the day. But I still call her on the telephone if we are away from each other for any length of time."

Every morning when he got up, he invariably logged on, posting diaries of his thoughts and activities, and even entering chat rooms under a pseudonym. "I don't announce myself when I go into my chat rooms, but I do have a pet name which they know as 'Sailor'! As in 'Hello, Sailor.' I just couldn't resist it," he revealed in an interview with Richard Wallace, which David insisted be conducted over the Internet.

"I love the chat rooms, because you get to hear what people genuinely think," he said. "The communication between me and my web audience has become more intimate than it's ever been. It is a feeling I enjoy because it is new to me. It is adventurous, it is a new position of what the artist is, it is a demystification."

David being David, he threw himself into exploring the Wild West of the Internet with a vengeance. "I was an obsessive, I'd surf the web all the time, just crazed," he admitted afterward.

However, after six months, he made the decision to cut down on his time surfing the Internet, "because I was on too much. Iman wasn't too happy because I just never came to bed. But now I'm very disciplined," he said. Then, in a comment that prefigured the cataclysmic effect of the Internet on relationships ten or fifteen years later, he added, "Once you start surfing at night, you can really break up a relationship. You've got to be very careful about that."

By the end of the nineties he had launched what the *Economist* called "a creative empire." Apart from signing a special edition Mini car, he had his own radio network on *Rolling Stone*'s Internet radio site. Barnesandnoble.com hired him to write online reviews of books, and he shocked the music business establishment by releasing his album *Hours* on the Internet. On September 11, 1996, he released his track "Telling Lies" exclusively on the Internet through his own site, Davidbowie.com, which 350,000 fans downloaded.

Later on, in a 1999 interview, he accurately prophesized, "The exciting part of music on the Internet is the impact it could have on delivery systems. . . . It would be good news for the consumer, too, who by choosing the individual tracks or making a compilation of various artists, would in a sense become the producer."

Then he went on to warn, "Record companies may resist the web until the last minute before being forced into action. My record company isn't exactly jumping on board. . . . I think if I was starting out in music now, I think I'd look on rock as a stodgy, traditional format and the Internet as what's happening tomorrow."

With that in mind, in September 1998, he launched Bowienet, a high-speed Internet service that offered customers e-mail addresses with the suffix @davidbowie.com, and a multitude of other Bowie-related elements: live chats, live video feeds, chat rooms, and question and answer sessions with David, himself.

Subscribers wishing to use Bowienet as their full Internet service provider paid a fee of $19.95 a month, and users who only wanted to avail themselves of content paid $5.95 a month. A great resource for all things Bowie, the site would survive for fourteen years.

On January 7, 1997, David celebrated his fiftieth birthday at Madison Square Garden, where he performed in aid of Save the Children with Lou Reed, Robert Smith, and many others. That same year, he performed at the Phoenix Festival in aid of Amnesty International's Refugee Campaign in Stratford-upon-Avon, England. And on January 31, 1997, Madonna inducted him into the Rock and Roll Hall of Fame, but, predictably, he didn't bother to show on the night. "I'm not really one for those awards shows," he commented. "That aspect of competiveness leaves me a little cold."

Afterward, hearing what Madonna had said about him, he professed to be deeply touched by her words. This is what she said that night: "Before I saw David Bowie live, I was just your normal, dysfunctional, rebellious teenager from the Midwest, and he has truly changed my life.

"I've always had a sentimental attachment to David Bowie, not just because I grew up with his music, but it's because it was the first rock concert that I ever saw and it was a major event in my life. I planned for months to go and see it.

"I was fifteen years old, it was the end of the school year, and leading up to the week of the show, I begged my father and he said, 'I absolutely refuse, over my dead body, you're not going there, that's where horrible people hang out,' so of course I had to go.

"So my best friend spent the night at my house and when we thought everyone was asleep, we snuck out of my window, which was no mean feat, as I was wearing my highest platform shoes and a long black silk cape. Don't ask.

"We couldn't drive, so we hitchhiked into Detroit and I don't know who was scarier . . . the drivers that picked us up, or us in our outfits. Anyway, we arrived at Cobo Hall and the place was packed and we fought our way to our seats. And the show began.

"And I don't think that I breathed for two hours. It was the most amazing show that I'd ever seen, not just because the music was great, but because it was great theater. And here's this beautiful, androgynous man, just being so perverse . . . as David Byrne so beautifully put it: so unconventional, defying logic and basically blowing my mind.

"Anyway, I came home a changed woman, as you can see, and my father was not sleeping and he knew exactly where I went, and he grounded me for the rest of the summer. But it was worth every minute that I sat and suffered in my house that summer. So I would just like to thank you, David Bowie—wherever you are—for inspiring me and I would like to accept your award. Thank you."

• • •

On April 1, 1998, he and Iman hosted a party thrown at artist Jeff Koons's SoHo studio, launching the book *Nat Tate: An American Artist: 1928–1960,* ostensibly a biography by William Boyd. The book was published by David's new art-house publishing company, 21, and in it, Boyd recounted the tragic story of Tate, who, after destroying 99 percent of his work, jumped off the Staten Island ferry and drowned.

Guests at the party, who all feted author William Boyd and toasted the memory of Nat Tate, included Charlie Rose, Jay McInerney, and assorted art world glitterati, all of whom listened respectfully as David read out an excerpt of the biography. However, a week later, *Independent* art critic David Lister revealed that Nat Tate was only a figment of Boyd's imagination, and that the book was a hoax in which Bowie willingly and knowingly participated.

In 1999, David signed to make an album, *Hours*, for Virgin Records. Publicist Mick Garbutt worked with him on it and, subsequently, on *Heathen* and then *Reality.* He said, "David's an absolute gentleman. He's polite and takes an interest in you. He is generally nice; he disarms you and asks you how you are. But unlike [John] Travolta, who wanted to know everything my mother was doing, David doesn't go into great depths.

"I've met him hundreds of times, and he has a gentleness about him. There is just an aura of otherworldliness about him. Obviously he has got those eyes, he has that look. There is a youthfulness about him, a sharpness."

At one stage, while David was promoting the album in England, Garbutt traveled up to Manchester, where he met David at BBC Manchester. "When I got there, I realized that I'd got David's schedule wrong," Mick remembered. "He knew that I had, but he didn't say anything to me in front of anyone. It was almost as if he didn't want to show me up in front of them, but he was obviously annoyed.

"I apologized to him, and he just nodded. He knew his schedule better than I did and it was a good thing that I rectified my mistake. All of us who work with David feel that we don't want to get anything wrong. We don't want to disappoint him. He commands loyalty more than any other artist I know."

When Garbutt flew to Manhattan to work with David further, he received another insight about him. "I remember I went to a studio on West Broadway, and David just sauntered in, wearing a black flat cap and didn't have an entourage with him. He was on his own. He'd just walked down West Broadway alone and just turned up at the studio, without any flunkies whatsoever."

In 1999, David played Wembley for NetAid, and Meg Mathews went with her then husband, Noel Gallagher of Oasis, to see him after the show, and remembered, "I went into his dressing room. We were having a laugh with him; it was very laid-back. I was a bit in awe. Gobsmacked. Noel was chatting away with him. David was very down to earth, really sexy voice, really polite. Gentlemanly, not a massive ego," she said.

In 1999, David was awarded an honorary doctorate of music by the Berklee College of Music and gave a fifteen-minute commencement speech, in which he told the story of John Lennon's fan-avoidance techniques. The rest of the speech was peppered with his customary wit and stellar advice for musicians of the future.

"Music has given me over forty years of extraordinary experiences. I can't say that life's pains or more tragic episodes have been diminished because of it. But it's allowed me so many moments of companionship when I've been lonely and a sublime means of communication when I wanted to touch people. It's been both my doorway of perception and the house that I live in. I only hope that it embraces you with the same lusty life force that it graciously offered me," he said.

On June 25, 2000, David headlined at Glastonbury 2000, performing in front of more than a hundred thousand fans, many of them cold and tired after three days at the festival. David kept them rapt and enthralled. Beforehand, though, he had been, "nervous as a kitten," but he swaggered through his two-hour show set and gave a masterly superstar performance.

NINETEEN

WHERE HE IS NOW

On February 13, 2000, David and Iman announced that she was pregnant with their first child. They had been trying since they first got married, and, as David put it, "It's been a long and patient wait for our baby, but both Iman and I wanted it to be absolutely right and didn't want to find ourselves working flat-out during the first couple of years of the baby's life. This is a wonderful time in both our lives."

In a more jocular vein, he said, "We are looking at names at the moment and all I can tell you is that it will be in keeping with the Somali-Bromley tradition." Alexandria Zahra Jones was born on August 15, 2000, and weighed in at seven pounds, four ounces. David was in the delivery room and cut the umbilical cord.

With the birth of Lexie, as her parents call her, his thoughts strayed to his own childhood, and to his half brother, Terry. "He was an autodidact. He would go to libraries and art museums and discover music on his own, and he would say, 'You gotta read these guys,' and 'You gotta listen to this.' I think I've passed that on to my son, and I do hope that I will do that for my daughter," he said.

His relationship with Zowie, now Duncan, had become even closer through the years, particularly as Duncan was exhibiting talent as a film director, although he had never shown any aptitude as a musician. After working for Jim Henson and attending the London Film School, like his father before him, he took a job in advertising and directed a campaign for French Connection. Despite his fractured childhood and lack of a mother's consistent love—so much in contrast with what the future held in store for Lexie—Duncan's creativity had flourished, just as his father had intended.

Apart from nurturing Lexie's creativity, from the first, David was concerned with practical matters, as well. Getting up before Lexie every morning, although he balked at changing her diapers, he read out loud to her and played with her, taking turns with Iman. He was a proud father and boasted, "Lexie has enormous energy. She's an absolutely extraordinary, vital child. And incredibly social." And, "She is wonderful and probably, I believe, the most intelligent child that has ever been born. She is terribly physical and I think she's mad for anything athletic. Running and dancing and getting bruises. She's a lovely, lively child."

Resolving not to tour so much, like he did when Duncan was growing up, he insisted, "I don't want to make the same mistakes with Lexie."

At the end of 2000, David made a cameo appearance in *Mr. Rice's Secret*, a low-budget independent film, playing the small part of Mr. Rice, the kindly neighbor of a small boy suffering from Hodgkin's disease. As Elvis Mitchell wrote in the *New York Times,* "Someone deserves the grand prize for persuading David Bowie to participate in this minor drama."

By way of an explanation, David said, "From the script, it was so thoughtfully and considerately conceived. Nothing smacked of the sensational. It could so easily have slipped into that hole given the subject matter. There was an active intelligence behind it all. . . . I have, on the whole, avoided Hollywood like the plague."

David was in America when, on April 2, 2001, his mother died in a nursing home in St. Albans, England. She was eighty-eight years old, and her death was sudden and a surprise to him. Since the mid-1980s, she had been spending three months each year at his home in Switzerland. But despite his largesse, true to form, Peggy had complained to her younger sister Pat that he was away for most of the time she had been there.

Whether or not he had ever cared about pleasing his mother, the die had long ago been cast. However, unlike in the case of his half brother, Terry, David did attend his mother's funeral, where Ken Pitt was in attendance, and so was his errant aunt Pat. Seeing her, David let the past fall away and hugged her as if bygones were bygones. Afterward, he made no comment about his mother, her life or her death.

Peggy had been demanding, flamboyant, unloving, fanciful, a writer of poetry, a stickler for cleanliness and perfect manners, a long-distant, relatively silent supporter of his career, unemotional, unloving and, in many ways, his doppelgänger, his other self. And now she was gone.

If he was suffering from the loss of his mother as he suffered in the wake of Terry's suicide, David never revealed his feelings, but instead, threw himself into work, as was his wont. He was up in Woodstock with Tony Visconti recording his first album of the new millennium, *Heathen*, when the planes hit the Twin Towers. He saw the news and immediately called Iman in their SoHo apartment just two miles from the World Trade Center. From the apartment, Iman had a full view of the towers but had missed the first attack. She was still on the phone with David when the second plane crashed into the buildings. According to David, "She said, 'Oh my God, another one has gone.' I said, 'You are under attack. Get the fuck out of there.'"

With Lexie in the stroller, she ran twenty blocks away from the apartment to shelter and safety in a friend's apartment. But to David's horror, after that the phones went down and they lost contact with each other. "I didn't speak to her until the nighttime," David remembered. "I was in a right state. I just had no idea if she and Lexie got out. It was so, so horrifying. It was incredibly traumatic, one of the nastiest days of my life."

In the wake of September 11, 2001, on October 20, 2001, he performed at a benefit concert at Madison Square Garden: the Concert for New York City, to honor the New York City Fire Department and the New York City Police Department, their families, those lost in the attacks, and those who had worked in rescue and recovery.

A year later, he released the *Reality* album via satellite, the world's largest interactive event of its time, and then embarked upon the Reality tour. Bassist Gail Ann Dorsey, who had played with him for the last decade, said, "We are starting to find our footing as a band. Of course, as soon as it settles down, David always mixes it up again. He gets bored, so that helps to keep us on our toes."

Although he was still a bona fide rock star, he underplayed his fame and fortune, dressing in J.Crew, declaring a year later, "I've been a pretty regular guy over the past fourteen years, in the way that I live my life and my ambitions, which are very few these days. It's about trying to keep my family unit together, really to try to create a secure and comforting nucleus for my daughter. If I'm looking further ahead, I'm usually looking through her eyes."

He had already rejected a life peerage in 2000 (which would have meant that he would have been made a baron for his lifetime, but that the title would not be passed on to his son), and in 2003, he was offered a knighthood by Queen Elizabeth II. He rejected that as well, explaining, "I'm indifferent to royalty. I can't remember the last time I thought about them. So I'm certainly not excited about the prospect of working for them. Accepting one of those things would make me feel owned, and I'm not owned by anybody. Not even the music industry," he said.

When asked how he felt about Mick Jagger, in contrast, accepting the knighthood, he shrugged and said, "It's not my place to make a judgment on Jagger; it's his decision but it's just not for me. Am I anti-monarchy? I'd only have a serious answer to that if I was living in this country."

In November of that same year, David gave a concert at Wembley Stadium, the site of so many past triumphs, and chalked up yet another.

He hadn't taken drugs for many years, and had also given up drinking. According to Tony Visconti, he and David went to AA: "David found it very useful. We talk about being each other's support system. If two people from the program sit together, that's technically an AA meeting. Every two or three days we talk about it, although we don't start and end with a prayer. I'll say, 'I'm coming up to my twelfth birthday,' and he says, 'Well it's been my twenty-third.' I ask, 'Do you miss it?' and he says, 'I don't miss it at all.'"

At the end of 2003, he did a shoot with waifish supermodel Kate Moss, a South London girl who grew up in Croydon, just six miles from Bromley, and, like him, had dabbled in cocaine and was also a smoker. Although twenty-eight years separated David and Kate, they immediately bonded, and afterward, she enthused, "I've just been clinging to David Bowie naked. It doesn't get better than that."

As for David, mindful of the age difference between them, he took on a paternal role, "She's so young and smokes like a chimney. And she's got such a gorgeous little body! It needs protecting," he said.

The following year, he and Iman paid over $1.5 million dollars for a sixty-four-acre estate outside Woodstock, New York. He fell in love with Little Tonche Mountain, as the property was called, when he was recording *Heathen* at a nearby studio. Afterward, he said of their new hideaway, "This is not cute, on top of this mountain: It's stark, and it has a spartan quality about it. In this instance, the retreat atmosphere honed my thoughts. I've written in the mountains before, but never with such gravitas."

In June 2004, he was performing at the Norwegian Wood festival in Oslo when a crazed fan flung a lollipop in his eye. The missile actually wedged itself in his eye socket, and, given the childhood injury to his eye, he was palpably shocked. Fortunately, there was no permanent damage to the eye.

By now he had been on the road for almost two years, promoting *Reality*, playing to audiences all over the world in a show that lasted two and a half hours. After playing Prague, where he was forced to cut the gig short because of a trapped nerve in his shoulder, he ended up in the German town of Scheeßel, where the pain in his shoulder increased.

Admitted to hospital, his trapped nerve was treated, but during a checkup doctors found that he had suffered a heart attack while performing onstage, and at Hamburg's St. George Hospital, chief cardiologist Karl-Heinz Kuck operated on him, fitting a special filter to his artery. Until the operation was over and a success, he said nothing to Iman, and she only heard the news four hours afterward.

Advised not to tour, he went home to Manhattan. Strangely enough, he had given up smoking six months before he had the heart attack, which then came out of left field for him—but now he also gave up coffee in favor of decaffeinated coffee. But he still couldn't convince himself to jettison performing forever, and in 2006, he performed with Alicia Keys at the Black Ball at the Hammersmith Ballroom in New York, in aid of the Keep a Child Alive organization. Afterward he thanked her, telling her that he wouldn't have been able to sing again had he not got over his fears by performing that night.

In 2006, he played the part of legendary inventor Nikola Tesla in the movie *The Prestige*. Scarlett Johansson was in the movie as well but, sadly for her, didn't have any scenes with David.

"My first ever crush was David Bowie in the movie *Labyrinth*," she confessed. "I actually met him a year or so ago, backstage at one of his concerts. I couldn't tell him he was my first love because I couldn't actually speak when he shook my hand."

But despite his acclaimed appearance in *The Prestige*, he was bored with making movies and decided not to do any more. "On set, I end up sitting outside the trailer talking with people about God knows what. What a waste of a day just to be in front of the camera for fifteen minutes," he said.

In January 2007, he celebrated his sixtieth birthday. According to Iman, he didn't freak out about it beforehand: "I guess that's because he's happy. We just lead a very simple family life," she said.

He had given up alcohol, was exercising on a daily basis, and said that he felt fantastic. That same year, he appeared in an episode of Ricky Gervais's *Extras*, in which he did a cameo as himself, turning on Ricky by singing the song "Pathetic Little Man," in a scene which some critics hailed as the funniest of the series.

His heart attack plus his mother's death had lent him intimations of mortality. "There's a realization of an end looming," he said. "And it becomes even more focused when you've got a small child.

"How long have I got left? That's the saddest thing in the world, because you have this realization that everything you love you're going to let go of and give up. I look at Lexie and think there's going to be a point when I'm not around for her. The thought of that is truly heartbreaking."

In 2010, he and Iman bought a three-bedroom villa in Saint Lucia. The villa was situated in the prime location of the Pitons, with a volcano on either side, and he and Iman loved the breathtaking views. Manhattan remained their primary home, and there, David was relaxed and unthreatened by fans or the public. "It's easy to get about. Nobody looks at me twice. In New York, they don't feel they have possession of you. They let you get on with your life," he said.

At home in Manhattan, David and Iman regularly entertain friends. They once threw a dinner party for singer Boy George, who said afterward, "Bowie was lovely, extremely charming. He cooked. I can't remember what."

According to George, the conversation switched to Russian art house flicks, about which he knew very little, then turned to brands of English tea, what David loved about London, and what he missed about England. And in a surreal moment, David, who loves Cadbury Flake Chocolate and Sunday fry-ups, which Iman makes for him each week, confided to George that he was also a massive fan of the British soap *EastEnders*.

At exactly 5 A.M. GMT on January 8, 2013, without any prior warning or fanfare, David released his new single "Where Are We Now?" accompanied by a video, to be followed by the release of his first new album in ten years, and his thirtieth studio album, *The Next Day*, two months later.

With his perfect sense of drama, David had released his single on the morning of his sixty-sixth birthday. Within hours, the download of the track skyrocketed to number one, and the album went straight to the top of the presales chart.

Mick Garbutt observed, "David is very aware that less is more. He doesn't need to have a PR team, which was certainly proved by what he did on January 8, releasing a record with no promotion.

"If you speak to people in the camp, they say that he had been in the studio for ages. Only David Bowie knew when he was ready. Then he gets more publicity."

As Chris Charlesworth, who had been David's RCA publicist, put it, "Most artists of his stature, if a new record was coming out after a long period of nothing, there would be a fanfare, a team of PRs, and six months, three months, and they would build up expectations of the record, and if it wasn't very good it would be a damp squib.

"But Bowie was very clever not saying a word to anyone. No one had a clue he was making a new record. The release of the record became a news story itself. Everyone was taken by surprise—he created more press by doing nothing."

Afterward, producer Tony Visconti said, with a certain amount of glee, "I've been listening to this on headphones, walking through the streets of New York, for the past two years. If people are looking for classic Bowie, they'll find it on this album. If they are looking for innovative Bowie, some new directions, they'll find that on this album too."

David was till adept at stirring up publicity through his anarchic approach to music: The release of *The Next Day* album was to lead to controversy, with YouTube removing the promo for the single from its site because it "contravened the terms of use." The offending video featured Gary Oldman playing a priest and Marion Cotillard playing a prostitute with stigmata, as if she has been crucified. David is on hand, in a smock. That video was followed by one for "The Stars (Are Out Tonight)" starring Tilda Swinton, a passionate David Bowie fan.

During the first minutes of David's sixty-sixth birthday, his son, Duncan proudly tweeted, "First off, it's midnight in NY. That means, a HUGE HAPPY BIRTHDAY is in order to my lovely, very talented dad!"

And then, "Would be lovely if all of you could spread the word about da's new album. First in ten years, and it's a good 'un."

Now, as always, Duncan was one of the greatest joys of David's life. "I just thank my good fortune that we get on so well now. Any bridges that had been broken—and I don't think many had been—are mended," David said, later adding, "We get on famously. He is enjoying what he is doing in his life, and I am really enjoying seeing him being fulfilled."

After Duncan married photographer Rodene Ronquillo in 2012, straight afterward she was diagnosed with breast cancer. Since then, she and Duncan have fought to raise awareness of the disease.

Fascinatingly, Duncan's professional fulfillment, and his greatest success until now, came from directing the science-fiction movie *Moon*, about an astronaut who is the only inhabitant of a space station on a three-year tour of duty just coming to an end. The movie won Duncan countless awards, plus the inevitable comparison between *Moon* and "Space Oddity." Through it all, David was unendingly proud of him.

Once fascinated by Howard Hughes, for more than a decade David has seemed intent on emulating Hughes's retreat from the world. Consequently, he turned down a plea to appear at the Olympics closing ceremony, although "Heroes" became the Games' unofficial anthem, played rousingly as Britain's team marched into the arena.

His absence at the event, which would have been the crowning glory of his career, was perhaps a testament to the fact that for the past two decades, America, not Britain, has been his home.

Toward the end of 2013, he did make a cameo appearance playing the piano and singing the song "I'd Rather Be High," from the album *The Next Day*, in a Louis Vuitton commercial. Starring twenty-five-year-old model Arizona Muse, and ostensibly shot at a glittering Venetian masque ball, the commercial shows David looking strained and ill at ease, yet in just the first two days after its release, there were 1,750,000 downloads.

In Manhattan, where David and Iman live in a $4 million SoHo loft apartment, he has a panic room where the family can lock themselves in the eventuality of a home invasion. There are terraces, woodburning fireplaces, and twenty-six-foot-high ceilings, and the living room of the apartment is painted hunter green and decorated with suede, leather, and dark wood paneling.

Sometimes David slips out of the apartment and, wearing a flat cap, a hooded jacket, and wraparound sunglasses, browses the books at McNally Jackson bookstore, but generally he spends most of his time in the apartment.

Although David and Iman have been seen dining at Indochine, they are very rarely photographed on the streets of the city together. Instead, he has been photographed with the ever-present Coco by his side, still a central figure in his life forty years since she first became his personal assistant. For while Iman is clearly nurturing of and loving toward David, he has never been the sole fulcrum of Iman's life, as he is of Coco's.

For a take on David, his marriage to Iman, and Coco's role in it, Tony Zanetta, who first became close to David during his marriage to Angie, and has watched his evolution over the last quarter of a century, observes, "Iman has her own light, and until David married her, he always seemed to need all the light on him, and everything else was secondary.

"Iman is a real powerhouse—she has her own thing going and she doesn't need him for anything. She is more active than he is in many ways; she's got her own business, she's a strong independent person. But perhaps because Coco supplies his other needs, she allows the marriage to flourish."

David Bowie is now the grand old man of rock, the epitome of a free-spirited, all-powerful, ever sexually charismatic rock god; yet he has never been dogged by paternity suits, or embroiled in any late-in-life scandals of any sort. Instead, he remains both elusive and reclusive.

The Victoria and Albert Museum exhibition *David Bowie* opened on March 23, 2013, ran until August 11, 2013, and attracted more than three hundred thousand visitors. The exhibit featured three hundred objects from his archive, including costumes, fashion photographs, handwritten lyrics, film, music videos, set designs, and David's own musical instruments.

Although David had opened up his archives (which he had housed in Switzerland for many years) to the Victoria and Albert Museum's curators, he never once met them. During the run of the exhibition there was constant speculation that David might attend the closing of the exhibition, which was the most successful ever mounted by the Victoria and Albert, but he did not.

Or did he? What if, on some chilly London night in March, with Coco by his side, David, in his flat cap and dark glasses, was smuggled into the exhibition after closing? And if he was, surveying the memorabilia of a career that has endured for over fifty years, would he not have felt like a drowning man, watching his entire life float in front of him?

A series of pictures of him as a ten-month-old child, glittering with personality, a different expression for every frame; the song sheet for "Liza Jane," with him grinning at the camera, fresh-faced, brash, confident; a picture of him as Pierrot, his turquoise leather boots; the lyrics of "Ziggy," scrawled in blue ballpoint pen in a school textbook, his writing full of loops, all attesting to his tendency toward fantasy; fashion dummies dressed in the Ziggy quilted costume; a picture of him and Angie at Haddon Hall, the epitome of *la jeunesse dorée*, yet with a waxwork quality about them—the potpourri of his life and career as one of the most influential artists of the twentieth and twenty-first century. Among the museum exhibits was a page from the performers' directory *Spotlight* that read "David Bowie, 5 ft 10 and a half inches. Kenneth Pitt Management, 35, Curzon Street."

But while there is no evidence that David Bowie ever once set foot in the exhibition dedicated to his life, his art, his times, late one evening, when the Victoria and Albert Museum had closed, a frail and emaciated ninety-year-old gentleman, David's former manager, Ken Pitt, was escorted into the exhibition.

And as he gazed at the memorabilia of David's life, the incontrovertible evidence of his kaleidoscopic creativity, his talent, and his glory, Ken Pitt's thoughts may well have strayed to an April afternoon in 1966 when he looked up at the stage of the Marquee Club and first set eyes upon the nineteen-year-old David Bowie, brimming over with talent, sex appeal, and charisma, never dreaming that one day in the near future, this glittering boy would become the man who changed the world.

Thanks to Steven Gaines; Vicki Hodge; Angela Bowie (whom I first interviewed in 1976 at Oakley Street); Mandy Rice-Davies; Meg Mathews; Claudia Skoda; John Eddowes; Lesley Joseph; Leslie Thomas; Maggie Abbott; Reverend Alan Dodds; Kim Fowley; Billy Sloane; Dana Gillespie; Betty Ann Grund; Bob Gruen; Mick Garbutt; Jonathan King; John Bloom; Ann Bloom; Noreen Taylor Greenslade; Ron Ross; Chris Charlesworth; Shirley Dunmall; Andy Peebles; Monique van Vooren; Asha Puthli; Jeff Griffin; Simon Napier-Bell; Si Litvinoff; May Routh; Laurence Myers; Steve Dube; Peter Gillman; Leni Gillman; Nicholas Defries; Stuart Lyons; Don Short; Joe Stevens; Tony Perry; Tony Zanetta; Leee Black Childers; Cherry Vanilla; Josette Caruso; Martin Samuels; Winona Williams; Glenn Hughes; Kenny Bell; Phil Lancaster; Suzi Ronson; Tony Hatch; June Millington; Jean Millington; Nick Dudman; Malcolm Diplock; George Tremlett; Dai Davies; Michael Armstrong; Arthur Stockwin; Audrey Stockwin; Nita Bowes; Yvonne Sewall; Eugene Chaplin; Tim Rice; Nic Roeg; Jean Rose (Random House); the Kensington and Chelsea Library; Clyde 1 radio station; Nick Pyke of *the Mail on Sunday*; Trudy Southern from the British Library; John Chittenden of Capital FM; Robin James from BBC/Getty Images; my thanks to Alexis Schumacher for her work, enthusiasm, and commitment to this book; Carole Mallett of Ravensbourne College; Melanie Aldridge from Alamy; Alison Stacey of the *Birmingham Mail*; Faye Rawlinson of Tim Rice's office; Jess Morris of Jess Morris PR; Kelly DiNardo; Brenda Evans; Lionel Bart Archive; IMDB; Christine Phillips of Barnardo's; Millie Seaward (Random House); the Carmarthenshire Antiquarian Society; *Sunday Mail Glasgow*; Campbell Thompson; Jayne Marsden of the *Yorkshire Post*; Bene Factum Publishing; Annette Witheridge; Sharon Churcher; Allan Hall; Patrick Goldstein of *the Berliner Morgenpost*; Casian Sala of Legastat; Grace Robbins; Daniel Knight from Q; Marion Charles Pigache; Dwina Murphy-Gibb; Roger Alton, executive editor of *The Times*; Chris Bott; Eddie Mulholland; Justine Hodgkinson; Ken McReddie Associates; Rebecca Michael; Maggie Abbott, who has written her memoirs, *Total Recoil*, and a novel, *The Acid King*, and whose second novel, *The Bimbo Syndicate*, is published as an e-book; Alessandro Nasini of the Royal Collection; Anthony Marotto of the APA Agency; Loraine Budge, Simone Harris, and Arthur Holden at the Bromley Central Library; Buddy at Photofest NYC; Charlotte Russell of the Yorkshire Agricultural Society; Cheryl Minnis of Infomart; Diana Thomas; Emily Stillwell of the Royal Agricultural Society of England; Fiona Hamalton; Isaida Miranda from City of Rochester, NY; Jayne Marsden; Kirsten Foster of Curtis Brown Group; Laura Gibbons of CDA London; Laura Wagg of the Press Association; Lori Di Costanzo from Clare Best; Melanie Aldridge of Alamy; Melissa Tagoe of Laura Ashley; Nicole Hormuth of Agentur Aussicht; Paul Kasler from the Pleasure Home; Reinhard Keck from Axel Springer; Ryan Chambers of Bauer Media; Sally Wall of the Yorkshire Agricultural Society; Todd Ifft of Photofest NYC; Theresa Dellegrazie, Corbis, Starr Hackwelder, Alamy, Princess Pratt, Alamy, Simon Flavin, Mirrorpix, Stephen Atkinson, Rex Features, Michelle Butnick-Press, Getty Images.

Tom Freeman of Freeman News Service; Tom McCartney; Martine King, archive manager at Barnardo's. Barnardo's, where David's father was press officer, works with more than 200,000 children, young people, and their families each year, and runs more than 900 services across the UK. "We believe in children and we believe every young person has a right to thrive. Our vision is to realize Thomas Barnardo's dream of a world where no child is turned away from the help that they need. We work to transform the lives of the UK's most vulnerable children and every year we help thousands of families to build a better future. But we cannot do it without you. Visit www .barnardos.org.uk to find out how you can get involved and show you believe in children."

With my thanks and admiration to my brilliant, cool, and perceptive publisher, Jen Bergstrom, and to Trish Boczkowski, editor extraordinaire, whose creativity and insight is unparalleled. And to the great team at Gallery Books: copy editor Polly Watson, production editor John Paul Jones, editorial assistants Elana Cohen and Paige Cohen. And to my agent, Daniel Strone, Chief Executive of Trident Media Group, always and forever the best agent on the planet, bar none.

SOURCE NOTES: AN OVERVIEW

INTRODUCTION

Monique van Vooren

Dana Gillespie

Angela Bowie

Claudia Skoda

Tony Zanetta

Leni and Peter Gillman

Joe Stevens

Asha Puthli

Kim Fowley

Andy Peebles

Mick Garbutt

Jean Millington

CHAPTER ONE: ABSOLUTE BEGINNING

Kim Fowley

Leni and Peter Gillman

Winona Williams

Suzi Ronson

CHAPTER TWO: STARBOY
Leni and Peter Gillman
Winona Williams
Suzi Ronson

CHAPTER THREE: SELLING HIMSELF TO THE WORLD
John Bloom
Ann Bloom
Leslie Thomas
Dana Gillespie
Simon Napier-Bell
Kenny Bell
Phil Lancaster

CHAPTER FOUR: SEXUAL LABYRINTH
Leni and Peter Gillman
Jonathan King
Caroline Stafford
Mandy Rice-Davies
George Tremlett
John Eddowes
Stuart Lyons
Leslie Thomas
Phil Lancaster
Kenny Bell
Michael Armstrong
Malcolm Diplock confirmed that his fateful meeting with David
     Bowie, which inspired David to write "The Laughing Gnome,"
     was "a long time ago."

CHAPTER FIVE: MODERN LOVE
Steve Dube
Lesley Joseph

Nita Bowes
Dana Gillespie
Angela Bowie
Michael Armstrong
Nicholas Defries provided the anecdote
    about orange crates.

CHAPTER SIX: ON THE WILD SIDE
Tony Zanetta
Michael Armstrong
Cherry Vanilla
Russell Juby
Nita Bowes
Dai Davies
Dana Gillespie
Nicholas Defries
Laurence Myers
Maggie Abbott
Jonathan King

CHAPTER SEVEN: STARMAN
Maggie Abbott
Suzi Ronson
Angela Bowie
Dana Gillespie
Kim Fowley
Dai Davies
Stuart Lyons
Tony Zanetta
Cherry Vanilla
Peter Gillman
Leee Black Childers

CHAPTER EIGHT: ZIGGY

Dai Davies

Laurence Myers

Chris Charlesworth

Nita Bowes

Angela Bowie

Ron Ross

Kim Fowley

Dana Gillespie

Cherry Vanilla

Tony Zanetta

Leee Black Childers

Yvonne Sewall-Ruskin

Suzi Ronson

June Millington

Jean Millington

CHAPTER NINE: SUPERSTARMAN

Tony Zanetta

Leee Black Childers

Josette Caruso

Suzi Ronson

Kim Fowley

Dai Davies

Nicholas Defries

Joe Stevens

Jeff Griffin

Angela Bowie

Vicki Hodge

Dana Gillespie

Russell Juby

Bob Gruen

Maggie Abbott
Chris Charlesworth
Jean Millington
June Millington

CHAPTER TEN: CHANGED
Steven Gaines
Maggie Abbott
Tony Zanetta
Suzi Ronson
Winona Williams
Jeff Griffin
Joe Stevens
Vicki Hodge
Jean Millington

CHAPTER ELEVEN: YOUNG AMERICAN
Dana Gillespie
Tony Zanetta
Winona Williams
Suzi Ronson
Cherry Vanilla
Jean Millington
Leee Black Childers
Maggie Abbott
Bob Gruen
Chris Charlesworth

CHAPTER TWELVE: FALLING
Steven Gaines
Maggie Abbott
Tony Zanetta

Winona Williams
Glenn Hughes
Cherry Vanilla

CHAPTER THIRTEEN: CRACKING ACTOR
Maggie Abbott
Si Litvinoff
Nick Dudman
Winona Williams
Glenn Hughes
May Routh
Chris Charlesworth
Nic Roeg

CHAPTER 14: BERLIN
Claudia Skoda
Winona Williams
Allan Hall
Don Short

CHAPTER FIFTEEN: JUST A GIGOLO
Winona Williams
Eugene Chaplin
Chris Charlesworth
Monique van Vooren
Andy Peebles
Nick Dudman
Jonathan King
Mandy Rice-Davies

CHAPTER SIXTEEN: ASHES
Leni and Peter Gillman
Melissa Hurley checked facts.

Winona Williams
Noreen Taylor-Greenslade

CHAPTER SEVENTEEN: HEROINE FOR MORE THAN JUST ONE DAY
Betty Ann Grund
Billy Sloane

CHAPTER EIGHTEEN: GOLDEN YEARS
Mick Garbutt
Chris Charlesworth
Meg Mathews

CHAPTER NINETEEN: WHERE HE IS NOW
Mick Garbutt
Chris Charlesworth
Tony Zanetta

Andersen, Christopher. *Mick: The Wild Life and Mad Genius of Jagger*. New York: Gallery Books, 2012.

Bego, Mark. *Tina Turner: Break Every Rule*. Lanham, MD: Taylor Trade Publishing, 2005.

——. *Elton John: The Bitch Is Back*. Beverly Hills, CA: Phoenix Books, 2009.

Björk. *Bjork*. New York: Bloomsbury, 2001.

Bloom, John. *Full Bloom*. London: John Bloom, 2013.

Bockris, Victor. *Lou Reed: The Biography*. New York: Vintage, 1994.

Bowie, Angela. *Free Spirit*. London: Angela Bowie/Solo, 1981.

——, and Patrick Carr. *Backstage Passes: Life on the Wild Side with David Bowie*. London: Orion, 1993.

Bowie, David, and Mick Rock. *Moonage Daydream: The Life and Times of Ziggy Stardust*. Guildford: Genesis Publications, 2002.

Brackett, Donald. *Dark Mirror: The Pathology of the Singer-Songwriter*. Westport, CT: Praeger Publishers, 2008.

Broackes, Victoria, and Geoffrey Marsh. *David Bowie Is*. London: V&A Publishing, 2013.

Buckley, David. *The Complete Guide to the Music of David Bowie*. London: Omnibus, 1996.

Buckley, David. *Strange Fascination: David Bowie: The Definitive Story*. London: Virgin, 1995.

Buell, Bebe. *Rebel Heart: An American Rock & Roll Journey*. New York: St. Martin's Press, 2001.

Cann, Kevin. *David Bowie: A Chronology*. London: Vermilion, 1983.

——. *David Bowie: Any Day Now, The London Years, 1947–1974*. New York: Distributed Art Publishers, 2010.

Carr, Roy, and Charles Shaar Murray. *David Bowie: An Illustrated Record*. Richmond: Eel Pie, 1981.

Cassidy, David. *C'mon, Get Happy: Fear and Loathing on the Partridge Family Bus*. New York: Warner Books, 1994.

Chandler, Charlotte. *Marlene: A Personal Biography*. New York: Simon & Schuster, 2011.

Chapman, Graham, John Cleese, Terry Gilliam, Eric Idle, Bob McCabe, and Michael Palin. *The Pythons: Autobiography by the Pythons*. New York: St. Martin's Press, 2003.

Charlesworth, Chris. *David Bowie: Profile*. London: Proteus, 1981.

Clarkson, Wensley. *Bindon: Fighter, Gangster, Actor, Lover—The True Story of John Bindon, a Modern Legend*. London: John Blake Publishing, 2005.

Clayson, Alan. *Mick Jagger: The Unauthorized Biography*. London: Sanctuary Publishing, 2005.

Cooper, Alice, and Steven Gaines. *Me: Alice, The Autobiography of Alice Cooper*. New York: Putnam Press, 1976.

Currie, David. *David Bowie: Glass Idol*. London: Omnibus, 1987.

——. *David Bowie: The Starzone Interviews*. London: Omnibus, 1985.

Davis, Stephen. *Watch You Bleed: The Saga of Guns N' Roses*. New York: Gotham Books, 2008.

Des Barres, Pamela. *Let's Spend the Night Together: Backstage Secrets of Rock Muses and Super Groupies*. Chicago: Chicago Review Press, 1987.

Dirie, Waris, and Cathleen Miller. *Desert Flower: The Extraordinary Journey of a Desert Nomad*. New York: HarperCollins, 1998.

Douglas, Edward. *Jack: The Great Seducer*. New York: HarperCollins, 2004.

Eno, Brian. *A Year with Swollen Appendices: Brian Eno's Diary*. London: Faber and Faber, 1996.

Faithfull, Marianne, and David Dalton. *Faithfull: An Autobiography*. New York: Cooper Square Press, 1994.

Fletcher, Winston. *Keeping the Vision Alive: The Story of Barnardo's 1905–2005*. Essex: Barnardo's, 2005.

Flippo, Chet. *David Bowie's Serious Moonlight: The World Tour*. New York: Dolphin/Doubleday & Company, 1984.

Foxe-Tyler, Cyrinda and Danny Fields. *Dream On: Livin' on the Edge with Steven Tyler and Aerosmith*. New York: Dave Books, 1997.

Frampton, Owen. "Our Way: The Autobiography of a Teacher of Art and Design." Unpublished manuscript.

Fujiwara, Chris. *The World and Its Double: The Life and Work of Otto Preminger*. New York: Faber and Faber, 2008.

Gillman, Peter and Leni. *Alias David Bowie: A Biography*. New York: Henry Holt and Co., 1987.

Giuliano, Geoffrey. *Lennon in America: 1971–1980, In Part Based on the Lost Lennon Diaries*. New York: Cooper Square Press, 2000.

Gross, Michael. *Model: The Ugly Business of Beautiful Women*. New York: William Morrow and Company, 1995.

Hampton Armani, Eddy. *The Real T: My 22 Years with Tina Turner*. London: Blake Publishing, 1998.

Harry, Debbie, Chris Stein and Victor Bockris. *Making Tracks: The Rise of Blondie*. Cambridge, MA: First Da Capo Books, 1998.

Haywood, Spencer, with Ostler, Scott. *The Rise, the Fall, the Recovery*. New York: Amistad Press, 1992.

Hemmings, David. *Blow-Up . . . and Other Exaggerations: The Autobiography of David Hemmings*. London: Robson Books, 2004.

Hopkins, Jerry. *Bowie*. London: Corgi, 1986.

Jackson, Laura. *Heart of Stone: The Unauthorized Life of Mick Jagger*. London: Blake Publishing, 1998.

John, Marc. *Beaming David Bowie*. Marc John, 2005.

Juby, Kerry, and Barry Miles. *In Other Words . . . David Bowie*. London: Omnibus, 1986.

Kensit, Patsy. *Absolute Beginner*. London: Sigdwick and Jackson, 2013.

Kent, Nick. *Apathy for the Devil: A Seventies Memoir*. Cambridge, MA: Da Capo Press, 2010.

Laing, R. D. *The Divided Self*. New York: Penguin Group, 1965.

Leigh, Wendy. *Speaking Frankly*. London: Frederick Muller Limited, 1976.

Lulu. *I Don't Want to Fight*. London: Time Warner Books, 2002.

Mayes, Sean. *We Can Be Heroes: Life on Tour with David Bowie*. London: Music Sales Ltd, 1999.

McNeil, Legs, and Gillian McCain. *Please Kill Me: The Uncensored Oral History of Punk*. London: Abacus, 1997.

Mendelsohn, John. *I Discovered David Bowie!* E-book.

Miles, Barry. *Bowie in His Own Words*. London: Omnibus, 1980.

——, and Chris Charlesworth. *David Bowie: Black Book*. London: Omnibus, 1988.

Morrissey. *Morrissey*. London: Penguin Classics, 2013.

Norman, Philip. *Mick Jagger*. London: HarperCollins, 2013.

Pafford, Steve. *BowieStyle*. London: Omnibus, 2000.

Paytress, Mark. *Bolan: The Rise and Fall of a 20th Century Superstar*. London: Omnibus Press, 2002.

——. *The Rise and Fall of Ziggy Stardust and the Spiders from Mars*. New York: Schirmer Books, 1998.

Pegg, Nicholas. *The Complete David Bowie*. Revised and expanded 3rd ed. London: Reynolds and Hearn, 2004.

Pitt, Kenneth. *Bowie: The Pitt Report*. London: Omnibus, 1985.

Pop, Iggy, and Anne Wehrer. *I Need More: The Stooges and Other Stories*. New York: Karz-Cohl, 1982.

Priore, Domenic. *Riot on Sunset Strip: Rock 'n' Roll's Last Stand in Hollywood*. Georgia: Jawbone, 2007.

Richards, Jonathan. *David Bowie: The Shirts He Wears*. London: Helter Skelter, 2005.

Roberto, Chris, and Lou Reed. *Walk on the Wild Side*. New York. Carlton Books, 2004.

Rock, Mick. *Glam!—An Eyewitness Account*. Vision On Publishing, 2001.

Roeg, Nicolas. *The World Is Ever Changing*. London: Faber and Faber Film, 2013.

Sandford, Christopher. *Bowie: Loving the Alien*. London: Little, Brown, 1996.

——. *Keith Richards: Satisfaction*. New York: Carrol & Graf, 2003.

Scovell, Jane. *Oona: Living in the Shadows: A Biography of Oona O'Neill Chaplin*. New York: Grand Central, 1999.

Seabrook, Thomas Jerome. *Bowie In Berlin: A New Career in a New Town*. London: Jawbone, 2008.

Sewall-Ruskin, Yvonne. *High on Rebellion: Inside the Underground at Max's Kansas City*. New York: Thunder's Mouth Press, 1998.

Spector, Ronnie. *Be My Baby*. New York: Harmony, 1990.

Spitz, Marc. *Bowie: A Biography*. New York: Three Rivers Press, 2009.

Stafford, David, and Caroline Stafford. *Fings Ain't Wot They Used T'Be: The Life of Lionel Bart*. London: Omnibus Press, 2011.

Thompson, Dave. *Moonage Daydream*. Medford, New Jersey: Plexus, 1987.

Thomson, Elizabeth, and David Gutman. *The Bowie Companion*. New York: Macmillan, 1993.

Tremlett, George. *David Bowie: Living on the Brink*. London: Century, 1996.

——. *The David Bowie Story*. London: Futura, 1974.

Trynka, Paul. *Iggy Pop: Open Up and Bleed*. London: Sphere, 2007.

——. *Starman, David Bowie, The Definitive Biography*. New York: Sphere/Little, Brown and Company, 2011.

Vanilla, Cherry. *Lick Me*. Chicago: Chicago Review Press, 2010.

Visconti, Tony. *The Autobiography: Bowie, Bolan and the Brooklyn Boy*. London: HarperCollins, 2007.

Weird and Gilly. *Mick Ronson: The Spider with the Platinum Hair*. Shropshire: Independent Music Press, 2003.

Welch, Chris. *Changes: The Stories Behind Every David Bowie Song 1970–1980*. London: Carlton, 1999.

Zanetta, Tony, and Henry Edwards. *Stardust: The Life and Times of David Bowie*. New York: McGraw-Hill, 1986.

ARTICLES ON BOWIE

Adams, Cindy. "Sex, Drugs and David Bowie." *New York Post*, January 6, 1993.

Aitkenhead, David. "David Bowie Names the 'Real' Ziggy Stardust." *Independent*, December 22, 1996.

Aizlewood, John. "Look Back in Pleasure." *Evening Standard*, October 3, 2002.

Aris, Brian. "The Wedding of David Bowie and Iman," *Hello*, June 13, 1992.

Bailey, Doug. "Jarvis and Bowie Light Up." *Big Issue*, December 8, 1997.

Bangs, Lester. "Johnny Ray's Better Whirlpool," *Creem*, January, 1975.

Bennetts, Leslie. "Role Model." *Town and Country*, June 2007.

Bohn, Chris. "Merry Christmas, Mr. Bowie." *New Musical Express*, April 16, 1983.

Bonner, Hilary. "My Secret Guilt by David Bowie." *Mail on Sunday*, May 15, 1983.

Booth, Samantha. "Souvenir Mugshots: Ugly Side of the Stars Who Have Been Nicked." January 27, 2010.

Boshoff, Alison. "After Eight Years of Waiting, Bowie Has a Daughter." *Daily Mail*, August 16, 2000.

——. "His Parents Were Both Bisexual Ego-Maniacs So How DID Zowie Bowie Turn Out So Normal?" *Daily Mail*, February 27, 2010.

——. "Price of Addiction." *Daily Mail*, April 15, 2000.

Bowienet. "Q&A with Coco Schwab." June 27–July 13, 2001.

Bowie, David. "Bowie Interviews Bowie." *Canadian National Post*, February 26, 2000.

——. "How I Nearly Lost My Eye." *Music Star*, Bowie Exclusive, 1973.

——. "My World." *Mirabelle*, August 11, 1973.

——. "The Truth About Me and Ziggy." *Evening Standard*, June 27, 2002.

—— and Ricky Gervais. "Q&A." *Observer*, September 21, 2003.

Brazier, Chris. "Bowie: Beauty Before Outrage." *Melody Maker*, September 4, 1976.

Bream, Jon. "Hunky Dory: All Is Well with David Bowie After Battling the Flu—and the Burden of His Own Legacy." *Minneapolis Star Tribune*, January 9, 2004.

——. "Post-Flu, David Bowie's Back in Action." *Minneapolis Star Tribune*, January 9, 2004.

Brown, Gary. "Monster Maestro." *Record Mirror*, August 9, 1980.

Brown, Mick. "Lindsay Kemp: The Man Who Taught Bowie His Moves." *Crawdaddy!*, September 1974.

Bryant, Tom. "Return of the Thin White Duke." *Mirror*, October 9, 2012.

Buckley, David. "60 Years of Bowie." *Mojo*, January 2007.

——. "New Music Night and Day." *Q/Mojo Special Edition*, 2005.

——. "Renaissance Man." *Mojo*, "Bowie: Loving the Alien," special issue, 2003.

Buford, Bill. "That Nat Tate Hoax." *Guardian*, April 10, 1998.

Cable, Amanda. "I Hope God Can Forgive Bowie." *Sun*, May 11, 1992.

Catchpole, Charles. "Cloak and Dagger Bowie Is a Wowie." *Sun*, February 27, 1982.

Cavanagh, David. "Changes Fifty Bowie." *Q*, February 1997.

Charlesworth, Chris. "David Bowie: Ringing the Changes." *Melody Maker*, March 13, 1976.

——. "Watch That Man." *Mojo*, "Bowie: Loving the Alien," special issue, 2003.

Cocker, Jarvis. "Jarvis and Bowie Light Up." *Interview*, December 8, 1997.

Cocks, Jay. "David Bowie Rockets Onwards." *Time*, July 18, 1983.

Cohen, D. R. "David Bowie Eats His Young." *Rolling Stone*, December 25, 1980.

Cohen, Howard. "Hunky Dory: David Bowie Content with His 'Reality.'" *Miami Herald*, September 8, 2003.

Cohen, Scott. "David Bowie: Artist, Stylist, Mythmaker, Innovator, Manipulator." *Details*, September 1991.

Coleman, Ray. "A Star Is Born." *Melody Maker*, July 15, 1972.

Cook, Judy. "Even When He Was Kissing Me, Warren Beatty Could Not Resist Staring at Himself in the Mirror." *Daily Mail*, August 16, 2008.

Cooper, Tim. "I've Beaten Vices Thanks to My Daughter." *Evening Standard*, November 20, 2003.

——. "Star Man." *Observer*, June 9, 2002.

——. "Thirty Years On, Bowie Brings Back the Stardust." *Evening Standard*, October 3, 2002.

Copetas, Craig. "Beat Godfather Meets Glitter MainMan." *Rolling Stone*, February 28, 1974.

Costa, Maddy. "David Bowie: Live Review, Royal Festival Hall." *Guardian*, July 1, 2002.

Cromelin, Richard. "The Return of the Thin White Duke," *Circus*, March 1976.

——. "David Bowie: The Darling of the Avant Garde." *Phonograph Record*, January 1972.

Crowe, Cameron. "All Access Bowie." *Rolling Stone*, May 18, 2006.

——. "Bowie Golden Years." *Playboy*, September 1976.

——. "Ground Control to Davy Jones." *Rolling Stone*, February 12, 1976.

Currie, David. "Tony Visconti: A Producer's Tale." *Starzone* 11, 1984.

Daily Mail. "Who's the Mug Now." July 23, 2010.

Daily Mirror. "Bashful Bowie," February 27, 1982.

Daily News. "David Bowie's in No Rush to Get to the Altar." January 29, 1990.

——. "Happy Twosome." February 3, 1987.

——. "Iman Plans $10M Lawsuit." March 13, 1983.

——. "Iman/Zulekha." March 0, 1990.

——. "Injuries Heal; Iman Back Clicking with Fashion Photogs." August 3, 1983.

——. "Man, Oh Man, Iman." May 2, 1993.

——. "Supermodel Iman's Drug Crusader Ex Spills the Beans About His Dream Marriage Gone Sour." July 29, 1983.

Dalton, Stephen, Rod Hughes. "David Bowie: Berlin? I Can't Express the Feeling of Freedom I Felt There." *Uncut*, April 2001.

Daly, Les. "Bowie Is So Cruel, Says His Auntie." *Sun*, June 4, 1982.

Das, Lina. "When Iman Fell to Earth." *Daily Mail*, June 10, 2006.

Davies, Andrew. "Starman Lost in Cyberspace." *Big Issue*, January 11–17, 1999.

Davies, Stephen. "Performance: David Bowie, Radio City Music Hall." *Rolling Stone*, March 29, 1973.

Deevoy, Adrian. "Boys Keep Swinging." *Q*, June, 1989.

Derogatis, Jim. "David Bowie's New Scary Monsters." *Chicago Sun Times*, January 9, 2004.

Dingwall, John. "Another Whirl." *Scottish Daily Record & Sunday*, November 10, 2006.

Dorsey, Gail Ann. "Diary of a Rock 'n' Roll Star." *Mirror*, November 14, 2003.

Dube, Steve. "I Can Understand David Bowie's Success, But Branson's? Never." *Western Mail* (Cardiff, Wales), January 29, 2008.

Du Noyer, Paul. "Contact." *Mojo*, July 2002.

——. "Do You Remember Our First Time?" *Word*, November 9, 2003.

——. "Please God Let It Be Me." *Q*, April 1990.

Ellen, Barbara. "David Is a Goliath." July 7, 2002.

Elms, Robert. "All You Have to Do Is Win." *Face*, May 1985.

Esquire. "David Bowie: Chameleon, 57, New York City." March 2004.

Ferris, Tim. "David Bowie in America—The Iceman, Having Calculated, Cometh." *Rolling Stone*, November 9, 1972.

Flanagan, Bill. "The Happy Wanderer." *GQ*, January 1997.

Flynn, Paul. "David Sticks the Boot In." *Guardian*, April 27, 2004.

Franks, Alan. "Keeping Up with the Jones." *Times Magazine*, September 9, 1995.

Fricke, David. "The Dark Soul of a New Machine." *Rolling Stone*, June 15, 1989.

Fulman, Ricki. "Iman's 300G (No-Hum) Job." *Daily News*, August 15, 1982.

Gallagher, William. "Bowie Thrills the Crowd with Cinema Gig." *BBC News Online*, September 9, 2003.

Gamboa, Glenn. "Stardust Memories." *Newsday*, February 21, 2001.

Gandee, Charles. "A Perfect Match." *Vogue*, June 1994.

Garnett, Daisy. "24 Hours with Iman." *Harper's Bazaar*, February 2002.

Gilbert, Matthew. "Portrait of an Artist, by an Artist." *Boston Globe*, August 18, 1996.

Gilbey, Ryan. "Screen Oddity." *Guardian*, April 28, 2012.

Gilmore, Mikal. "How Ziggy Stardust Fell to Earth." *Rolling Stone*, February 2, 2012.

Glaister, Dan. *Guardian*, February 19, 1996.

Goldstein, Patrick. "Berlin Will Die: David Bowie Show." *Berliner Morgenpost*, September 19, 2013.

——. "David Bowie Ist Wieder Da—Und In Berlin," *Berliner Morgenpost*, January 9, 2013.

——. "Von Station zu Station: David Bowie's Berlin," *Berliner Morgenpost*, March 2, 2013.

Greenleaf, Vicki, and Stan Hyman. "Bowie's Hunger." *Us*, June 6, 1983.

Griffin, Jon. "Regrets? Mott a Bit." *Sunday Mercury* (Birmingham, UK), July 22, 2012.

Gundersen, Edna. "Bowie, Beyond Fame and Fashion." *USA Today*, May 14, 1995.

——. "Turning to Face the Change." *USA Today*, October 5, 1999.

Hall, Carla. "The Iman Mystique." *Washington Post*, June 6, 1987.

Harrington, Richard. "David Bowie, Unmasked." *Washington Post*, April 26, 1987.

Hauptfuhrer, Fred. "Rock's Space Oddity, David Bowie Falls to Earth and Finds His Feet in Film." *People*, September 1976.

Heller, Zoe. "Bowie Today." *Harper's Bazaar*, August 2002.

Hendrickson, Matt. "Bowie's Golden Hours." *Rolling Stone*, September 30, 1999.

Hilburn, Robert. "Bowie Has Comeback, Broadway Debut, Too." *Los Angeles Times*, September 21, 1980.

——. "Bowie: Now I'm a Businessman." *Melody Maker*, February 28, 1976.

——. "Bowie Puts the Past on Ice." March 21, 1976.

——. "Coming Clean—Bowie on the Big Three: Drugs, Love & Music." *Newsday*, April 6, 1993.

——. "David Bowie Has Dropped the Disguises." *Los Angeles Times*, May 29, 1983.

——. "David Bowie: Home Edition." *Los Angeles Times*, April 19, 1987.

——. "Pop Music David Bowie: The Man Who Fell . . . Then Got Up Again." *Los Angeles Times*, April 4, 1993.

New Musical Express, November 5, 1974.

Hi! Magazine. "The All New Adventures of David Bowie." June 7, 1975.

Hinckley, David. "The Picture of David Bowie." *Daily News Magazine*, August 2, 1982.

Hislop, Christopher. "Hot Shots: Joe Stevens Reflects on His Time Photographing David Bowie." Seacoastonline.com, January 20, 2013.

Hoare, Philip. "Obituary: John Bindon." *Independent*, November 6, 1993.

Hofman, Katja. "Life Etc: I Was a Teenage Groupie (But My Daughter Says I'm All Right Now): Josette Spent the Seventies in Bed With Rock Gods. And She Didn't Learn a Thing." *Independent*, August 5, 2001.

Holden, Stephen. "Rock Kings, Drag Queens: A Common Strut." *New York Times*, June 1, 1998.

Holloway, Danny. "David Bowie: 'I'm Not Ashamed of Wearing Dresses,'" *New Musical Express,* January 29, 1972.

Hoskyns, Barney. "Profile: David Bowie." *Independent*, June 15, 2002.

Hughes, Rob. *Uncut*, December 2005.

Independent on Sunday. "The Listener: David Bowie: Ch-ch-ch-changes." March 19, 2000.

Interview, September 1995.

Itzkoff, Dave. "Bowie: The Fashion Rocks Q&A." *Lucky Magazine*, October 2005.

Jeffries, Stuart. *Guardian*, December 14, 2001.

Jerome, J. "A Session with David Bowie." *Life*, December 1992.

Jewell, Derek. *Sunday Times*, May 9, 1976.

Jones, Allan. "Goodbye to Ziggy and All That." *Melody Maker,* October 29, 1977.

——. "The Great White Hope Versus the Thin White Duke." *Melody Maker*, April 21, 1979.

Jones, Cliff. "David Bowie / Nine Inch Nails, Meadowlands Arena Live Review." *Mojo*, December 25, 1995.

Jones, Dylan. "Bowie: The Most Stylish Man." *GQ*, October 2000.

Times, October 9, 1994.

Jones, Leslie-Ann. "Marc Bolan and David Who?" *Mail on Sunday*, October 28, 2012.

——. "My Night in Bowie's Bed." *Daily Mail*, June 14, 2007.

Jones, Tricia. "Is the Lad Too Sane for His Own Good?" *i-D*, May 1987.

Kane, Peter. "Bowie: Cash for Questions." *Q*, July 2000.

Kavanagh, Julie. "The New Strings." *W*, April 1976.

Kent, Nick. "Iggy Pop: Iggy Said It, Iggy Had the Power, Iggy Had the Disease." *New Musical Express*, March 12, 1977.

Kimmelman, Michael. "Talking Art with David Bowie." *New York Times*, June 14, 1998.

Konner, Linda. "Where I Grew Up—Iman." *Glamour*, September 1989.

Langton, James. "I'm Iman. Now Back Off." *Evening Standard*, November 12, 2001.

Leogrande, Ernest. "Bowie Fits Snugly on Broadway." *Daily News*, September 29, 1980.

Levin, Angela. "Bunny Girls, Tips from Sinatra and the Day I Turned Down Marilyn." *Daily Mail*, November 26, 2001.

Lewin, David. "Revealing the Many Profound Brilliant and Sometimes Shocking Personalities That Make Up a Folk Hero of Today." *Sunday Mirror*, July 20, 1975.

Loder, Kurt. "David Bowie." *Rolling Stone*, April 23, 1987.

Lott, Tim. *Record Mirror*, September 9, 1977.

Mackinnon, Angus. "The Elephant Man Cometh and Other Monstrous Tales." *New Musical Express*, September 13, 1980.

Maconie, Stuart. "Ziggy's Stardust Changed Our Lives." *Mirror*, June 7, 2012.

Mail on Sunday. "Sabrina and the Prince of Rock." July 3, 1983.

Malins, Steve. "Duke of Hazard." *Vox*, October 1995.

Marshall, William. "The Immortal David Bowie." *Daily Mirror*, July 15, 1982.

Maychick, Diana. "Soup for a Songster." *New York Post*, July 21, 1983.

McLaren, Leah. "Ground Control to David Bowie." *Globe & Mail* (Toronto), March 23, 2013.

McNeill, Phil. "The Axeman Cometh . . ." *Wire*, October 1991.

Melody Maker. "Bowie's Milton Keynes Hunger." April 9, 1983.

——. "A Message from Dave." February 26, 1966.

Mendelsohn, John. "David Bowie? Pantomime Rock?" *Rolling Stone*, April 1, 1971.

Mirror. "Bowie Mum Dies in Home." April 3, 2001.

Moline, Karen. "Iman: 'Women Are Responsible to the Children.'" *Self*, September 1990.

More, Sheila. "The Restless Generation: 2 Heroes of Our Time." *Times*, December 11, 1968.

Morgan, Piers. "David Bowie and Iman." *Hello*, November 23, 1991.

Murray, Charles Shaar. "And the Singer's Called Dave . . ." *Q*, October 1991.

——. "The Bowie Experiment." *New Musical Express*, June 9, 1973.

——. "David at the Dorchester: Bowie on Ziggy and Other Matters." *New Musical Express*, July 22, 1972.

——. "David Bowie: Bowie-ing Out at the Chateau." *New Musical Express,* August 4, 1973.

——. "David Bowie: Gay Guerillas and Private Movies." *New Musical Express*, February 24, 1973.

——. "David Bowie: The Byronic Man." *Face*, October 1984.

——. "David Bowie: Who Was That (Un) Masked Man?" *New Musical Express*, November 12, 1977.

——. "The Man Who Fell to Earth." *Arena*, May / June 1993.

——. "On the Set with Bowie." *Record Mag*, December 1984.

——. "Sermon from the Savoy." *New Musical Express*, September 29, 1984.

——. "Tin Machine: Versus." *Q*, October 1991.

——. "Ziggy Played Guitar." *Independent on Sunday*, June 9, 2002.

Murray, James. "Bad Guy Bowie—Warts and All." *Daily Express*, March 2, 1982.

Music Star. "A Star Called Davie Bowie," Special issue, 1974.

Musto, Michael. "Night of the Bowie Zombies." *Soho Weekly News*, May 4, 1978.

Nathan, Sara. "Duncan Jones Wedding." *Daily Mail*, May 20, 2013.

——. "Two Years Recording in Secret." *Daily Mail*, January 9, 2013.

Newsday. "New Lines from Iman." March 12, 1987.

——. *Newsday*. February 22, 1981.

——. *Newsday* March 27, 1989.

New Musical Express, January 10, 1976.

New Musical Express, March 19, 1977.

New York Post. "AIDS Test Ordered for Rock Star in 'Rape' Flap." October 31, 1987.

——. "Bowie Beats Dallas Rape Charge." November 19, 1987.

——. "David Bowie to Bow as 300-Year-Old Man." June 10, 1982.

——. "Fit to Be High—David Bowie's Seen the Valleys, Prefers the Peaks." September 12, 2003.

——. "Golden Years." May 15, 1995.

——. "Hurley: House-Warmer." January 10, 1989.

——. "Iman: Battered." March 3, 1983.

——. "Model Took Risk at Height of Her Career." April 23, 1985.

——. "Squeaky Clean." July 25, 1987.

Norman, Philip. "No Hiding Face." *Sunday Times*, September 19, 1999.

Norwich, William. "Florence Silence." *New York Post*, June 5, 1992.

Odell, Michael. "Clash of the Titans." *Q*, October 2003.

O'Grady, Anthony. "David Bowie: 'Rock and Roll Is Dead.'" *RAM*, July 26, 1975.

——. "Dictatorship: the Next Step?" *New Musical Express*, August 23, 1975.

O'Hagan, Sean. "Major Tom.com." *Observer*, January 16, 2000.

Orshoski, Wes. "Bowie Gets Back to 'Reality.'" *Billboard*, October 6, 2003.

Pagnozzi, Amy. "Key Bowie Musician Jumps off Bandwagon." *New York Post*, May 18, 1983.

Paphides, Peter. "Cyberspace Oddity." *Time Out*, December 1998.

Pareles, Jon. "David Bowie, 21st Century Entrepreneur." *New York Times*, June 9, 2002.

Parsons, Tony. "Bowie, What's He Like." *Arena*, Spring/Summer 1993.

Paterson, Tony. "Berlin Gets Bowie Fever." *Independent*, March 9, 2013.

Penman, Ian. "What Was That All About?" *Guardian*, November 7, 1996.

People. "Iman Business Woman." May 8, 2000.

——. "She's from Africa and She's a Stunner—and Everything Else About Iman Is In Dispute." November 3, 1976.

Perry, Andrew. "Jumping Through the Hooples Again." *Daily Telegraph*, October 31, 2013.

Petridis, Alexis. "David Bowie: Odeon Cinema, Brighton." *Guardian*, September 10, 2003.

——. "A Star Is Reborn." *Guardian*, May 31, 2002.

Pond, Steve. "Beyond Bowie." *Live!* March 1997.

Raven, Paul. "Popping the Question: David Bowie." *Mirabelle*, September 1972.

Reed, Lou. "David Bowie." *Rolling Stone*, April 15, 2004.

Reed, Rex. "Bowie Rocks the Crowds at the Fest." *New York Post*, May 13, 1983.

——. "David Bowie—He Is Far Out." *Sunday News*, June 13, 1976.

Reilly, Rachel. "Hothouse Property Gossip, Bowie Hits His Peak in St. Lucia." *Daily Mail*, June 14, 2010.

Reilly, Sue. "Tall, Dark and Handsome." *People*, April 21, 1980.

Reynolds, Simon. "The Singer Who Fell to Earth." *New York Times*, March 10, 2013.

Rice, Anne. "David Bowie and the End of Gender." *Vogue*, November 1983.

Roberts, Chris. "David Bowie with La La La Human Steps." *Melody Maker*, July 9, 1988.

Robinson, John. *"New Musical Express*, December 2, 2000.

Robinson, Lisa. "Bowie's 'So Long' to the Solo Songster." *New York Post*, June 11, 1989.

——. "Bowie Took from the Best." *Spin*, August 1990.

——. "Clockwork Orange in Black & White." *Creem*, May 1976.

——. "David Bowie." *Hit Parade*, June 1978.

——. "Gossip-Loving Bowie Plays Up Rumors." *New York Post*, October 10, 1997.

Robinson, Tony. "Pop Star's Wife in Drama at Snow Chalet." *Sunday Mirror*, January 15, 1978.

Rock, Mick. "The Bowie Scene." *Music Scene*, July 18, 1973.

——. "David Bowie Is Just Not Serious." *Rolling Stone*, June 8, 1972.

Rook, Jean. "Bowie Reborn." *Daily Express*, February 14, 1979.

Rose, Cynthia. "David Bowie." *City Limits*, June 3, 1983.

Rush, George. "Bowie, Iman Hear Patter of Little Feet." *Daily News*, February 14, 2000.

Russell, Rosalind. "David Bowie: Bent on Success." *Disc and Music Echo*, May 6, 1972.

Sandall, Robert. "David Bowie: The Star Looks Very Different Today." *Sunday Times*, August 31, 2003.

——— "Demolition Man." *Times*, 1995.

Sanneh, Kelefa. "A Regular Guy and Friends, Just Touring." *New York Times*, August 2, 2002.

Savage, Jon. "The Gender Bender." *Face*, November 7, 1980.

Scaggs, Austin. "Bowie's Heroes." *Rolling Stone*, September 2003.

Scrudato, Ken. "David Bowie—Life on Earth." *Soma*, July 2003.

Sessums, Kevin. "You Get Better with Age—Iman." *Parade*, May 17, 2009.

Sexton, Paul. "Still the Starman." *Scotland on Sunday*, June 13, 2004.

Sheaves, Becky. "David Bowie Saved My Life." *Daily Mail*, October 17, 2006.

Shreyer, Steve, and John Lifflander. "David Bowie: Spaced Out in the Desert." *Creem*, December 1975.

Simpson, Dave. "David and Me." *Guardian*, February 23, 2003.

——. "David Bowie Live Review, Manchester Arena." *Guardian*, November 18, 2003.

——. "Ground Control." *Guardian*, June 5, 2002.

Simpson, Kate. "Interview." *Music Now!*, 1969.

Simpson, Richard. "Bowie and Moss Band Together for Photo Copy." *Evening Standard*, September 4, 2003.

——. "Bowie Feeling Hunky Dory." *Evening Standard*, July 28, 2004.

Sinclair, David. "All the Old Dude Had, He's Still Got." *Times*, November 18, 2003.

——. "Blonde on Blonde." *Independent*, July 13, 2006.

——. "A Star Who Will Never Fall to Earth." *Times*, July 1, 2002.

Sischy, Ingrid. "Rock's Major Chameleon Sheds His Skin Like Never Before." *Interview*, June 2002.

Sklar, Rachel. "Bowie Motivated by Fatherly Fear." *Canadian Press*, June 5, 2002.

Sloane, Billy. "I Missed My Son Growing Up . . . I'm Not Going to Make the Same Mistake With My Daughter." *Scottish Sunday Mail*, November 23, 2003.

Snow, Mat. "Mr. Bowie Changing Trains." *Mojo*, October 1994.

Spencer, Neil. "Space Invader." *Uncut*, August 1998.

Sporkin, Elizabeth. "Elegant, Ageless, Iman." *USA Today*, January 12, 1987.

Stahl, Jerry. "Bowie." *Esquire*, May 1993.

Stasio, Marilyn. "Bowie Blazing on Broadway." *New York Post*, September 29, 1980.

Stein, Bruno. "Flying Saucers, Hitler and David Bowie." *New Musical Express*, February 1975.

——. "World Problems Solved in US Hotel Room." *Creem*, February 1975.

Stout, Alan K. "Bowie Knifes into NEPA." *Times Leader*, May 26, 2004.

Stout, Gene. "Getting Ziggy With It?" *Seattle Post-Intelligencer*, April 11, 2004.

Street-Porter, Janet. "Leave Me Out of This Bowiemania." *Independent*, January 13, 2013.

Sullivan, Caroline. "David Bowie, Reality." *Guardian*, September 12, 2003.

——. "Kitsch 'n' Synch Adds Up to Art." *Guardian*, November 16, 1995.

Sullivan, Chris. "The Gods of Glam." *Independent*, August 2, 2005.

Sutherland, Steve. "Alias Smiths and Jones." *New Musical Express*, March 27, 1993.

——. "Bowie: Boys Keep Swinging." *Melody Maker*, March 24, 1990.

——. "Bowie, Ch-Ch-Ch-Changes?" *Melody Maker*, March 31, 1990.

——. "The Man Who Fell Back Down to Earth." *Melody Maker*, March 26, 1983.

——. "Metallic KO." *Melody Maker*, May 27, 1989.

——. "One Day, Son, All This Could Be Yours . . ." *New Musical Express*, March 20, 1993.

——. "Tin Machine: Metal Gurus." *Melody Maker*, July 1, 1989.

——. "Tin Machine: The Industrial Blues." *Melody Maker*, July 8, 1989.

Sweeting, Adam. "The Star Who Fell to Earth." *Guardian*, March 3 & 4, 1990.

——. "Tin Machine Live Review." *Guardian*, November 12, 1991.

Swenson, John. *Rolling Stone*, May 5, 1977.

Teeman, Tim. "After a Silent Decade, Bowie Is Back," *Times*, January 12, 2013.

Thomas, D. "Bowie's Profile." *Extra*, March 9, 1986.

Thompson, Ben. "I've Been on a Diet Since I Was Eight." *Daily Mail*, April 14, 2010.

Tobler, John. "Secret Never Seen: An Interview with David Bowie," *ZigZag*, January 1978.

Trebay, Guy. "David Bowie Style." *W*, October 2004.

Trebbe, Anne. "Iman: No Model Mom But 'I Try.'" *USA Today*, March 18, 1983.

Trong, Stephanie. "David Bowie Is So Wise That Stephanie Trong Wants Him to Be Her Personal Spiritual Guide for Eternity." *Jane*, August 2002.

Tulich, Katherine. "Family Man Hits the Road." *Sydney Morning Herald*, September 15, 2003.

Turner, Steve. "The Great Escape of the Thin White Duke." *Independent*, May 4, 1991.

Tyler, Andrew. "Cherry Vanilla—Cherry Sauce." *Disc and Music Echo*, April 21, 1973.

Udovitch, Mim. "Q&A." *Rolling Stone*, November 11, 1999.

——. "Q&A with David Bowie." *Rolling Stone*, August 8, 2002.

Us. "Bowie, David: Rock's Chameleon Talks About His Latest Ch-ch-ch-changes." August 10, 1987.

USA Today. "A Leader in Fashion." May 21, 1995.

Vanity Fair. "Proust Questionnaire." August 1998.

Varmi, Anuji. "Bowie's Starman: Drummer Phil Helped Young Rock Legend In Road to Fame," *Sunday Mercury* (Birmingham, UK), June 26, 2011.

Verna, Paul. "New York Metro." *Mix*, September 1, 2003.

Vogue. "Iman." 1989.

Waris. "A World Apart—Iman." *Vogue*, June 1998.

Watts, Michael. "Confessions of an Elitist." *Melody Maker*, January 22, 1972.

——. "David Bowie: From Brixton to Berlin." *Melody Maker*, February, 1978.

——. "Oh You Pretty Thing." *Melody Maker*, January 22, 1972.

Welch, Chris. "Beckenham Arts Lab." *Melody Maker*, September 1969.

Wells, Steven. "The Artful Codger." *New Musical Express*, November 25, 1995.

West, Carinthia. "Night and Day: *Marie Claire* Spends 24 Hours with Iman." *Marie Claire*, December 1996.

Wheeler, Steven P. "David Bowie: Man of a Thousand Phases." *Music Connection*, September 1995.

White, Timothy. "David Bowie: A Fifteen Year Odyssey of Image and Imagination." *Musician*, May 1983.

——. "Turn and Face the Stranger," *Crawdaddy*, February 1978.

Wigg, David. "David's Generosity Helped My Mother and Me Survive." *Daily Mail*, August 12, 2011.

Wild, David. "Bowie's Wedding Album," *Rolling Stone*, January 21, 1993.

Wills, Judith. "At 17 She Became a Secretary on a Pop Magazine." *Daily Mail*, August 4, 2008.

Woods, Vicki. "Rock of Ages." *Vogue*, December 1999.

——. "Who Says Supermodels Rarely Ace Their Second Acts?" *Vogue*, April 2000.

Young, Charles M., *Rolling Stone*, May 19, 1977.

STUDIO ALBUMS

1967 *David Bowie*

1969 *Space Oddity*

1970 *The Man Who Sold the World*

1971 *Hunky Dory*

1972 *The Rise and Fall of Ziggy Stardust and the Spiders from Mars*

1973 *Aladdin Sane*

1973 *Pin Ups*

1974 *Diamond Dogs*

1975 *Young Americans*

1976 *Station to Station*

1977 *Low*

1977 *Heroes*

1979 *Lodger*

1980 *Scary Monsters (and Super Creeps)*

1983 *Let's Dance*

1984 *Tonight*

1987 *Never Let Me Down*

1989 *Tin Machine*

1991 *Tin Machine II*

1993 *Black Tie White Noise*

1995 *Outside*

1997 *Earthling*

1999 *'Hours . . .'*

2002 *Heathen*

2003 *Reality*

2013 *The Next Day*

LIVE ALBUMS

1974 *David Live*

1978 *Stage*

1983 *Ziggy Stardust: The Motion Picture*

1992 *Tin Machine Live: Oy Vey, Baby*

1994 *Santa Monica '72*

2008 *Live Santa Monica '72*

2008 *Glass Spider Live*

2009 *VH1 Storytellers*

2010 *A Reality Tour*

Bandslam (2009)
David Bowie

August (2008)
Cyrus Ogilvie

SpongeBob SquarePants (TV Series) (2007)
Lord Royal Highness
- Atlantis SquarePants (2007) . . . Lord Royal Highness (voice)

Arthur and the Invisibles (2006)
Maltazard (English version, voice)

The Prestige (2006)
Nikola Tesla

Extras (TV Series) (2006)
David Bowie
- David Bowie (2006) . . . David Bowie

Nathan Barley (TV Series) (2005)
David Bowie
- Pilot (2005) . . . David Bowie (uncredited)

Zoolander *(2001)*
David Bowie

Empty (Short) *(2000)*
Man

The Hunger (TV Series) *(1999–2000)*
The Host / Julian Priest
- The Suction Method (2000) . . . The Host
- The Falling Man (2000) . . . The Host
- Double (2000) . . . The Host
- The Seductress (2000) . . . The Host
- Approaching Desdemona (2000) . . . The Host

Mr. Rice's Secret *(2000)*
Mr. William Rice

Omikron: The Nomad Soul (Video Game) *(1999)*
Boz / The Dreamers (voice)

B.U.S.T.E.D *(1999)*
Bernie

Il Mio West *(1998)*
Jack Sikora

Basquiat *(1996)*
Andy Warhol

Full Stretch (TV Series) *(1993)*
David Bowie
- Ivory Tower (1993) . . . David Bowie

Twin Peaks: Fire Walk with Me *(1992)*
Phillip Jeffries

The Linguini Incident *(1991)*
Monte

Dream On (TV Series)   *(1991)*
The Second Greatest Story Ever Told (1991) . . . Sir Roland Moorecock

The Last Temptation of Christ   *(1988)*
Pontius Pilate

Labyrinth   *(1986)*
Jareth the Goblin King

Absolute Beginners   *(1986)*
Vendice Partners

Into the Night   *(1985)*
Colin Morris

Yellowbeard   *(1984)*
The Shark (uncredited)

Merry Christmas, Mr. Lawrence   *(1983)*
Maj. Jack "Strafer" Celliers

The Hunger   *(1983)*
John Blaylock

The Snowman (Short)   *(1982)*
Older James (Rereleased Version)

Baal (TV Movie)   *(1982)*
Baal

Just a Gigolo   *(1978)*
Paul Ambrosius von Przygodski

The Man Who Fell to Earth   *(1976)*
Thomas Jerome Newton

Pierrot in Turquoise or The Looking Glass Murders (TV Short)   *(1970)*
Cloud

The Virgin Soldiers   *(1969)*
Soldier (uncredited)

Theatre 625 (TV Series)   *(1968)*
- The Pistol Shot (1968)

The Image (Short)   *(1967)*
The Boy

1972–73: Ziggy Stardust tour: *The Rise and Fall of Ziggy Stardust* and *the Spiders from Mars* and *Aladdin Sane*

1974: Diamond Dogs tour: *Diamond Dogs*

1976: Isolar—1976 tour: *Station to Station*

1978: Isolar II—1978 world tour: *Low* and *"Heroes"*

1983: Serious Moonlight tour: *Let's Dance*

1987: Glass Spider tour: *Never Let Me Down*

1990: Sound+Vision tour: *Sound+Vision*

1995–96: Outside tour: *Outside*

1996: Outside summer festivals tour

1997: Earthling tour: *Earthling*

1999: The Hours . . . tour: *"Hours . . ."*

2000: Mini tour

2002: Heathen tour: *Heathen*

2003–04: A Reality tour: *Reality*

Cavett, Dick, *The Dick Cavett Show*, December 4, 1974, ABC

Hall, Arsenio, *The Arsenio Hall Show*, 1993, CBS

Harty, Russell, *Russell Harty Plus*, 1973, ITV

Harty, Russell, *Russell Harty Plus*, 1975, ITV

O'Donnell, Rosie, *The Rosie O'Donnell Show*, 1997, NBC

Parkinson, Michael, *Parkinson*, 2003, BBC1

Rose, Charlie, *The Charlie Rose Show*, March 31, 1998

Michelmore, Cliff, *Tonight*, November 15, 1964, BBC2

The Sacred Triangle: Bowie, Iggy and Lou, 1971–1973, 2010

Whately, Francis, *David Bowie: Five Years*, UK, 2013

Pennebaker, D. A., *Ziggy Stardust and the Spiders from Mars*, UK, 1973

BBC Documentary, *David Bowie: Dancing in the Streets*, UK, 1996

Cracked Actor, BBC, January 26, 1975